Summary of Contents

HTML Utopia
Designing Without Tables Using CSS

by Dan Shafer

HTML Utopia: Designing Without Tables Using CSS
by Dan Shafer

Copyright © 2003 SitePoint Pty. Ltd.

Editor: Georgina Laidlaw
Technical Editor: Kevin Yank
Cover Design: Julian Carroll
Printing History:
  First Edition: May 2003
Latest Update: December 2004

Notice of Rights

Notice of Liability

Trademark Notice

Published by SitePoint Pty. Ltd.

424 Smith Street Collingwood
VIC Australia 3066.
Web: www.sitepoint.com
Email: business@sitepoint.com

ISBN 0-9579218-2-9
Printed and bound in the United States of America

About the Author

Dan Shafer is a highly respected Web design consultant. He cut his teeth as the first Webmaster and Director of Technology at Salon.com, then spent almost five years as the Master Builder in CNET's Builder.com division.

Dan gained widespread recognition as a respected commentator on the Web design scene when he hosted the annual Builder.com Live! conference in New Orleans. He has designed and built more than 100 Websites and is regarded as an expert in Web user experience design and implementation.

The author of more than 50 previous titles on computers and technology, Dan lives in Monterey, California, with his wife of almost 25 years, Carolyn, and their Shiitzu dog, Albert Einstein.

About the Technical Editor

As Technical Director for SitePoint, Kevin Yank oversees all of its technical publications—books, articles, newsletters, and blogs. He has written over 50 articles for SitePoint on technologies including PHP, XML, ASP.NET, Java, JavaScript, and CSS, but is perhaps best known for his book, *Build Your Own Database Driven Website Using PHP & MySQL*, also from SitePoint. Kevin now lives in Melbourne, Australia. In his spare time he enjoys flying light aircraft and learning the fine art of improvised acting. Go you big red fire engine!

About SitePoint

SitePoint specializes in publishing fun, practical and easy-to-understand content for Web Professionals. Visit http://www.sitepoint.com/ to access our books, newsletters, articles and community forums.

This book is dedicated to One Mind,
in the knowing that It is all there is.

Table of Contents

Preface

I was already in my 50s when the World Wide Web burst upon the scene. Having spent most of my life to that point as a writer and editor, I naturally gravitated to the publishing side of the coin, rather than remaining content to be an amazed consumer of all the wonderful information and connections that began to flow from it.

As I saw the first version of the first graphical Web browser before it was officially released, some might say I've been there from the beginning. And one thing that bothered me from that beginning, as an author and publisher, was the inability to disentangle content from presentation. The interconnectedness of it all meant that, to produce a Website, you needed not only something to say, and some graphical designs to make the site look good, but you also needed to be a bit of a programmer. Initially, this "programming" was a pretty lightweight task to someone like me who had a broad but thin programming background. HTML markup, when all was said and done, wasn't really programming. Still, it was more than just writing words. And it was more than using a word processor to format words.

Designers who had clear ideas of how they wanted their Web pages to look were frustrated and stymied by the need to create complex sets of deeply nested tables even to *approximate* their visions. And, as designers came up with increasingly complex ideas, and Web browsers diverged further and further from standards and compatibility, the Web threatened to collapse under its own weight. Serious designers began lobbying for a complete break from HTML to some new approach to the Web. Chaos reigned.

I was at CNET's Builder.com at the time, chronicling all of this, as well as participating in it both as a designer and as a pundit. I was one of the founding members of the Web Standards Project, or WaSP[1], and I helped found the major conference where Web designers and creators gathered at *Builder.com Live!* in New Orleans. So I had a front-row seat as we gradually figured out the best way to deal with this problem.

The Holy Grail of the Web, then, was the notion that authors should write, designers should design (and code HTML) and programmers should... well... program. Those boundaries were not clean in the first few years of the Web.

---

[1] http://www.webstandards.org/

Then, along came Cascading Style Sheets (CSS), the subject of this book. The governing forces of the Web, through the World Wide Web Consortium, better known as the W3C[2], addressed the problem and proposed that we divide presentation instructions, and structural markup with content, into two separate kinds of files.

Things haven't been the same since, thank goodness! Now we really can (mostly) separate what we say from how it gets presented to the user in a Web browser. I wager that most Web developers today are fairly comfortable with CSS and would no more think of embedding presentation instructions in their HTML than they'd consider mixing 23 fonts on the same Web or print page.

Since CSS emerged, there have been dozens of books written about it. So when SitePoint approached me about doing a CSS book, my first thought was, "Who needs another CSS book?" But as they began to reveal their vision to me, it made sense. It was indeed time for a book that took a different tack, based on the extensive experience of the Web design community.

So, this book is different in two primary ways.

First, it focuses on the question of how to accomplish with CSS some of the successes Web designers have spent significant time and energy to create using nested tables. Said another way, this book doesn't try to start from scratch and become a CSS tutorial. Instead, it's a sort of introductory CSS design guide.

Second, it starts at the outside and works its way in. Most, if not all, other CSS books, focus first on the little pieces: the attributes, values, and tags that comprise the syntax of CSS. They then explain how to put those pieces together into a Website.

This book begins by looking at how CSS should influence the entire design of a site, and how to put the CSS framework in place before you begin to deal with individual HTML elements and their styling.

Who Should Read This Book?

As I wrote this book, I had in mind Web designers with at least a little experience building sites, who are curious about how CSS can help them become more effective designers. It is, then, aimed at a beginner to intermediate designer. I shall assume a strong grasp of HTML, but that's about it.

---

[2] http://www.w3.org/

The Book's Website

Located at http://www.sitepoint.com/books/css1/, the Website supporting this book will give you access to the following facilities:

The Code Archive

As you progress through the text, you'll note a number of references to the code archive. This is a downloadable ZIP archive that contains complete code for all the examples presented in the book. You'll also find a copy of the *Footbag Freaks* Website[4], which we use as an example throughout the book.

Updates and Errata

No book is perfect, and I expect that watchful readers will be able to spot at least one or two mistakes before the end of this one. The Errata page on the book's Website will always have the latest information about known typographical and code errors, and necessary updates for new browser releases and versions of the CSS standard.

The SitePoint Forums

If you'd like to communicate with me or anyone else on the SitePoint publishing team about this book, you should join SitePoint's online community[5]. In fact, you should join that community even if you *don't* want to talk to us, because there are a lot of fun and experienced Web designers and developers hanging out there. It's a good way to learn new stuff, get questions answered (unless you really enjoy being on the phone with some company's tech support line for a couple of hours at a time), and just have fun.

The SitePoint Newsletters

In addition to books like this one, SitePoint publishes free email newsletters, including *The SitePoint Tribune* and *The SitePoint Tech Times*. In them, you'll read about the latest news, product releases, trends, tips, and techniques for all aspects of Web development. If nothing else, you'll get the useful CSS articles and tips,

---

[4] http://www.footbagfreaks.com/
[5] http://www.sitepointforums.com/

but if you're interested in learning other technologies, you'll find them especially useful. Sign up to one or more SitePoint newsletters at http://www.sitepoint.com/newsletter/.

Your Feedback

If you can't find your answer through the forums, or if you wish to contact us for any other reason, the best place to write is <books@sitepoint.com>. We have a well-manned email support system set up to track your inquiries, and if our support staff is unable to answer your question, they send it straight to me. Suggestions for improvements as well as notices of any mistakes you may find are especially welcome.

Acknowledgements

A huge vote of thanks and appreciation goes to Kevin Yank, Technical Editor of this book. SitePoint as a publisher has a radically different approach than any other publisher I've dealt with. Kevin taught me a lot about CSS, argued with me about details when necessary, and generally made a major and measurable contribution to the technical quality of this book. In particular, he wrote the impressive Appendix C. Needless to say, errors remain my responsibility, but I can tell you that any errors that slipped through are my fault, and not due to a lack of understanding on Kevin's part. He must eat, sleep, and breathe W3C specs.

Also immensely influential on this book was Editor Georgina Laidlaw. She kept the project as on schedule as it could be, acted as a liaison between Kevin and I, and copy-edited the text to make sure my propensity to write incredibly long sentences was curbed. Plus, she was a joy to work with.

Julian Carroll, Designer, created the graphic design for the book, did almost all the graphics work, and designed the *Foothag Freaks* sample Website[7] to boot. He also wrote the article that was the original inspiration for this book: *HTML Utopia! Design Websites Without Tables*[8].

Mark Harbottle, SitePoint's CEO, approached me with the concept, negotiated the deal, and remained flexible during sometimes difficult periods as the book

---

[7] http://www.footbagfreaks.com/
[8] http://www.sitepoint.com/article/379

evolved and grew and shrank and missed deadlines. He was never anything less than a professional and a gentleman.

Jeff Soulé, a bright technology guy who also happens to be married to my lovely oldest daughter Sheila, read some of the chapters of the book as it was being written, learned some CSS in the process, and offered several helpful suggestions that led to clearer explanations of some points.

Two world-class Web designers, Eric Meyer and Jeffrey Zeldman, helped me through, with their writing, their examples, and their dogged determination that CSS be understandable to, and usable by, all Web designers.

Finally, my wife, Carolyn, continues to stand by her man despite long hours, blue air, bouts of self-doubt and depression, periods of inexplicable and incomprehensible joy, and reams of techno-speak. She is, as always, my primary inspiration and life teacher, without whom none of this would be possible or make sense.

Introduction to CSS

Getting the Lay of the Land

We can look at Cascading Style Sheets (CSS) from a number of contextual perspectives. I prefer to view them as a correction to a fundamental mistake that was made at the beginning of Web Time, back in the old days of the early 1990s, when Tim Berners-Lee and the first pioneering Web builders first envisioned the beginnings of the Web.

What was that mistake?

To meet the requirements of the Web's initially limited purpose, it was not necessary to separate content from presentation. Even though some thought it was a good idea, there was no really compelling, practical reason to recognize this distinction. After all, the Web's early intent was simply to allow a small number of nuclear physicists using disparate systems at various locations to share vital experimental data.

Berners-Lee didn't envision the massively popular, wildly commercialized, extensively morphed Web that emerged from his core ideas in the early 1990s—I doubt that anyone could have.

So, the mistake was a lack of foresight, rather than an oversight. But it was a mistake nonetheless.

CSS in Context

Almost as soon as the Web became popularized by the emergence of the first graphical Web browser (the forerunner to Netscape Navigator), graphic designers became aware of a problem. The method by which the Web browser displayed information stored in HTML files was not within the designer's control. No, it was the users who were in primary charge of how the Web pages they visited would appear on their systems.

While there were many, including myself, who thought this was A Good Thing, professional designers were beside themselves with concern. From their perspective, this constituted a fundamental flaw. "Users don't know anything about good design", they argued. If the designers couldn't control with great accuracy things like colors, fonts, and the precise, pixel-level positioning of every design element on the Web page, their creations could easily end up as ugly travesties in the user's browser.

While a few decided to look upon this as a challenge posed by the new medium, most designers, accustomed to print and other fixed layouts that afforded them complete control over what the user saw, found ways to bend the Web to their will.

Lest I incur the ire of every designer reading this book, let me hasten to add that I don't think this was A Bad Thing. It is certainly the case that designers know more about how content should be displayed for users than do the users themselves. Things like spacing, color combinations, and other design elements affect readability and usability. My point has much less to do with who should have been in charge, than it does with the actions to which designers were more or less forced to resort, in order to achieve at least some measure of control.

Soon, expert designers discovered that they could use tables to gain significant control over the presentation of content to users. By carefully laying out tables within tables within tables, they could position quite precisely any design element that could be contained within a table cell. And that encompassed almost everything.

The first desktop publishing-style Web page design tool, NetObjects Fusion, enabled designers to lay out pages with a high degree of precision. It generated complex, table-based HTML, which resulted in Web pages that were as close as possible to the designer's original vision.

We never looked back.

But tables weren't intended to be used as layout tools, so while they were marginally effective, they were also horribly inefficient. We'll explore some of the shortcomings and disadvantages of using tables for layout tasks a little later in this chapter; for now, just know that everyone, including the designers who used the techniques, understood pretty well how clumsy a solution they really were.

The Basic Purpose of CSS

CSS emerged as a standard for Web page design, in large part, as a reaction to the overuse of excessively complex tables to force precision layout upon a medium that was not originally intended for such a purpose. While this is a bit of an oversimplification of the facts, it's hardly an unfair one.

After a brief series of skirmishes at the beginning of the Web's development, the question of who should control the overall appearance of a page or site ended with the designers as victors. In fact, hardly a shot was fired. Users, after all, eventually care most about usability, accessibility and convenience, rather than the nitty-gritty details of design techniques.

Though flush with their victory, designers found themselves hard-pressed to identify very good, standards-compliant ways to provide their customers—and their customers' users—with great designs that were also effective and efficient. Thus, they were forced to rely largely on tables.

As the snarl of tables grew to resemble a giant thicket, even the design community became uneasy. Maintaining a Web page that consists of a half-dozen or more deeply intertwined tables is a nightmare. Most designers prefer not to deal with code—even simple HTML markup—at such a level of detail.

Into the breech stepped the World Wide Web Consortium, better known as the W3C[1], a body founded by Tim Berners-Lee to oversee the technical growth of the Web. They saw that separating the content of a site from its form (or appearance) would be the most logical solution. This would enable content experts—writers, artists, photographers, and programmers–to provide the "stuff" that people come to a site to see, read, or experience. It would also free the design experts—artists, graphic designers, and typographers–to determine the site's aesthetics independently of its content.

The result was CSS.

---

[1] http://www.w3.org/

Why Most—But Not All—Tables Are Bad

Why are tables such a bad idea as a design mechanism? There are numerous reasons, but the ones we're most concerned with in this context are:

- ❏ They result in load times that are longer than necessary.

- ❏ They encourage the use of inefficient "placeholder graphics" that further slow performance.

- ❏ Their maintenance can be a nightmare in which even minor changes "break" the entire layout.

Tables Mean Long Load Times

Most people don't know that Web browsers are deliberately designed to ensure that each table downloads as a single entity. So, none of the material that's contained in a table will be displayed until all the contents of that table are downloaded to the client machine and available for display.[1]

When the original, intended purpose of tables is taken into account, this makes sense. Tables were designed to display... well, tables of data. Each cell contained a value that was being compared to, or related with, the values of other cells in the table. Isolated bits of data appearing quasi-randomly would not do; the table was a single, integrated entity.

When designers began to rely on tables to contain all or most of the content of a Web page, they were also saddled with the consequences of this design decision. In addition to the *apparent* delay that many users experience as a result of tables displaying all at once, the sheer volume of HTML code that is required to create today's Web page layouts with nested tables can also add *actual* load time due to increased page size. Table-based layouts almost certainly account for more user concern over long page load times than any other single factor.

Avoiding this significant load time would obviously be A Good Thing.

---

[1] Cascading Style Sheets Level 2 (CSS2) includes a property called `table-layout` that alters this behavior, with several important caveats. Refer to Appendix C for details.

Use of Transparent Images Slows Us Down

Even with the availability of tables as layout mechanisms, designers could not quite attain the detailed level of control over page design that they wanted. Sometimes, for instance, a designer might need a bit more breathing room around one part of a table cell (something for which table design does not allow). This kind of precision was unachievable.

Early on, some designer came up with the notion of creating a `transparent.gif` image file—a tiny GIF image that had no visible content. By creating table cells to contain these transparent images, we could force extra room both vertically and horizontally into tables whose cells were designed to remain in close proximity to one another.

The problem is, given a table with dozens (or even hundreds) of these images, and depending on a variety of other factors, the performance impact of transparent GIFs on a Web page can be significant. More importantly, however, this technique will often restrict the page to a fixed pixel size, and it clutters the page with images that have no actual meaning for the content of the page. As we'll see later, this severely impacts the ability for users with disabilities to make sense of your site.

Maintaining Tables Is a Nightmare

The third reason that most tables are bad is that maintaining a complex array of deeply nested tables is a nightmare. If you use tools such as Macromedia Dreamweaver or Adobe GoLive to manage your sites and their designs, you can generally ignore the messiness of the nested tables that make the design possible. But even these tools are not foolproof, and when they "mess up" (to use a highly technical term), amending the unsightly pages they create can be quite a challenge.

If you're like most designers, and you wouldn't be caught dead using an HTML-generating tool because you feel you gain more control and understanding if you hand-code everything, then you'll be familiar with this problem.

The difficulty arises because, by necessity, tables have a fairly complex set of tags, even if they aren't embedded within other tables. And when we have nested tables, well, we've got a clear case of the uglies, all right.

The situation is further complicated by the fact that, unlike programming editors, HTML editors generally do not force or support the clean indentation of code. So, finding the start and end points for a given table, row, or even cell turns out to be what software folks call a "non-trivial task." While it's true that a competent HTML coder or designer could make this problem more tractable, it's never really solvable, no matter what we do.

When it's OK to Use a Table

There is one notable exception to the cardinal rule that Tables are A Bad Thing.

If you have tabular data, and the appearance of that data is less important than its appropriate display in connection with other portions of the same data set, then a table is in order.

In general (though there are undoubtedly some exceptions to this rule as well), this means that the use of tables should be confined to the presentation of numeric or textual data, not graphics, multimedia data types, forms, or any other interactive user interface components.

What Is CSS, Really?

OK, now that we've established that an important role of CSS in our lives as designers is to free us from the drudgery (and treachery) of using tables for page layout, let's take a look at what CSS really is.

The most important word in the Cascading Style Sheets label is the middle one: **style**. The cascading issue becomes important only when we get into fairly complex style usage, while the word "sheet" is even a tad misleading at times. So, even though we mean Cascading Style Sheets in the broadest and most accurate sense, we'll focus not on the cascading or sheet-like nature of these beasts, but on their role in determining the styles of our Web pages and sites. Styles are defined in the form of **rules**. These rules tell any Web browser that understands them (i.e., that supports CSS) how to display specific types of content structures when it encounters these structures in delivering a Web page to a user.

To understand how styles affect Web page appearance, we need to be sure we understand what happens to a Web page in the absence of any style rules.

Figure 1.1 shows the general process of interaction between a client (Web browser), and a server where a Web page or site is located. Note that the browser automatically determines how information provided by the server is displayed to the user, unless it is specifically told otherwise. In other words, each browser has a default way of displaying all HTML-tagged content. So, a first-level heading enclosed in the <h1></h1> tag set will always be displayed using a relatively large font in black. The "default" font that's used may vary between browsers, and can be affected by user-defined settings as well.

Figure 1.1. Normal Browser Page Display Behavior

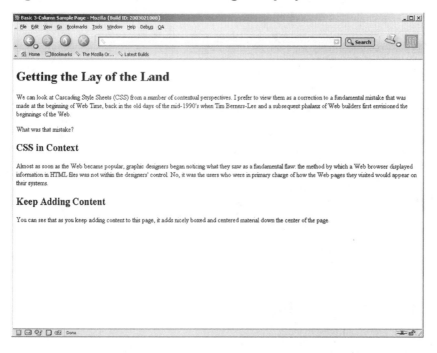

Figure 1.2 depicts what happens when a style rule exists for a particular type of HTML structure. The rule overrides the browser's default handling of that element, and the style takes over. Even if the user has defined his or her own settings for this element, those wishes will generally not be honored (though there are some intriguing exceptions to this, which we'll discuss much later in this book).

Figure 1.2. Browser Displaying Page With Style Rule in Effect

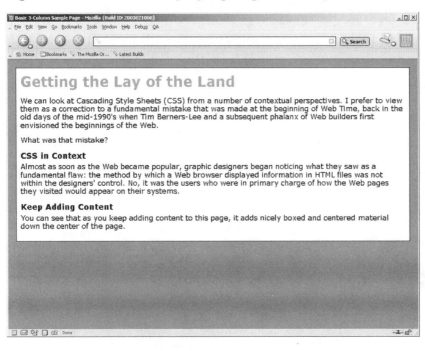

Parts of a CSS Rule

Every style, whether it's embedded in a separate style sheet or not, consists of one or more **rules**. Figure 1.3 shows a CSS rule with all the parts labeled.

Each rule has exactly two parts:

 A **selector** that defines the HTML element(s) to which the rule applies

 A collection of one or more **properties**,[2] which describes the appearance of all elements in the document that match the selector

---

[2]Many books and articles about CSS call them "attributes," or use the two terms interchangeably. In this book, I used the W3C endorsed terminology of "properties", and reserve the name "attributes" for attributes of HTML tags.

Figure 1.3. Parts of a CSS Rule

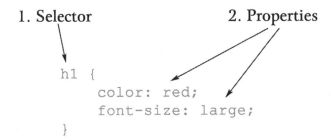

Each property consists of a pair of values separated by a colon. The first item of the pair defines the specific property that's being modified. The second item describes the value that the property takes on. Each property-value pair must be followed by a semicolon, with one exception: The semicolon following the last property is optional and may be omitted. In this book, however, we will always add this optional semicolon. I encourage you to adopt this habit as well, as it's much easier to train yourself to always add that semicolon than it is to remember when it is required and when it isn't. It also makes it easier to add properties to an existing style rule.

Here are a few examples of increasingly complex CSS rules, with the parts identified so that you can fix this syntax clearly in your mind. Essentially, this is the only real syntax issue you must learn in order to master CSS, so it's important!

```
h1 {
  color: red;
}
```

The selector, h1, indicates that this rule applies to all h1 headings in the document. The name of the property that's being modified is color, which applies to the font color. The value we want the color property to take on is red. Chapter 7 and Chapter 9 explore fonts and coloring in CSS in great detail.

```
p {
  font-size: 14px;
  color: green;
}
```

The selector, p, indicates the style rule should be applied to all paragraphs in the document. There are two property name-value pairs in the rule. The first, font-size, sets the size of the font in all paragraphs in the document to 14 pixels. A pixel is one dot on your screen, and is the most common measurement used in CSS. See Chapter 3, for an explanation of this and other measurement issues in CSS. The second property is color and is set to green. The result of this rule is that all paragraphs in the document will appear in a green, 14-pixel-high font.

```
p {
    font-family: 'New York', Times, serif;
}
```

Again, this rule deals with paragraphs, as is evidenced by the p selector. This time, the selector affects the font family that is used to display text. The new wrinkles in this example are that it includes a list of values for the font-family property, and one of those values is enclosed in quotation marks.

The font-family property is one of a handful of CSS properties to which you can assign a *list* of possible values, rather than a single, fixed value. When you use a list, commas must separate its individual members. In this case, the font-family property list tells the browser to use New York as the font if the user's machine has it installed. If not, it directs the browser to use Times. And if neither of these fonts is available on the user's system, then the browser is told to default to the font used for serif type. Again, this subject is covered in more depth in Chapter 7 and Chapter 9.

Whenever the name of a property value in a CSS rule includes spaces (as is the case with the font named "New York"), you must put that value into quotation marks. Many designers use single quotation marks for a number of reasons, not the least of which is that they're easier to type, but you can use either single or double quotation marks.

Types of CSS Rules

There are several possible ways to categorize and think about CSS rules.

First, there is the question of what types of style properties the rules define. Second, there is the requirement of describing the type(s) of HTML elements that the rules affect. Finally, there is the issue of whether the styles are "inline", "embedded" or "external."

Let's take a brief look at each of these categorizations, so that you have a good overview of the organization of CSS rules before you embark on a detailed study of their actual use.

What Properties Can CSS Rules Affect?

CSS rules can include properties that affect virtually every aspect of the presentation of information on a Website. A complete reference to these properties is presented in Appendix C.

What Elements Can CSS Affect?

Stated another way, this question asks "How specifically can a CSS rule target a piece of information on a Web page for special presentation?" CSS allows the designer to affect all paragraphs, but how can you confine that impact to certain, specific paragraphs? Is this even possible?

The answer, unsurprisingly, is yes. Through various combinations of selector usage, the designer can become quite specific indeed about the circumstances under which a style rule is enforced. For example, you can assign rules so that they affect:

❑ all elements of a specific type

❑ all elements of a specific type that are assigned to a common group or class

❑ all elements of a specific type that are contained within other elements of a specific type

❑ all elements of a specific type that are both contained within another specific element type and assigned to a common group or class

❑ all elements of a specific type only when they come immediately after an element of some other type

❑ only a specific element of a specific type which is assigned a unique ID

Chapter 3, includes a detailed discussion of all the CSS selectors you can use to achieve this kind of precision targeting.

Where Can CSS Styles Be Defined?

Finally, you can define CSS styles in any of three places, in conjunction with a Web page.

Inline CSS

First, you can define a style entirely within an appropriate HTML tag. This type of style is referred to as an **inline style** because it is defined in line with the document's HTML code. You can assign a `style` attribute to almost all HTML elements. For example, to make a second-level heading in a document appear in red text and all capital letters, you could code a line like this:

```
<h2 style="color: red; text-transform: uppercase;">An Unusual
   Heading</h2>
```

If you follow the advice in this book, you won't use many inline styles. As you'll learn, separating content from presentation is one of the big advantages of CSS, and embedding styles directly in HTML tags defeats that purpose. Inline styles are mainly useful for rapid prototyping—quickly applying style properties to a particular element to experiment with an effect before giving the properties a more permanent place in an embedded or external style rule.

Embedded CSS

Specifying style properties in an **embedded style** is probably the method that's most common today, particularly among beginning Web designers or those just learning the techniques involved in CSS design. It's not my favorite, but it does have the singular virtue of being easy to deal with, so you'll see it used from time to time in this book.

To embed a style sheet in a Web page, you place a `style` block in the `head` of the document's HTML, as shown here in bold:

```
<!DOCTYPE html PUBLIC "-//W3C//DTD XHTML 1.0 Transitional//EN"
   "http://www.w3.org/TR/xhtml11/DTD/xhtml1-transitional.dtd">
<html xmlns="http://www.w3.org/1999/xhtml">
<head>
<title>CSS Style Sheet Demo</title>
<meta http-equiv="Content-Type"
   content="text/html; charset=iso-8859-1" />
<style type="text/css">
<!--
```

```
h1, h2 {
  color: green;
}
h3 {
  color: blue;
}
-->
</style>
</head>
...
```

The CSS rules contained in the `style` block apply to all the designated parts of the current document. In this case, the first rule directs the browser to display all level 1 and 2 headings (`h1`, `h2`) in green. The second rule displays all level 3 headings (`h3`) in blue.

Notice the HTML comment delimiters (`<!-- -->`) just inside the `<style>` tags. These prevent ancient browsers that do not support CSS from interpreting the style rules as document content and displaying them in the browser window. All CSS capable browsers will ignore the comment delimiters. Even though it's probably safe (or nearly so) to omit these symbols today, as so few ancient browsers are still in use, it does no harm to include them. I recommend you do so, just because it's good form.

The second thing to notice about the `style` element's syntax is that each rule starts on a new line, and each property specified within the rule appears indented within braces on its own line. This is not, strictly speaking, required, but it's a good rule of thumb that improves the readability of your code, especially if you're used to the look of JavaScript code.

External CSS

Finally, you can define CSS rules in a file that's completely separate from the Web page. You can then link to this file by including a `<link>` tag in the `head` portion of any Web page on which you want to implement the styles contained in that file.

```
<!DOCTYPE html PUBLIC "-//W3C//DTD XHTML 1.0 Transitional//EN"
  "http://www.w3.org/TR/xhtml11/DTD/xhtml1-transitional.dtd">
<html xmlns="http://www.w3.org/1999/xhtml">
<head>
<title>CSS Style Sheet Demo</title>
<meta http-equiv="Content-Type"
  content="text/html; charset=iso-8859-1" />
```

```
<link rel="stylesheet" type="text/css" href="corpstyle.css" />
</head>
...
```

In this example, the file `corpstyle.css` contains a set of **external styles** that have been linked to this page. Here's what the contents of this file might look like:

```
h1, h2 {
  color: green;
}
h3 {
  color: blue;
}
```

This is my personal preference for the way we should deal with *all* CSS usage, for a number of reasons.

First, this is the least "locked-in" of the three basic methods designers can use to insert styles into a Web page. If you define an external style sheet file, you can bring it to bear on as many pages on your site as you want, simply by `linking` to the style sheet from each page on which you want it used. Making a change to a style that appears on every page of your site becomes a simple matter of modifying the shared `.css` file. If you use embedded or, worse yet, inline styles, you'll have to copy and paste them into other documents if you want to use them.

Second, and closely related to the first advantage, is that this method is the easiest way to ensure the maintainability of your CSS styles. If you define all your site's styles in external files, implementing a site-wide style change is a simple matter of making one edit in a single file. All the pages that use that style sheet will display the new styles immediately, following this one change. With the other techniques, you have to either remember which styles are defined on which pages, or use search mechanisms to help you deal with the decentralized styling rules.

Third, external style sheets are treated as separate files by the browser. When the browser navigates to a new page, using the same style sheet, the external style sheet does not need to be downloaded again. Pages that use external styles are therefore quicker to load.

Last, but not least, external style sheets are simply more professional. By using them, you demonstrate an understanding of the importance of the first two issues I've just raised, and you make it much easier to discuss them, share them with colleagues, analyze their effects, and, in general, to work with them as if they were a serious part of the site's design, rather than an afterthought.

Why Bother?

Well, now that you have a basic overview of what CSS is all about, why we have it, and why I think it's an important technique for Web designers to adopt, where's the proof? Let's look at an example of a small, but not overly simplistic Web page (see Figure 1.4).

Figure 1.4. Sample Web Page Demonstrating Embedded Styles

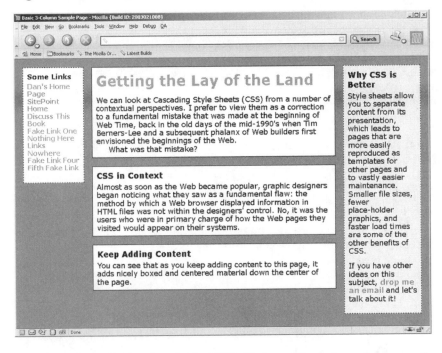

Using embedded CSS, here's the HTML that will produce that page. Look ma, no tables! Don't let the complexity of the code intimidate you—by the end of Chapter 3, you should be able to infer the meaning of most of it without my help. For now, you can download the code archive from the book's Website[2] and marvel at the results in your browser. The file is called `ch1sample.html`.

---

[2] http://www.sitepoint.com/books/

```
<!DOCTYPE html PUBLIC "-//W3C//DTD XHTML 1.0 Transitional//EN"
  "http://www.w3.org/TR/xhtml11/DTD/xhtml1-transitional.dtd">
<html xmlns="http://www.w3.org/1999/xhtml">
<head>
<title>Basic 3-Column Sample Page</title>
<meta http-equiv="Content-Type"
  content="text/html; charset=iso-8859-1" />
<style type="text/css">
<!--
body {
  background-color: teal;
  margin: 20px;
  padding: 0;
  font-size: 1.1em;
  font-family: verdana, arial, helvetica, sans-serif;
}
h1 {
  font-family: verdana, arial, helvetica, sans-serif;
  margin: 0 0 15px 0;
  padding: 0;
  color: #888;
}
h2 {
  font-family: verdana, arial, helvetica, sans-serif;
  margin: 0 0 5px 0;
  padding: 0;
  font-size: 1.1em;
}
p {
  font-family: verdana, arial, helvetica, sans-serif;
  line-height: 1.1em;
  margin: 0 0 16px 0;
  padding: 0;
}
.content>p {
  margin: 0;
}
.content>p+p {
  text-indent: 30px;
}
a {
  color: teal;
  font-family: verdana, arial, helvetica, sans-serif;
  font-weight: 600;
  text-decoration: none;
}
```

```
a:link {
  color: teal;
}
a:visited {
  color: teal;
}
a:hover {
  background-color: #bbb;
}

/* All the content boxes belong to the content class. */
.content {
  position: relative;
  width: auto;
  min-width: 120px;
  margin: 0 210px 20px 170px;
  border: 1px solid black;
  background-color: white;
  padding: 10px;
  z-index: 3;
}

#navleft {
  position: absolute;
  width: 128px;
  top: 20px;
  left: 20px;
  font-size: 0.9em;
  border: 1px dashed black;
  background-color: white;
  padding: 10px;
  z-index: 2;
}

#navright {
  position: absolute;
  width: 168px;
  top: 20px;
  right: 20px;
  border: 1px dashed black;
  background-color: #eee;
  padding: 10px;
  z-index: 1;
}
-->
</style>
```

```
</head>
<body>

<div class="content">
  <h1>Getting the Lay of the Land</h1>
  <p>We can look at Cascading Style Sheets (CSS) from a number of
     contextual perspectives. I prefer to view them as a
     correction to a fundamental mistake that was made at the
     beginning of Web Time, back in the old days of the mid-1990's
     when Tim Berners-Lee and a subsequent phalanx of Web builders
     first envisioned the beginnings of the Web.</p>
  <p>What was that mistake?</p>
</div>

<div class="content">
  <h2>CSS in Context</h2>
  <p>Almost as soon as the Web became popular, graphic designers
     began noticing what they saw as a fundamental flaw: the
     method by which a Web browser displayed information in HTML
     files was not within the designers' control. No, it was the
     users who were in primary charge of how the Web pages they
     visited would appear on their systems.</p>
</div>

<div class="content">
  <h2>Keep Adding Content</h2>
  <p>You can see that as you keep adding content to this page, it
     adds nicely boxed and centered material down the center of
     the page.</p>
</div>

<div id="navleft">
  <h2>Some Links</h2>
  <p>
    <a href="http://www.danshafer.com/"
       title="Dan Shafer's Personal Web Site">Dan's Home
       Page</a><br/>
    <a href="http://www.sitepoint.com/"
       title="SitePoint Home Base">SitePoint Home</a><br/>
    <a href="http://www.sitepointforums.com/"
       title="Discussion Board for This Book">Discuss This
       Book</a><br/>
    <a href="" title="">Fake Link One</a><br/>
    <a href="" title="">Nothing Here</a><br/>
    <a href="" title="">Links Nowhere</a><br/>
    <a href="" title="">Fake Link Four</a><br/>
```

```
      <a href="" title="">Fifth Fake Link</a><br/>
  </p>
</div>

<div id="navright">
  <h2>Why CSS is Better</h2>
  <p>Style sheets allow you to separate content from its
     presentation, which leads to pages that are more easily
     reproduced as templates for other pages and to vastly easier
     maintenance. Smaller file sizes, fewer place-holder graphics,
     and faster load times are some of the other benefits of
     CSS.</p>
  <p>If you have other ideas on this subject,
     <a href="mailto:dan@danshafer.com">drop me an email</a> and
     let's talk about it!</p>
</div>

</body>
</html>
```

Summary

You should now understand the historical and technological contexts in which CSS has emerged, what major problems it is designed to solve, and how it works at a surface level. You should also know why tables are a bad idea as a Web page layout device, even though they have other, perfectly valid uses.

In addition, you can identify both the parts of a CSS rule and at least three ways of categorizing CSS style rules in general.

Chapter 2 drills more deeply into the prospective issues surrounding CSS. It clears up some of the misconceptions you may have about this technology, and describes some of the important issues you'll have to take into consideration because of the way Web browsers work (or don't) with CSS rules.

2

Putting CSS Into Perspective

In Chapter 1, we took a 10,000-foot view of CSS. We began by looking at why using tables for Web page layout is generally a bad idea. Then, we examined the types of CSS rules, and which aspects of a Web page style sheets could affect.

This chapter provides an overview of CSS's place in the Web development cosmos. First, we'll discuss what CSS is good for, and what it *can't* do for you. We'll spend a little time examining the role of CSS in making Websites more accessible to people with special needs, and those who access the Web outside a conventional browser.

After a quick look at how CSS interacts with the ever-shifting world of Web browsers, we'll discover how we can create CSS that accommodates browsers that don't provide full support for CSS standards, either because they predate the standard, or they just haven't been designed properly.

What is CSS Good For?

Recall from Chapter 1, that one of the key advantages of CSS is that it separates the *content* of a Website from its *appearance* or *presentation*. This separation is important because it allows us to create Websites that enable writers and artists to create the *information* the Website is intended to convey, while leaving the *design* of the site—how it looks and how it behaves—to designers and programmers.

It follows, then, that CSS would be useful for defining the *appearance* of a site, but not necessarily for dictating its *behavior*.

Like many such generalizations, however, this statement turns out to be true only most of the time. Why? Because the dividing line between appearance and behavior is necessarily fuzzy.

For example, as we'll see in Chapter 11, CSS can be used effectively to create context-sensitive menus, along with other elements of the interface with which your users will interact. You may be familiar with menu designs whose interactivity relies heavily on JavaScript, or some other scripting language, but we'll learn some techniques that avoid scripting, while allowing us to do some fairly creative things with navigation.

While Part III of this book provides detailed instructions and examples of how you can alter the appearance of colors, fonts, text, and graphics using CSS, the rest of this section provides some idea of the *kinds* of tasks for which you can use CSS. My intention here is less to teach you how to do these things, than it is to whet your appetite and start you thinking about the possibilities...

Color and CSS

You can use style sheet rules to control the color of any HTML element that can be displayed in color. The most common elements for which you'll find yourself setting the color are:

❏ text

❏ headings (which are really a special form of text)

❏ page backgrounds

❏ background colors of text and headings

This may not seem like much, but knowing when and how to apply color to these elements—and, perhaps more importantly, how to *combine* the use of color in interconnected elements—can really expand your Web design capabilities.

The simple act of changing the color of all the text on a page, and then providing a colored background for that text, can turn a fairly ordinary-looking Web page (Figure 2.1) into one that has a completely different feel to it. Figure 2.2 shows what the page in Figure 2.1 looks like if we simply choose holiday-appropriate colors—yellow text on a black background. Figure 2.3 shows the opposite effect: black text on a yellow background. While you could argue that these alternative layouts aren't as readable as the black-and-white original in Figure 2.1, you'd have to admit that the two variations are more interesting to look at.

Figure 2.1. Black and White Version of Fall Holiday Page

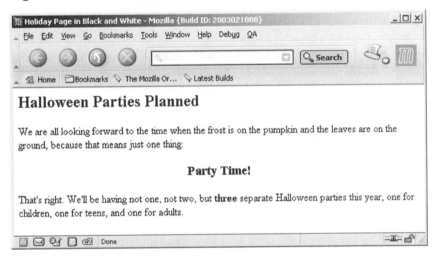

Figure 2.2. Yellow on Black Version of Fall Holiday Page

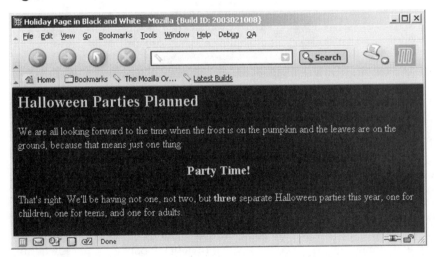

Here's the style rule that creates the effect in Figure 2.2. As you can see, it's pretty straightforward, yet the result of its use is certainly dramatic.

```
body {
  color: yellow;
  background-color: black;
}
```

As we'll see in Chapter 7, naming the colors you want is just one of several ways to define color in CSS. And, yes, I know orange would be more appropriate than yellow here, but `orange` isn't one of the 16 standard keyword color names that are currently available in CSS. More on this in Chapter 7.

Figure 2.3. Black on Yellow Version of Fall Holiday Page

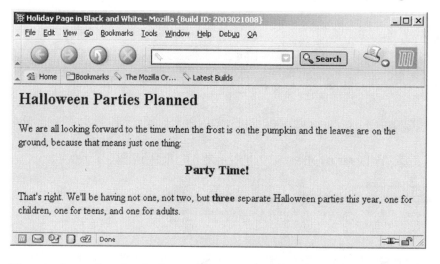

Here is the style rule that creates the effect in Figure 2.3. No surprise: it's the opposite of the code used to generate the look in Figure 2.2.

```
body {
  color: black;
  background-color: yellow;
}
```

Maybe you find the use of a starkly contrasting color for the entire background of a page a bit overwhelming. Figure 2.4 shows you another variation on the text color theme. Here, we've provided yellow text on a black background only behind the headings on the page. The rest of the page's background color, and all non-heading text, remains unchanged from the original design in Figure 2.1.

Figure 2.4. Yellow on Black in Headings Only of Fall Holiday Page

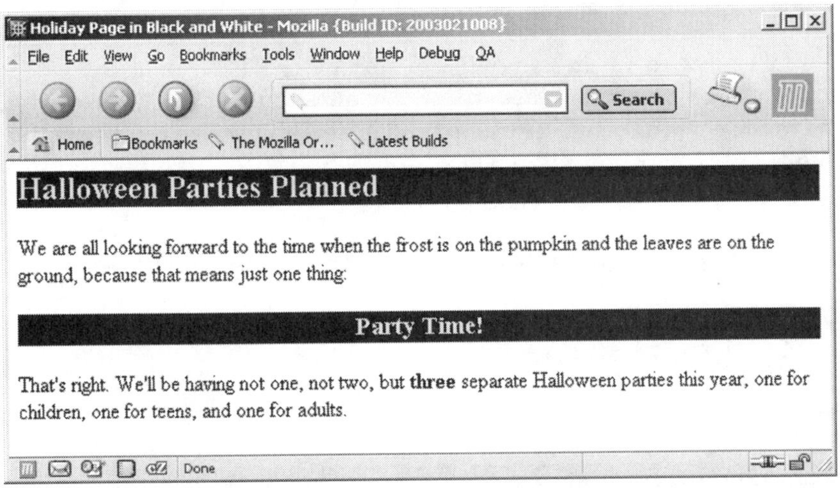

Here's the style rule that generates the heading effect shown in Figure 2.4.

```
h1, h2, h3, h4, h5, h6 {
  color: yellow;
  background-color: black;
}
```

Notice that we didn't have to do anything fancy, like put the headings inside a <div> tag, or create a rectangular box around them. In the view of the Web browser, the heading is a **block level element**, which occupies the full width of the space in which it resides, by default. So, if you give a heading a background-color property, that property will apply to the entire horizontal block that contains the heading.

There's a range of other advantages CSS provides to the color-conscious designer, but we'll leave those details to Chapter 7. Our purpose here is merely to touch upon the variety of things you can expect CSS to accomplish.

Fonts and CSS

In Chapter 1, we saw a number of examples that used fonts in CSS style rules. From that exposure, you're probably comfortable with defining the fonts in which body text and headings of various levels should be displayed.

You can apply fonts to smaller amounts of text by enclosing that text within <span> tags (a subject we'll treat in detail in Chapter 9), and then applying style properties to the span. You can use this approach, for example, to create an effect called "drop caps" (see Figure 2.5), which some graphic designers like to use at the beginning of the first paragraph of a page or section.

Figure 2.5. Drop Cap Style Applied to First Letter on Page

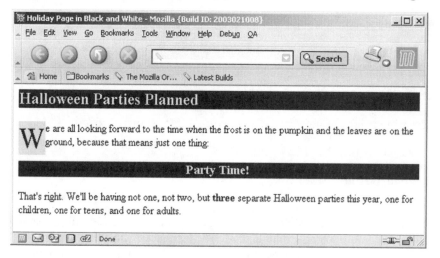

These examples involve the creation of span elements, and there are a number of issues to consider before you use these techniques—see Chapter 8 and Chapter 9, for all the gory details.

By choosing contrasting font, color, and background-color properties for a single character, you can also achieve some good effects, as shown in Figure 2.6, where a storybook feel is created.

Figure 2.6. Drop Cap Style Combined With Font and Colors

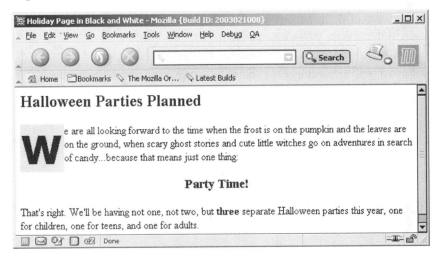

Figure 2.7. A List Showing Off Its Importance

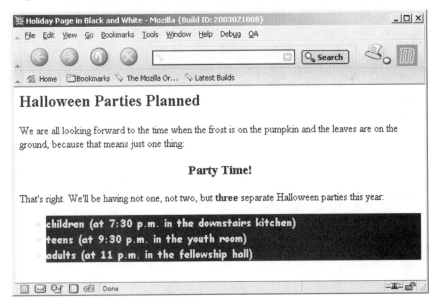

One type of HTML text element to which it is sometimes quite useful to apply font rules, is the list. We generally create lists in an effort to call specific attention to several items that are related to one another, and using a font style to set the list off even more clearly from the text can be a good design technique. Figure 2.7 shows a list that has been set in a contrasting font from the main text of the page, and made bold as well. You can see how the list stands out from the page, calling attention to itself as being particularly important.

Pseudo-Class Animation and CSS

One of the more interesting effects you can create with CSS involves the use of the "hover" effect on text. By defining a CSS style rule that changes the appearance of text when the user pauses the mouse over that text, you can create an effect that looks a bit like animation.

However, this effect works only on text that's a link (though this is changing with the emergence of next-generation browsers). You can determine what will happen to a text link over which the user pauses with the mouse, by setting the a:hover style, as shown here:

```
a:hover {
  color: green;
  font-size: 22px;
}
```

Figure 2.8 shows what happens when the user positions the cursor over a link to which this style rule is applied. While you can't tell that the color of the text has changed, you can easily see that the text is larger than the other links around it.

Figure 2.8. Pseudo-Animation in a Hovered Link

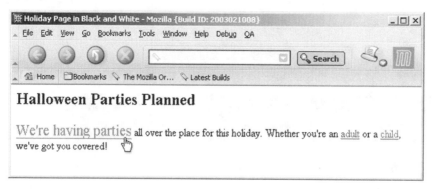

This effect feels a bit like an animated graphic in a menu where the buttons are programmed to change when the user's mouse hovers over them—it's an intriguing technique that we'll learn more about in Part III.

Images and CSS

Images are placed on a Web page using the HTML <img> tag. With CSS, we can only affect relatively minor aspects of an image's display, but that doesn't mean we can't control anything interesting.

Like any other object in a Web page, an image can always be enclosed inside a <div> tag and positioned arbitrarily on the page (this subject forms much of the focus of Part II). We can also affect the border around an image, as well as its alignment, again by embedding the image in a div element, and then using a style to alter the appearance of the div.

At least theoretically, you can create CSS style rules that apply to all the images on a page. I say "theoretically" because this appears to be one of the largest pits into which browser compatibility falls. I'll have more to say about this problem later in this chapter.

However, provided you're willing to live with less-than-perfect renditions of your pages in older and broken browsers, you can specify the border around images, as well as their alignment on the page, by providing style rules connected directly to an img element, like this:

```
img {
    display: block;
    margin-left: auto;
    margin-right: auto;
    border: 10px green groove;
}
```

One thing CSS is particularly helpful for is forcing text to flow gracefully around inline images. Using the float property (which is covered in detail in Chapter 6), you can "float" an image on a page in such a way that the text placed alongside it will wrap around it properly.

Figure 2.9 shows what would happen to an image placed on a page alongside text, in the absence of any CSS instructions. The image appears at the left edge of the page and it is aligned with one line of text, which shares its baseline with the bottom of the image. Subsequent lines of text appear below the image.

Figure 2.9. Image Mixed With Text Without CSS Styles

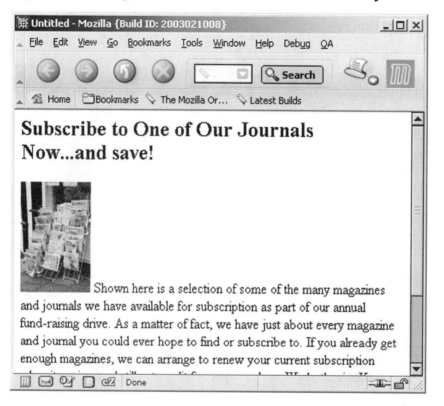

Figure 2.10, on the other hand, shows what happens if we position the image using the `float` property properly. Note how the text flows smoothly around the side and then under the image. This is almost certainly closer to the design effect we want than the example shown in Figure 2.9.

Figure 2.10. Image Mixed With Text With Help of `float`

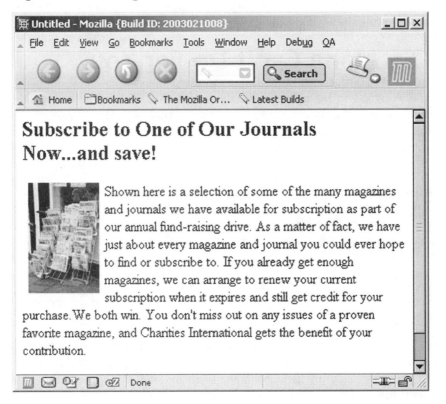

Of course, this same effect can be achieved with a simple HTML attribute (as can many of the effects we've seen so far), but to do so would rob us of the differentiation between content and presentation, and the many benefits of CSS that go with it. The point I want to make here is that using CSS is a choice. Just because you *can* do something the old way in straight HTML doesn't mean you *should*.

Multiple Style Sheets, Users, and CSS

It is possible to define more than one style sheet for a given Web page or site. In the event that you do so (and we'll learn how to do this below in the section called "CSS and Web Accessibility"), modern browsers will allow the user to choose which style sheet to use in creating his or her specific user experience.

With a bit of scripting, which we won't cover in this book, you can automate that selection process and create an adaptable site that several different categories of users can experience appropriately.

What CSS Alone Can't Do For You

CSS is not designed to provide clever ways to interact with users, or to make dynamic or context-sensitive changes to the appearance of a page. For example, displaying a popup menu when the user hovers the mouse cursor over a page element (e.g. a menu bar) can't be done with CSS alone. Carrying out this kind of design requires the use of JavaScript or some other scripting language.

The reason for this is simple: it's the same reason that a plain HTML page needs scripting to cause interactive and dynamic page changes. An HTML page is static. Once it's been served by the server on which it resides and displayed in the user's browser, you can't change it without an intervening program of some sort.

CSS does not make an HTML page dynamic. For example, even though you can use CSS to position elements on a page and control their visibility, these properties are fixed as soon as the page is displayed in the browser.

As I indicated in the preceding section, although you can define multiple style sheets for a given page (e.g. one for hand held devices, one for people with vision problems, etc.), you cannot use CSS *alone* to make sure the appropriate style sheet is used for a particular type of user.

You *can*, however, create completely separate copies of a page, each with a unique URL and associated style sheet. Here, for example, is a minimal style sheet embedded in a Web page, which we can arbitrarily store at the default `index.html` location, where virtually all Web servers expect to find the base page.

```
<style type="text/css">
body {
  font-family: verdana, arial, helvetica, sans-serif;
  background-color: #ffffcc;
  color: teal;
}
</style>
```

This style definition would be contained in the head portion of the page's HTML. It defines only the basic font and the colors to be used on the site.

Now, let's say that we know we have some people coming to the site whose vision is impaired, though not severely. We want to be sure that all of the type on the page is larger for these users. A *partial* solution might be to modify the above style sheet to look like this (changes in bold):

```
<style type="text/css">
body {
  font-family: verdana, arial, helvetica, sans-serif;
  font-size: 130%;
  background-color: #ffffcc;
  color: teal;
}
</style>
```

This approach, which has some pitfalls that we'll discuss later in this chapter, increases the size of all type on the page by 30%. Figure 2.11 shows a page with the first style provided above, while Figure 2.12 shows the same page with the second style sheet rule.

Figure 2.11. Normal Font Size in Sample Page

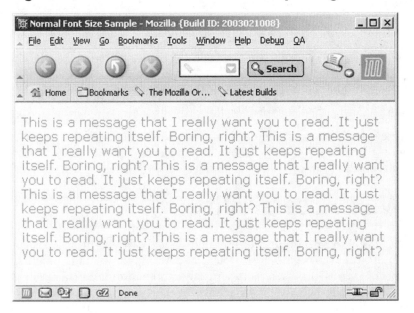

Figure 2.12. Page from Figure 2.11 with Type Size Increased 30%

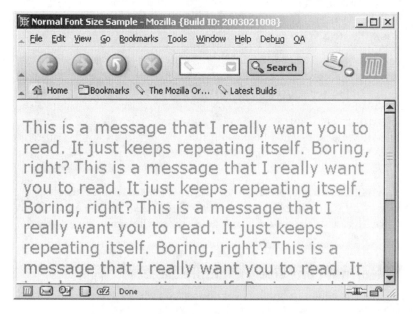

Now, we can make a copy of the page to which these styles are being applied, replace the style in the copy with the updated version shown above, and save the resulting page under a new URL (e.g. `bigtype.html`). Then, we can spread the word that if users have vision problems, and want to see our site more comfortably, they should load `http://www.mysite.com/bigtype.html`.

You can imagine other instances where this approach might be useful: using the same page content against different graphical backgrounds, for different schools, classes, or clients comes to mind.

CSS and Web Accessibility

Accessibility has been an important focus of a great deal of thought and design on the Web, almost from the beginning. People with various physical impairments, who needed specific kinds of browser support, have generally found themselves well served by various Web accessibility initiatives and products (see Recommended Resources, for a listing of some of the more important sites related to this topic).

While CSS cannot, obviously, provide an ideal solution for all special needs, you can take advantage of CSS to solve *some* accessibility problems.

In the preceding section, I provided a brief example of using CSS to increase the size of the type on your Web pages, which made it fairly easy to offer a site for people who are vision-impaired. I also said that the minimal approach I outlined there had some pitfalls. Let's look briefly at those now.

Many people who have vision problems have set the preferences in their Web browser to compensate. Modern browsers allow users a fair amount of control over such factors as font sizes, and background and link colors, for example. If you create a style sheet like the one I described in the preceding section, and a user who has set his or her font size to be larger than usual visits your site, strange results could arise. In theory, this shouldn't happen, but as one wag put it, "In theory, there's no difference between theory and practice, but in practice, there is."

Another issue is that you could set up a false expectation. By having a page on your site that displays an increased type size, you might lead people to expect that most users with vision difficulties will be comfortable with your pages. But there are limits to how much explosion you can apply to type without causing formatting and other problems, and some of these limitations could result in your disappointing users who have special needs.

Here's an interesting solution that you might find to be a good starting point from which to address this particular physical limitation. Create your main Web page with a message letting users know that there are larger type-sized versions of your site available. Use multiple style sheets to accomplish this. The message might say something like:

"If you have trouble seeing the type on this page because of a vision problem, you can select an alternative view. Just select "Use Style" (or similar) from the View menu in your browser and choose a larger magnification."

Support for Alternate Style Sheets

As of this writing, support for alternate style sheets is still patchy among current browsers. For instance, Microsoft Internet Explorer (version 6 for Windows and version 5 for Mac OS) provides no support for this at all. Browsers that *do* support alternate style sheets include Mozilla, Netscape 7, and Opera 7.

For practical purposes, therefore, you will have to provide a more rudimentary method of switching style sheets, if support for this feature is critical to the success of your site. You can have multiple versions of your site's pages, each pointing to a different linked style sheet, as described in the section called "What CSS Alone Can't Do For You", or you can use a server-side scripting language to allow users to register their preference and generate the `<link>` tag dynamically for each and every page.

To demonstrate how this works, I've taken the two styles defined in the previous section (the second of which specifies that type is to be 130% larger than the standard) and made them external style sheets. They're linked into the page so that modern browsers will see the alternative styles and offer them to the user.

I've also done something a little tricky. The first paragraph on each page, which tells the user about the availability of alternative style sheets, needs to differ depending on whether the user is already looking at the page with big type (and perhaps wondering what in the world is going on!), or the standard page. So I defined those two paragraphs as `div` elements and then, depending on which style sheet is loaded, I've changed the `display` property accordingly. The style sheets are called "Basic" and "Large Type." Here's how you include them on a Web page so that browsers that understand how to do so will offer them as alternatives:

```
<link rel="stylesheet" title="Basic" href="basic.css"
  type="text/css"/>
<link rel="alternate stylesheet" title="Large Type"
  href="largetype.css" type="text/css"/>
```

Here are the CSS rules that make up the "Basic" style. The key is in the `display` property:

```
body {
  font-family: verdana, arial, helvetica, sans-serif;
  background-color: #ffffcc;
  color: teal;
}
.large {
  display: none;
```

```
}
.norm {
  display: block;
}
```

Compare that to the CSS rules here for the "Large Type" style sheet:

```
body {
  font-family: verdana, arial, helvetica, sans-serif;
  font-size: 130%;
  background-color: #ffffcc;
  color: teal;
}
.norm {
  display: none;
}
.large {
  display: block;
}
```

The HTML for the page is shown here. I've deliberately minimized the content for the page so the listing doesn't get too long:

```
<!DOCTYPE html PUBLIC "-//W3C//DTD XHTML 1.0 Transitional//EN"
   "http://www.w3.org/TR/xhtml1/DTD/xhtml1-transitional.dtd">
<html xmlns="http://www.w3.org/1999/xhtml">
<head>
<title>Multi-Style Page</title>
<meta http-equiv="Content-Type"
  content="text/html; charset=iso-8859-1" />
<link rel="stylesheet" title="Basic" href="basic.css"
  type="text/css"/>
<link rel="alternate stylesheet" title="Large Type"
  href="largetype.css" type="text/css"/>
</head>
<body>

<div class="norm">
<p>If you have trouble seeing the type on this page because of a
  vision problem, you can select an alternative view. Just select
  'Page Style' from the View menu in your browser and then choose
  a larger magnification.</p>
</div>

<div class="large">
<p>Since you're looking at this page using the Large Type version
```

```
    of the layout, things may look a bit big to you. You can switch
    back to the normal size of type by going to the View menu in
    your browser and selecting "Page Style" and then choosing the
    "Basic" version of this page.</p>
</div>

</body>
</html>
```

Figure 2.13 shows the page loaded using the "Basic" style. Notice the text at the top of the page.

Figure 2.13. Sample Page with Basic Style Loaded

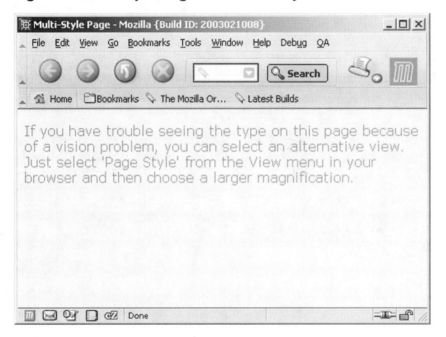

Figure 2.14 shows the page loaded using the "Large Type" style. As you can see, the first paragraph has changed appropriately.

Figure 2.14. Sample Page with Large Type Style Loaded

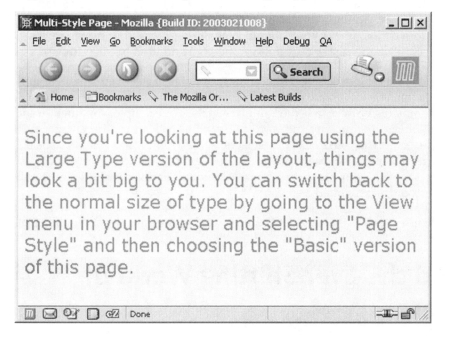

This design begs the question as to how a user with impaired vision could read the text that would make him or her aware of the availability of the "Large Type" style. But I figure that if drive-up windows at fast food restaurants can have Braille menus, I'm still in relatively safe user experience territory here!

One of the advantages CSS brings to the accessibility table is in the form of enabling Web designers to avoid practices that cause problems for users with special needs. For example, we commonly use `blockquote` and `table` tags, not to mark up quotations and tabular data, but for layout purposes. This "tag misuse" seems harmless, but when a browser that's designed, for example, to read a Web page aloud to a blind user encounters these misused tags, the results can be unintelligible to the user.

Another way that CSS supports accessibility is in the ability to specify fonts accurately and flexibly. Prior to the emergence of CSS, many Web designers, who wanted to specify a particular font for a layout, would use a graphical representation of the font because they couldn't be sure the user's system would have the appropriate font—or a reasonable facsimile to substitute. But the ability of CSS to specify gradually and gracefully degrading font families, eradicates the necessity for this use of graphics. This, in turn, makes it possible for Web browsers that read the text on a page in a synthesized voice, to do so. These browsers skip graphics, so they won't help the user understand text that's displayed in a graphical form (though, of course, a good Web designer would be sure to include, with images, meaningful `alt` tags that can be read and used by such browsers).

Using CSS properties such as `text-indent`, `text-align`, `word-spacing` and `font-stretch`, you can create designs that would otherwise cause browsers used by vision-impaired visitors to behave unintelligibly. For example, you might want the visual effect of spreading the word W E L C O M E over a broad space. If you do this simply by separating the letters of the word, a browser that speaks the content of the site will say each letter separately. If, on the other hand, you use `font-stretch`, you can keep the word pronounceable, while gaining the visual effect of the separated letters.

These are just some of the ways CSS can be used to improve the accessibility of your site.

CSS and the Ever-Shifting World of Browsers

The CSS "standard" is relatively recent, and the latest version, CSS2, is even newer. So, it's not surprising that older browsers don't do as good a job of supporting CSS as the newer ones. As the browser manufacturers release new versions of their products, CSS support gets better. Unfortunately, but understandably, a good many users refuse to upgrade their browsers every time a new release appears.

As a Web designer, you have to decide, usually in concert with your client or manager, how much you're willing to worry about support for older browsers. Regardless of how you answer that question, a helpful rule to keep in mind is this: wherever possible, design your pages so that a user with a browser that does not provide good CSS support will still be able to view the site.

Table 2.1 summarizes the browsers that most Web designers today aim to support to some degree. I've grouped the browsers into "ancient," "old," "recent," and "new" categories based on these criteria:

❑ Ancient browsers provide zero support for CSS. Any style tags in your Web pages or external style sheets are simply ignored.

❏ Old browsers provide marginal and often imperfect support for CSS and should not be counted on to render your styles correctly.

❏ Recent browsers provide nearly complete support for CSS1 and render at least some CSS2 features correctly as well.

❏ New browsers support all of CSS1 and most, if not all, of CSS2.

Table 2.1. Browsers Categorized by CSS Support

CSS Support Category	Browsers
Ancient	Netscape Navigator 3 and earlier Internet Explorer 2 and earlier Opera 3.5 and earlier
Old	Internet Explorer 3 and 4 Internet Explorer 5 for Windows Netscape Navigator 4 Opera 4
Recent	Internet Explorer 5 for Macintosh Internet Explorer 5.5 for Windows Opera 5
New	Internet Explorer 6 for Windows Netscape 6 and 7 Mozilla 1 Opera 6 and 7

There are many minor browsers and variations that aren't listed in Table 2.1. If you need to examine any particular browser, visit the W3C's CSS site[1] for a more complete listing.

In an intranet situation where you can control browser selection, you can freely use CSS1 and major portions of CSS2's interesting functionality. If you're designing pages for a public site, however, you probably still need to be concerned with supporting the older browsers listed in Table 2.1. The rest of this chapter is devoted to the basic design and coding issues you'll encounter as you work

[1] http://www.w3.org/Style/CSS/

with older browsers. Appendix C, provides a more complete reference to browser idiosyncrasies; our focus here is on techniques for dealing with the most common issues you're likely to encounter.

Accommodating Older Browsers

If you prepare a Web page using CSS techniques and publish it on the Web, users with ancient browsers are likely to experience it as a completely plain-looking page. Depending on the degree to which you apply CSS to your Web design, the user may see only a page whose text is formatted as the defaults in his or her browser dictate. This isn't necessarily A Bad Thing, but you can go further in supporting these ancient browsers if you want, or need, to do so.

First, you can use a browser-detecting JavaScript, sometimes called a "sniffer", to detect visitors to your site who use ancient browsers. You can then either direct them to a place to download a more current browser—and essentially slam the door in their faces, or warn them that they're going to have a less-than-satisfactory experience because of their browser's age. HotScripts.com[2] lists a number of sniffer scripts you can download for free. There are dozens of these scripts, so there's no sense in writing your own.

Alternatively, you could create a separate, decent-looking layout with straight HTML, and use scripting to redirect the user to this alternative page. That's a lot of work to go through, and statistically it will almost certainly not be worth it unless your circumstances are unusual. For example, your target audience is one of those government offices or educational institutions where ancient browsers are still the rule for budgetary or other reasons.

You can get a pretty good idea of the mix of browsers on the Web by visiting Chuck Upsdell's well-maintained BrowserNews site[3]. As he warns, you must use generic statistics carefully; they can be easily skewed. Ultimately, you'll want your Web host to perform some traffic analysis on your site, so you can see the profile of users who visit it.

Second, you can take advantage of the way HTML and CSS work together to create a page that looks good in an ancient browser, without interfering with the layout a new browser would produce by following CSS style rules. For example, you can include in your document's <body> tag some of the now-deprecated attributes that CSS overrides, as shown here:

---

[2] http://www.hotscripts.com/JavaScript/Scripts_and_Programs/Redirection/Browser_Based/
[3] http://www.upsdell.com/BrowserNews/stat.htm

```
<body text="#ffff00" link="green" vlink="green" bgcolor="#cc00cc"
  background="nightsky.jpg">
```

Now, if you include for this page a style sheet that supplies values for some or all of these properties, a new browser with CSS support will use those values in preference to the ones hard-coded in the <body> tag. But, a browser that ignores the CSS, will be perfectly happy with the values embedded in the tag.

If, using this technique, you want to specify fonts to be applied to text elements and headings, you'll have to enclose the text element you want to affect within a <font> tag, rather than embedding the font information within the element's tag. Otherwise, the provision of a specific local style for a particular piece of content would override your embedded and external style sheet instructions. Here's an example of the right way to use this technique—this allows ancient browsers to display your page the way you want, while newer browsers use CSS:

```
<font face="Verdana, Arial, sans-serif" size="3">
<h1>Company News and Views</h1></font>
```

Here's the wrong way, where the <font> tag will override any CSS applied to the <h1> tag:

```
<h1><font face="Verdana, Arial, sans-serif" size="3">
Company News and Views</font></h1>
```

You may also find it advantageous to use HTML comment symbols at the beginning and end of your <style> container, as shown in the code fragment below. This will cause at least the ancient browsers, plus some older versions, to ignore your <style> information completely, rather than simply ignoring the tags and displaying the rules as text on your page.

```
<style type="text/css">
<!--
   ...style rules go here...
-->
</style>
```

As I said earlier, these techniques are not only time consuming; they are concessions to the lack of support for Web standards. I recommend you avoid them if at all possible.

In fact, I'd be remiss if I didn't tell you that what you should really do is get on board the Web Standards Project (WaSP) Browser Upgrade Initiative[4]. Founded

---

[4] http://webstandards.org/act/campaign/buc/

in 1998, The Web Standards Project (WaSP) fights for standards that reduce the cost and complexity of development, while increasing the accessibility and long-term viability of any site published on the Web. I was one of the charter members of the WaSP Steering Committee when I was at CNET Builder.com, and I remain a firm believer in what they've done—and continue to do—to make our lives as Web designers easier.

Dealing with Broken Browsers

OK, this section should really be called "Tip-Toeing Your Way around Netscape Navigator 4." A long time ago, in a galaxy far, far away, during the Browser Wars, Netscape version 4 managed to foul up support for just enough CSS for most Web designers to consider it the bane of their existence.

Although Netscape Navigator 4.x accounts for only 2-5% of all browsers on the Web as of this writing, it was among the most widely-disseminated browsers of its time. This means it crops up in lots of places, often when you don't expect it. The Web community's opinion about support for Netscape 4 remains divided. It won't shock you to find that I'm on the side that argues we shouldn't go out of our way to support such a messy product.

On the other hand, this decision isn't always left in the hands of Web designers. Sales, marketing, advertising, and tech support folks may have a different view. So if you find yourself required to support Netscape 4 visitors, you have a challenge ahead! Here's a recipe that will lead to at least some significant success.

1. Refer to Appendix C, which provides a complete reference to which CSS properties work in which browsers.

2. With that information in front of you, browse through the HTML of your Web pages, searching for tags that are problematic in Netscape 4.

3. As you identify style problems, fix them using the techniques outlined above. Shielding by using deprecated tags is the most common.

4. Here's the tricky part. Create a separate, external style sheet that contains the styling for those areas with which Netscape 4 has problems. Now, in the head portion of your document, import this style sheet with a different syntax, called the **import at-rule** approach, as shown here:

```
<style type="text/css">
@import url(notfornav4.css);
</style>
```

Netscape 4 doesn't support this syntax for style sheet import, so it simply skips over that step—and the style sheet containing the styles that will break your layouts in Netscape 4 is never imported.

We'll talk more about dealing with browser idiosyncrasies in Chapter 12.

Summary

In this chapter, I described the primary uses of CSS, explained a few things for which CSS is not well suited, and spent some time talking about how CSS techniques can make your Web pages more accessible to people with special needs.

I also explained how ancient, old, recent, and new browsers support CSS in varying degrees, and how you can accommodate both older and broken browsers. Finally, I outlined a technique for ensuring that the newer browsers will show your pages correctly, regardless of the degree to which your pages implement CSS.

Chapter 3, focuses in greater detail on the how of CSS: how rules are included in tags, embedded in pages and loaded from external files, and how the various locations of CSS figure into determining which rules get applied in what sequence. I'll also explain the various selectors and structures of CSS rules, and the units and values you'll use in all rules that require specific measurements. That will conclude our detailed overview of CSS and lay the groundwork for its application to our site design project, which begins in Chapter 4.

3

Digging Below The Surface

This chapter completes our look at the "mechanics" of CSS: the background you need to have to work with the technology. It covers six major topics:

❏ Quick review of the three methods for assigning CSS properties to HTML documents

❏ Use of shorthand properties to group values for a related set of properties in a single statement

❏ Workings of the inheritance mechanism in style sheets

❏ Structure of a style, including variations on the use of selectors for determining with great precision exactly what is affected by a style

❏ Units and values that can appear in styles to express sizes, locations, and other properties, and how they are used

❏ CSS comments, which can be used to place human-readable notes in your CSS code

Applying CSS to HTML Documents

In Chapter 1, I introduced the three methods for applying style sheet properties to HTML documents. I will briefly review them here to jog your memory.

❑ **Inline styles**: We can use the `style` attribute, which is available for the vast majority of HTML elements, to directly assign CSS properties to HTML elements.

```
<h1 style="font-family: 'Comic Sans'; color: blue;">
  Welcome</h1>
```

This method is best reserved for when you want to try out quickly one or more CSS properties to see how they affect an element. You should never use this method in a practical Web site, as it misses almost every advantage that CSS has to offer.

❑ **Embedded styles**: We can use the `<style>` tag in the `head` portion of any HTML document to declare CSS **rules** that apply to the elements of the page.

```
<style type="text/css">
<!--
h1, h2 {
  color: green;
}
h3 {
  color: blue;
}
-->
</style>
```

This form of CSS offers many advantages over inline styles, but is still not as flexible or powerful as external styles (see below). I recommend you only use embedded styles when you are certain the styles you are creating will only be useful in the current page. Even then, the separation of code offered by external styles can make them a preferable option, but embedded styles can often be more convenient for quick-and-dirty, single-page work.

❑ **External styles**: We can use a `<link>` tag in the `head` portion of any HTML document to apply a set of CSS rules in an external file to the elements of the page.

```
<link rel="stylesheet" type="text/css" href="mystyles.css" />
```

The recommended method for applying CSS to HTML, external styles offer the full range of performance and productivity advantages that CSS can provide.

Using Shorthand Properties

Most property names take a single item as a value. When you define a property with a collection of related values (e.g. a list of fonts for the font-family property), the values are separated from one another by commas and, if any of the values include embedded white space or reserved characters such as colons, they may need to be enclosed in quotation marks.

In addition, there is a special set of properties called **shorthand properties**. Such properties let you use a single property declaration to assign values to a number of related properties. This sounds more complicated than it is.

The best-known shorthand property is font. CSS beginners are usually accustomed to defining font properties one by one:

```
h1 {
  font-weight: bold;
  font-size: 12pt;
  line-height: 14pt;
  font-family: Helvetica;
}
```

But CSS provides a shorthand property, font, that allows this same rule to be defined much more succinctly:

```
h1 {
  font: bold 12pt/14pt Helvetica;
}
```

All shorthand properties are identified as such in Appendix C.

How Inheritance Works in CSS

Before you can grasp some of the syntax and behavior of CSS rules, you need a basic understanding of the inheritance CSS uses.

Every element on an HTML page belongs to the document's inheritance tree. The root of that tree is *always* the html element, even in documents that fail to include the html tag explicitly.

Commonly, the html element has only two direct descendants in the inheritance tree: head and body.

Figure 3.1 shows a simple HTML inheritance tree for a small document.

Figure 3.1. Sample HTML Inheritance Tree Diagram

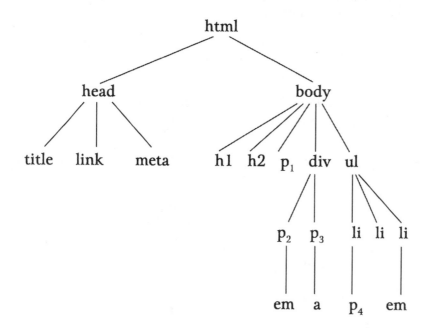

As you can see, the document has in its head the standard title and link elements, the latter of which probably links to an external style sheet. It also includes a meta element (most likely to set the document's character set).

The body consists of five elements: an h1, an h2, a p element (labeled p1 so we can refer to it easily), a div and a list (ul) element. The div element, in turn, contains two paragraph elements, one of which has an emphasis (em) element, and the other of which contains an anchor (a) element. The ul element includes three list item (li) elements, one of which includes an emphasis (em) element, while another contains a paragraph element labeled p4.

Paragraph element p1 is a direct descendant of the body.

Each element in an HTML document has a parent element (with the exception of the root html element), and is said to be a child of its parent element. In Figure 3.1, for example, p2's parent is the div. p2 would be described as a child of the div.

Some elements in an HTML document—and most of them in a complex document—are descendants of more than one element. For example, in Figure 3.1, the paragraph element p1 is a descendant of body and html. Similarly, paragraph elements p2 and p3 are descendants of the div element, the body element, and the html element. Paragraph element p4 is tied with several other elements in the document for the most ancestors: an li, the ul, the body, and the html elements. This notion of element hierarchy is important for two reasons.

First, the proper use of some of the CSS selectors you'll work with depends on your understanding of the document hierarchy. There is, for example, an important difference between a descendant selector and a parent-child selector. These are covered in detail in the section called "Selectors and Structure of CSS Rules".

Second, many properties for which you don't supply a specific value for a particular element will take on the value assigned to the parent element. This means, for example, that if you don't explicitly define a font-family property for the h1 element in the document diagrammed in Figure 3.1, it will use the font defined in the body tag. If no explicit font-family is defined there either, then both body text and the h1 heading use the font defined by the browser as the default. In contrast, setting the width property of an element will *not* directly affect the width of child elements. font-family is an **inherited property**, width is not.

Inherited properties, properties that are inherited from ancestors by default, are indicated in Appendix C. In addition, you can set any property to the special value inherit, to cause it to inherit the value assigned to the parent element.

This inheritance issue can be tricky to understand when you deal with fairly complex documents. It is particularly important when you're starting with a site that's been defined using the traditional table layout approach, in which style information is embedded in HTML tags. When a style sheet seems not to function properly, you'll frequently find the problem lies in one of those embedded styles from which another element is inheriting a value.

Selectors and Structure of CSS Rules

Recall from Chapter 1, that every CSS style rule consists of two parts: a selector, which defines the type(s) of HTML element(s) to which the style rule applies, and a series of property declarations that define the style.

So far, we've seen only simplistic selectors. Typically, they've contained only one element:

```
h1 {
  font-size: 18px;
  text-transform: capitalize;
}
```

We have encountered one or two instances where a single rule is designed to apply to more than one *kind* of HTML element:

```
h1, h2, h3 {
  font-size: 18px;
  text-transform: capitalize;
}
```

These are the most basic selectors in CSS. There are many others. Table 3.1 summarizes all the selector types available in CSS, roughly from simplest to most complex. The remainder of this section describes each type of selector in detail, in the order in which they appear in Table 3.1. Selector types that are defined for the first time in the CSS2 specification or that have changed between CSS1 and CSS2 are marked with "(CSS2)."

Table 3.1. Types of CSS Selectors

Selector Type	Use or Meaning	Example(s)
universal selector (CSS2)	Apply rule to all elements in document.	`*` (no selector)
element type	Apply rule to all HTML elements of the selector's type.	`h1` `p`
class selector	Apply rule to all HTML elements of the type preceding the period (or all, if none is specified) whose definition makes them part of the class following the period of the selector.	`.articletitle` `h1.important`
ID selector	Apply rule to only one element in the entire document: the one whose `id` attribute matches the string following the pound sign (hash mark) in the selector.	`#special3` `p#special52`
pseudo-element selector (CSS2)	Apply rule to occurrences of the pseudo-element.	`p:first-letter` `p:first-line` `h1:first-child`
pseudo-class selector (CSS2)	Apply rule to occurrences of the pseudo-class, whose appearance may change as the user interacts with the page.	`a:hover` `a:active` `a:focus` `a:link` `a:visited` `body:lang(d)`
descendant selector	Apply rule to all elements of the type listed last in the selector, but only when they occur within the other element type(s) given.	`p em` `p.wide em`

Selector Type	Use or Meaning	Example(s)
parent-child selector (CSS2)	Apply rule to all elements of type specified to the right of the ">" that are *children* of the elements to the left of the ">" (stricter form of the descendant selector).	`body > p`
adjacent selector (CSS2)	Apply rule to all elements of type specified to the right of the "+" that are physically adjacent (in the HTML code, not necessarily on the visible page) to elements of the type to the left of the "+".	`h1+h2` `p+h3`

attribute selector (CSS2)	Apply rule to all elements with attributes matching the profile specified in square brackets.	`p[align]`
		`input[type="text"]`
		`img[alt~="none"]`
		`body[lang|="en"]`

Universal Selector

The universal selector has no real practical value by itself. A style rule with no selector applies to all elements of all types on a Web page, so the asterisk is superfluous.

However, the universal selector can come in handy in specific situations involving, for example, attribute selectors, which I explain later in this section.

In this example, all elements in the page are given a text color of red:

```
* {
  color: red;
}
```

Element Type Selector

The single element selector is the most common selector. It specifies one HTML element type with no qualifiers or enhancements.

In the absence of other style rules applying to the element type provided in the selector, this rule applies to all such elements on the page.

In this example, we specify the text and background colors (black and white, respectively) for the document by assigning these properties to the body element:

```
body {
  color: black;
  background-color: white;
}
```

Class Selector

To apply a style rule to a potentially arbitrary group of elements in a Web page, you'll need to define a class in the style sheet, and then identify through their HTML tags the elements that belong to that class.

Defining a class in a style sheet requires that you precede the class name with a period. No space is permitted between the period and the name of the class. The following style sheet entry defines a class named special. Because there's no HTML element name associated with the class, any type of element on a page using this style sheet can be identified with the class, as you'll see in a moment.

```
.special {
  font-family: verdana, arial, sans-serif;
}
```

If you want to include only elements of a particular type in your class, you can use the more specific selector shown here:

```
p.special {
  font-family: verdana, arial, sans-serif;
}
```

The above style rule would apply only to paragraph elements that were identified as being members of the class called special.

Within the HTML markup, you can indicate that an element belongs to a class by using the element's class attribute:

```
<p class="special">Paragraph of stuff.</p>
```

An HTML element can belong to multiple classes if you wish, simply by listing the classes (separated by spaces) in the class attribute:

```
<p class="special exciting">Paragraph! Of! Stuff!</p>
```

If you define an element-specific class such as the `p.special` example above, and then associate that class (in this case, `special`) with an element of any other type, the style rule simply does not apply to that element.

ID Selector

The ID selector permits you to identify single instances of HTML elements where you wish to override the style properties set in, for example, a class style rule. Like a class selector, an ID selector requires definition in the style sheet and explicit inclusion in the HTML tag. Use the "#" symbol to identify an ID selector[1]. IDs must be unique within a document; no two HTML tags in a single document should have the same ID.

This style sheet rule defines a rule for an element with the ID `unique`:

```
#unique {
   font-size: 10px;
}
```

The code below shows how to indicate the element to be affected by the above rule using the HTML `id` attribute:

```
<h4 id="unique">This will be a very tiny headline</h4>
```

For example, if you had five `<div class="sidebar">` items on your page, but you wanted to style differently the one responsible for displaying your site's search box, you could do so like this:

```
div.sidebar
{
    ...
}
#searchbox
{
    ...
}
```

---

[1] You can optionally confine the ID's use to an element of a specific type by preceding the # with the HTML element's tag name (e.g. `div#searchbox`). But, as you can have only one element with the specific ID in your document, it seems silly to confine it to a specific element type.

Now, if both of these rules define a `background-color` property, and your search box tag was `<div id="searchbox" class="sidebar">`, then the search box would get all the `sidebar` properties assigned to it, but it would take its `background-color` from the `#searchbox` rule. The guidelines for cascading overlapping rules (discussed in Chapter 9), in combination with the ID selector, let you avoid having to redefine all the `sidebar` properties in a special `searchbox` class.

However, you *could* just as easily define a class and apply it to the exceptional element (the search box, in this example). This is more flexible, although perhaps not as efficient in terms of code space. For example, after you've identified a class or other rule that applies to all level three headings except one, and if you've used an ID selector for the exception, what do you do when a redesign or content change requires even one more such exception? The ID selector solution breaks down immediately in that situation.

It appears from my testing that not all of the newer browsers enforce the rule that the ID be unique in the document. Instead, they apply the ID rule to *all* elements in the document that carry the ID. That makes the ID essentially equivalent to the class selector. This is clearly not what the CSS specification had in mind, but it is how many of the browsers I've tested behave.

Pseudo-Element Selector

This and all the remaining selectors in this section require a browser that supports the CSS2 specification.

The pseudo-element and pseudo-class selectors are unique among the CSS selectors in that they have no equivalent HTML tag or attribute. That's why they use the prefix "pseudo", meaning "false."

So far, the CSS specification has defined only three pseudo-elements: `first-letter`, `first-line`, and `first-child`. While the first two of these phrases mean something to us humans, it's ultimately up to each browser to interpret them when rendering HTML pages using these pseudo-elements. For example, does `first-line` mean "first sentence" or does it mean first physical line displayed, a value that changes as the user resizes the browser? The `first-child` pseudo-element, on the other hand, is not browser-dependent. It refers to the first descendant of the element to which it is applied, in accordance with the HTML document hierarchy described in the section called "How Inheritance Works in CSS".

To define a pseudo-element selector for a style rule, precede the pseudo-element name with a colon. Here's an example:

```
p:first-letter {
  font-face: Gothic, serif;
  font-size: 250%;
  float: left;
}
```

This creates a drop-caps effect for the first letter in every paragraph on the page. The first letter in each paragraph will be a Gothic letter 2.5 times larger than the usual type used in paragraphs. The `float` style property, which we discuss in Chapter 6, ensures the remaining text in the paragraph wraps around the enlarged drop-cap correctly.

Pseudo-Class Selector

The pseudo-class selector is exactly like the pseudo-element selector, with one exception. A pseudo-class selector applies to a whole element, but only under certain conditions.

The current release of CSS2 defines the following pseudo-classes:

- ❑ `:hover`

- ❑ `:active`

- ❑ `:focus`

- ❑ `:link`

- ❑ `:visited`

- ❑ `:lang()`

A style sheet, then, can define style rules for these pseudo-classes like this:

```
a:hover {
  color:#ffcc00;
}
```

All anchor tags will change their color when the user hovers over them with the cursor. As you can see, this means the pseudo-class selector comes into play only when the user interacts with the affected element.

The `:lang()` pseudo-class[2] refers to the setting of the `lang` attribute in an HTML element. For example, you can define a paragraph in a document as being written in German, with a tag like this:

```
<p lang="de">Deutsche Grammophone</p>
```

If you wanted, for example, to change the font family associated with all elements in the document written in German, you could write a style rule like this:

```
:lang(de) {
  font-family: spezialitat;
}
```

Don't confuse this `lang` attribute with the `language` attribute that applies to tags related to the *scripting* language being used in a script or on a page.

Descendant Selector

Recall that all HTML elements (except the `html` element) are descendants of at least one other HTML element. To apply a CSS style rule to an element that's a descendant of another type of element, use the descendant selector.

A descendant selector, such as the one shown in the following style rule, restricts the applicability of the rule to elements that are descendants of other elements. The descendant selector is read from right to left to determine its scope. Spaces separate the element types.

```
li em {
  font-size: 16px;
  color: green;
}
```

The style rule describes a 16-pixel-high font size and a color of green to be applied to any text contained in an em element (emphasis) *only* where the emphasized text is a descendant of a list item.

In the fragment below, the first `em` element will be displayed in green, 16-pixel characters, while the second will not, as it doesn't appear within a list item.

```
<ul>
<li>Item one</li>
```

---

[2]Be aware that browser support for the `:lang()` pseudo-class is still very scarce. It is covered here mainly for the sake of completeness.

```
<li>Item <em>two</em></li>
</ul>
<p>
An <em>italicized</em> word.
</p>
```

It's important to note that the descendant relationship need not be an immediate parent-child connection. In Figure 3.1, for example, the following style rule would apply to the anchor element (a) even though it explicitly focuses on a elements that are descendants of div elements. This is because, in this case, the a element is the child of a paragraph that's contained in a div element.

```
div a {
    font-style: italic;
}
```

Parent-Child Selector

The parent-child selector causes a style rule to apply to element patterns that match a specific sequence of parent and child elements. It is a special case of the descendant selector discussed in the preceding section. The key difference between the two is that the pair of elements in a parent-child selector must be directly related to one another in a strict inheritance sequence.

A parent-child relationship is specified in a selector with the "greater-than" sign (>).

The following style rule:

```
body > p {
    font-weight: bold;
}
```

will *not* apply to the p2, p3 or p4 elements in Figure 3.1 because these paragraph elements aren't children of a body element. Even though they are *descendants* of body, they are not *children*. Only p1, which is a direct child of the body tag, will be affected by the rule.

As of this writing, Internet Explorer for Windows (up to and including version 6) distinguishes itself by being the only major browser that does not support parent-child selectors in its latest version. Because of this, careful use of descendant selectors is far more common, and the parent-child selector is often abused to specifically create styles that do not apply to Internet Explorer for Windows.

Adjacent Selector

Adjacency is unrelated to inheritance. Adjacency refers to the sequence in which elements appear in an HTML document. As it happens, adjacent elements are always siblings, but it's their placement in the document, rather than their inheritance relationship, that is the focus of this selector. This is demonstrated in this HTML fragment:

```
<h1>This is important stuff!</h1>
<h2>First important item</h2>
<h2>Second important item</h2>
```

The first h2 heading is *adjacent* to the h1 heading. The second h2 heading is not adjacent to the h1 heading. Neither h2 heading inherits from the h1 heading.

The adjacent selector uses the + sign as its connector, as shown here:

```
h1 + h2 {
  margin-top: 11px;
}
```

This style rule would put an extra 11 pixels of space between the bottom of an h1 heading and an immediately-following h2 heading. It's important to recognize that an h2 heading that follows a paragraph under an h1 heading would not be affected.

As of this writing, Internet Explorer for Windows (up to and including version 6) remains the only major browser that does not support adjacent selectors in its latest version. Because of this, the adjacent selector has not yet found widespread use in practical Web design.

Attribute Selectors

The group of selectors I'm lumping together as "attribute selectors" are among the most interesting of all the CSS selectors, because they almost feel like programming techniques. Each attribute selector declares that the rule with which it is associated is applied only to elements that have a specific attribute defined, or have that attribute defined with a specific value.

There are four levels of attribute matching:

❑ [*attribute*] – matches if the attribute is defined at all for the element(s)

- ❏ [*attribute*="*setting*"] – matches only if the attribute is defined as having the value of *setting*

- ❏ [*attribute*~="*setting*"] – matches only if the attribute is defined with a space-separated list of values, one of which exactly matches "`setting`"

- ❏ [*attribute*|="*setting*"] – matches only if the attribute is defined with a hyphen-separated list of "words" and the first of these words begins with *setting*

You might, for example, want to apply style properties to all single-line text input boxes (`<input type="text" />`) in your document. Perhaps you want to set their text and background colors to white and black, respectively. This style rule would have that effect:

```
input[type="text"] {
  color: white;
  background-color: black;
}
```

The third variation of the attribute selector described above searches the values assigned to an attribute, to see whether it contains the word you've specified (i.e. a value in a space-separated list).

For example, during the development of a Website, various graphic designers may have inserted temporary placeholder `alt` text tags, with the idea of returning to them later to finish them. You could call attention to the existence of such tags with a style rule like this:

```
img[alt~="placeholder"] {
  border: 8px solid red;
}
```

This selector will find all `img` tags whose `alt` attributes contain the word "placeholder" and will put an 8-pixel red border around them. That ought to be hard to miss!

The fourth variation is really useful only when you're dealing with the `lang` attribute. It enables you to isolate the first portion of the `lang` attribute, where the human language being used is defined. The other portions of the hyphen-separated value are ignored. It would be pretty rare to use this version, but it comes in handy when the language defined is `en-cockney` and you're really only interested in whether the language is English.

As you would expect by now, attribute selectors are not supported by Internet Explorer for Windows. As with other advanced selector types, this has prevented widespread adoption of attribute selectors, despite their obvious usefulness.

Selector Grouping

To apply a style rule to elements in an HTML document of several different types, use selector grouping. Separate with a comma each element type to which the rule is to be applied.

Here's a simple example of this type of selector:

```
h1, h2, h3 {
    font-family: verdana, arial, sans-serif;
    color: green;
}
```

The elements in the selector list need not be all of the same type or even of the same level of specificity. For example, the following style rule is perfectly legal. It applies a specific style to level 2 headings (h2) and to paragraphs whose class is defined as special:

```
h2, p.special {
    font-size: 22px;
}
```

You may include a space between the comma-separated items or not.

Expressing Measurements

Many of the properties you define in a CSS rule include measurements. These measurements tell the rule how tall or wide something is to be. Fonts, spacing, and positioning are the primary places you'll use such measurements.

There are two types of measurements: absolute and relative. An absolute measurement (e.g. setting a font-size to 18px, or 18 pixels) tells the browser to render the affected content as 18 pixels in height[3]. Technically, it actually tells the browser to use the specified font and scale its character height, so that the font's

---

[3]Again, if I wanted to be terribly precise, I would say that a pixel is actually a relative measurement, because its meaning is relative to the display medium on which the page is produced. But, in this context, "relative" means "relative to some other value in the style rule or in the HTML" and in that sense, pixels are absolute.

overall height is 18 pixels. Chapter 8, includes an explanation of font height and width.

Using relative measurements, on the other hand, instructs the browser to scale a value by some percentage or multiple, relative to the size of the object before the scaling takes place.

This example defines a style rule, in which all fonts in paragraphs on the page should be scaled to 150% of the size they would have been without this style:

```
p {
   font-size: 150%;
}
```

If you knew that, in the absence of such an instruction, all paragraphs on the page display their text at a size of 12 pixels, you could also accomplish the same thing this way:

```
p {
   font-size: 18px;
}
```

I recommend that you generally use the relative sizing values whenever you can. This technique works better when the user has set preferences for font sizes, and in situations where multiple style sheets could be applied. It's also more accessible, as visually impaired users can more easily increase the font size on the page by configuring their browsers' preferences.

All **length values** (the term CSS2 uses to describe any size measurement, whether horizontal or vertical) consist of an optional sign ("+" or "-") followed by a number (which may be a decimal value) followed by a unit of measurement. No spaces are permitted between the number and the unit of measurement.

Absolute Values

Table 3.2 shows the absolute values supported in CSS style sheets, and where it's not obvious, their meanings.

Table 3.2. Absolute Values in Style Sheets

Style Abbreviation	Style Meaning	Explanation
in	inch	Imperial unit of measure; 2.54cm
cm	centimeter	
mm	millimeter	
pt	point	1/72 inch
pc	pica	12 points (1/6 inch)
px	pixel	One dot on the screen

When a length of zero is used, no unit of measurement is needed. 0px is the same as 0. It doesn't make sense to give a unit of measurement when the length is zero units, for zero is the same distance in any unit of measurement.

Wherever you need to supply an absolute measurement for the size or position of an element in a style sheet rule, you can use any of the above abbreviations interchangeably. All of the following should produce precisely the same result:

```
font-size: 1in;
font-size: 2.54cm;
font-size: 25.4mm;
font-size: 72pt;
font-size: 6pc;
```

Pixels pose an entirely different set of issues. If you use the pixel as your unit of measurement (as we have, with few exceptions, so far), you'll find that your fonts maintain their size ratio with graphics on your page, as the page is displayed on different monitors, with varying resolutions and screen sizes.

In general, pixels are *not* the most appropriate measurement to use; nevertheless, they are the most common. Most designers probably prefer to work with pixels because they want maximum control over the user experience. And clients often insist on using pixel measurements, believing that this is the best way to replicate on-screen a design they've seen on a printed page.

A pixel is one point on a screen that can be on or off, blue or green (or whatever color combination is needed). For example, if you set your computer's display to a resolution of 800 pixels by 600 pixels—one of the most common screen resolution settings—then a pixel corresponds to 1/600 of the screen height. On a typical 15-inch display, the height is about 10.5 inches and the width is a little more than 13 inches[4]. A 12-pixel-high font display on that monitor would turn out to be about 1/50 of the 10.5-inch height of the display, or just a bit more than 1/5 inch.

If the user sets his or her resolution to 1024 pixels by 768 pixels, the same 16-pixel high font displays at 78% the height, or 0.16 inches. What if the user's on a 13-inch display instead of a 15-inch display? You begin to see the problem with using pixels.

So, if pixels are problematic, why have we used them so far? There are three reasons.

First, they are easily the most common absolute value measurements used on Web pages, despite the problems they seem to pose. Even though some Web purists argue against the use of pixels, there really is no perfect, absolute measurement that will work well in all circumstances. In such situations, people tend to stay with what they know and what works for them. In this case, that's pixels.

Second, pixels are the measurement used in virtually all computer software. This means users expect the text on their displays to get smaller if they increase the resolution and larger if they decrease it. Text that worked "better" and didn't undergo such transformation would jar the typical user.

Finally, whenever a measurement is being applied to something other than a font, pixel measurements are generally the best way to describe distance. Only fonts are measured in non-pixel units, primarily because they have lives of their own in print and other media. Everything else on a computer display is measured in pixels by default, so using pixels for positioning, and to describe the size of such elements as graphic images is appropriate.

Relative Values

Because of the problems posed by the use of *any* absolute value, the most flexible and least controlling way to approach measurements for style rules is to use relative units of measurement. Principally, these are em and %, although some people prefer to use the more obscure ex measurement. The "em" measurement is so named because it refers to the height of a capital "M" character in the given font, but in practice it is equal to the font-size of the current font. The "ex" measure-

---

[4]High school math would lead you to predict a 9- by 12-inch screen, but, unfortunately, 15 inch monitors don't normally have a full 15 inches of diagonal screen space. Perhaps computer manufacturers don't study Pythagoras.

ment is based on the height of the lower-case "x" character in a font (more commonly known as the **x-height** of the font) and is far less common than the em.

Both the em and the percentage generate font sizes based on the inherited or default size of the font for the object to which they're applied. In addition, ems and percentages are 1:100 equivalent. A size of 1em is identical to a size of 100%.

This description begs the question, "What's the default or inherited font size for a particular HTML element?" The answer is: it depends.

Prior to the emergence of Opera 5 for Windows, browsers set the default values for all fonts as part of their startup process. Users had no control. The browser defined a default. The Web designer overrode defaults willy-nilly. The user took what was presented.

Then, along came the idea of user choice. Not surprisingly, this development was facilitated by the emergence of CSS. Essentially, what the developers of the Opera browser did was create a local style sheet that the user could modify, and set his or her defaults to use. They also defined a nice graphical user interface through which the user could set preferences for these styles.

This was great for users, but Web designers found themselves in a quandary. If, for example, you assumed that browsers were going to default body text to a 12 point font size[5] (which was the *de facto* standard before the user-controlled preferences era), you could set a style to apply a 1.25em scaling to the text and get a 15 point font size for the text in question. It was nice and predictable.

Now, however, a 1.25em scaling applied to a font tells the browser to increase the size of the font to 1.25 times (125% of) its default size. If the user has set up his or her browser to show standard text at a height of 16 points, your 1.25em transformation brings the size up to 20 points.

When you stop and think about it, though, that's probably just fine. The user who chooses a larger base font size probably needs to see bigger type. If you want type that would otherwise be at 12 points to display at 14 for some good reason, then it's not unreasonable to expect that this new user will benefit in the same

---

[5]Just in case you were wondering, pixel sizes and point sizes are not equivalent, and the ratio between the two varies between browsers and operating systems. For example, the 12 point default font size used by most Windows browsers was rendered at 16 pixels on that platform. 12pt is equivalent to 16px on Windows browsers.

way from seeing the font used in this particular situation increase from his or her standard 16 points to 20.[6]

Most of the time, there's not really a reason to muck with the user's settings for font sizes, so changing them arbitrarily isn't a good idea. Before you apply this kind of transformation to a text segment on your Web design, ask yourself if it's really necessary. My bet is that nine times out of ten, you'll find it's not.

I would be remiss if I didn't point out that there are some inherent pitfalls in using relative font sizes, of which you should beware. Under some circumstances, relative font values can combine and multiply, producing bizarre results indeed.

For example, if you define style rules so that all text that is bold is displayed at 1.5 ems and all text that is italic is displayed at 1.5 ems, text that is bold *and* italic will display at 2.25 ems (1.5 x 1.5). This problem arises with child elements, which inherit from their parent container elements the *computed* values for measured properties and not the *relative* values. This is relatively easy to avoid, but if you overlook it, the results can be quite startling.

CSS Comments

More than likely, you are familiar with the concept of **comments** in HTML:

```
<!-- this is an HTML comment -->
```

Comments allow you to include explanations and reminders within your code. These are entirely ignored by the browser, and are normally included solely for the developer's convenience. If you've ever had to make changes to code that hasn't been touched in a few months, I'm sure you can appreciate the value of a few well-placed comments that remind you of how it all works.

CSS has its own syntax for comments. In HTML, a comment begins with <!-- and ends with -->. In CSS, a comment begins with /* and ends with */:

```
<style type="text/css">
/* This rule makes all text red by default.
   We include paragraphs and table cells for
   older browsers that don't inherit properly. */
body, p, td, th {
  color: red;
```

---

[6]If that's not the case, you probably want to rethink your reason for boosting the font size in the first place.

```
}
</style>
```

If you know much JavaScript, you'll recognize this syntax, which can be used to create multiline comments in that language as well. Unlike JavaScript, however, CSS does not support the single-line double-slash (//) comment style.

Summary

This chapter ends our overview of CSS technology. This chapter covered more of the syntactical and structural rules of CSS styles. Along the way, it explained the basic ideas involved in HTML document inheritance.

In Part II, which starts with Chapter 4, we'll launch into a full-scale project. Beginning with a traditional table-based layout for a Website, we'll start to focus on how to lay out the page using CSS rather than tables.

Page Layout with CSS

4

CSS Web Site Design

The development of any Website begins with its design. Typically, you'll have a statement from your client, or at least a rough idea in your head, of the intended capabilities of the site. If you're a by-the-book sort of developer, this may even take the form of a detailed specification document, which may describe the use cases (i.e. things that visitors can do) the site needs to support, the official specifications and recommendations the site must observe, and the list of browsers and platforms that must be able to access the site.

At this stage, it is customary for the designer to create a series of mock-ups, progressing from paper sketches, to prototype designs in a graphics application, to actual Web pages in HTML. If you have some experience in traditional site design, you probably produce even your very first paper sketches with a mind to the HTML code that will eventually replicate those layouts on screen.

As you move from tables to using CSS as your primary page layout tool, you'll have to learn a whole new set of design principles upon which to base your initial mock-ups. In this and the next few chapters of this book, I'll guide you through those principles so that you can come to grips with the new limitations, and let your imagination run wild with the new possibilities.

It is human nature to resist change. When you encounter things that CSS *can't* do, you'll be tempted to cling tightly to the heavy handed control offered by table-based design, rather than to brave the new world of CSS layout, where the layout of a hundred pages can hinge on a single rule. In this chapter, I'll endeavour to coax you out of your comfort zone by explaining some of the "big picture" advantages of CSS-based design, and present some success stories of Websites that have taken the plunge and are reaping the rewards of CSS layout.

Advantages of CSS Design

In the past few chapters, I've touched on a number of the powerful features of, and reasons for, using CSS for site layout. In this section, I'll formalize those arguments and present them all in one place. Not only do I hope to convince *you* of the merits of CSS, but I hope to give you the tools to sell *others* on the technology.

In the cutthroat world of freelance Web development, you will often be called upon to explain why you will do a better job than other developers bidding on the same project. If CSS layout is one of the tools in your Web design arsenal, the sites you build will benefit from the advantages presented here. Many of these advantages go well beyond ease of development, and translate directly to extra value for your clients. Let them know about this—it just might make the difference between winning the contract and losing out to a designer who lives and breathes table-based design.

Increased Stylistic Control

The *prima facie* selling point of CSS, and the reason most Web developers first choose to dabble in the technology, is that it lets you control many aspects of the appearance of your site that you simply cannot control with pure HTML. There is, for example, a waning fad of removing the underlines from hyperlinks and indicating them with some other style distinction (such as bold or colored text, or perhaps adding the underline when the mouse hovers over a link) that was sparked by the introduction of CSS. For a complete reference to the style properties that can be controlled with CSS, see Appendix C.

In addition to the sheer *number* of controllable style properties, CSS lets you apply them more uniformly to the range of HTML page elements that are available. With HTML, for instance, if you want to put a visible border around an area of the page, you need to use a table to do it, because you can add borders only to tables. CSS not only gives you greater control over the look of the border (solid, embossed, dotted, or dashed, thick or thin, red or green, etc.), but also lets you add a border to *any* page element—not just tables. The design rationale behind CSS is to give the designer as many options as possible, so any style property that exists can usually be applied anywhere that it could potentially make sense to do so.

CSS simply has more style properties, that can be applied to more page elements, than HTML has ever offered. If you had to choose between CSS and HTML as a means for specifying the design of your site, based only on which would afford you the most visual control, CSS would win hands down. Despite this, common practice is to use HTML for design wherever possible, and to resort to CSS whenever an effect is needed that HTML cannot produce. While the visual appearance of sites designed with this rationale is just as good, you miss out on all the other advantages of CSS.

Centralized Design Information

As I've already explained, the best way to use CSS in the design of a Website is to write one or more .css files to house all your style code, and then **link** it to the appropriate pages with the HTML <link> tag. With this approach, everything to do with the *look* of your site can be found in one place, and is not jumbled up with the *content* of your site.

The idea is that you should be able to change the content of your site without affecting its look, and vice versa. In traditional Web design, where HTML tags and attributes are used to specify how things look in the browser, the code for these two aspects of your site is mixed together, so anyone who wants to modify one of these must understand both, or risk breaking one while making changes to the other. The look and the content of the site are said to be **coupled**.

This principle of keeping code that serves different purposes in different places is known in the programming world as **decoupling**. If a site's style and content are decoupled, a Web designer can modify the look of the site by editing the .css file(s), while a content editor can add content to the site by editing the .html files.

Even more significant than facilitating organization and teamwork, this separation of code reduces **code duplication**. In HTML-based design, if you want the title at the top of every article on your site to be displayed in a large, red font, you have to put a <font> tag inside the relevant <h1> tag on every article page of your site. With CSS-based design, you can specify the font properties for the <h1> tags in one place, which saves you typing. And should you decide to change the appearance of these headings, you have only to modify the CSS file instead of each and every HTML file, which saves your *sanity*! These differences are illustrated in Figure 4.1.

Figure 4.1. CSS Centralizes your Design Code

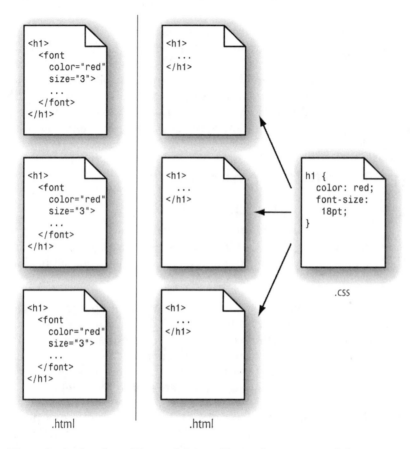

If you look closely at Figure 4.1, you'll see that on top of the organizational advantages described above, the browser has less code to download. On heavily-designed sites, or sites with hundreds of pages or more, this reduced download time can have a significant impact both on the user experience, and on your bandwidth costs.

Semantic Content Markup

When you use .css files to decouple the content and look of your site, as I've just described, a curious thing begins to happen to your HTML code. Because CSS affords you complete control over the appearance of page elements, you begin to choose tags because they describe the *structure* and *meaning* of elements of the page, instead of how you want them to look. Stripped of most or all of the presentational information, your HTML code is free to capture the **semantics** of your site's content.

There are a number of reasons why this is a desirable state of affairs, not the least of which is how easily you can find things when you're making changes to the content of your site. The easiest way to spot a CSS site is to use the "View Source" feature in your browser—if you can make sense of the code there within 10 seconds, chances are that you're not dealing with a site that uses table-based layout and other non-semantic HTML.

Search engine optimization (SEO) is greatly assisted by semantic HTML, because the fewer presentational tags the search engine has to wade through in analyzing your site, the greater your site's **keyword density**—an important metric in determining your site's ranking. As we'll see, CSS lets you control the position of an element in the browser window, largely independent of its position in the HTML document. So, if you have a newsletter subscription form or some other lengthy chunk of HTML that won't mean a whole lot to a search engine, feel free to move its code to the end of your HTML document and use CSS to ensure that it is displayed near the top of the browser window.

Increasingly supported by modern browsers is a feature of the HTML <link> tag[1], which lets you restrict a linked style sheet so that it affects only the page when it's displayed by a certain type of browser or display. For instance, you could link three .css files to a page: one that defined the appearance of the page on a desktop browser, another that dictates how the page will look when printed, and yet another that controls the display on mobile devices such as Internet-connected Personal Digital Assistants (PDAs). Only by using semantic markup, and allowing the CSS to take care of the display properties, is this sort of content repurposing possible.

Last, but certainly not least, are the vast improvements to accessibility that a site can garner by using semantic markup. We'll discuss these in detail in the next section.

Accessibility

Should you ever have the opportunity to observe a visually impaired individual browsing the Web, I highly recommend the experience. Alternatively, get yourself

---

[1] Specifically, the **media** attribute.

some screen reader software, switch off your monitor, and see for yourself what it's like.

Heavily designed Websites that make use of tables, images, and other nonsemantic HTML for layout are extremely difficult to use when the most natural way to experience a Website is to listen to it read aloud, from top to bottom. It's not uncommon for a modern Website to inflict 30 seconds or more of nested tables opening and closing, unidentified images for layout, and other nonsense, before the actual content begins. Now, if you think that sounds mildly annoying, imagine having to listen to it for each and every page of the sites that you visit!

Semantic HTML nearly eliminates this aural garbage, because it ensures that every tag in the document has a structural meaning that's significant to the viewer (or listener). An aural browser ignores the visual formatting properties defined in the CSS, so the user need not be bothered listening to them.

On a site that used semantic markup, for example, a visually impaired user would never have to wonder if a word was bold because it was more important, or just because it looked better that way. Elements that were displayed in bold for design reasons would have that property assigned using CSS, and the aural browser would never mention it. Elements that needed additional impact or emphasis would be marked up using the semantically meaningful <strong> and <em> tags, which are displayed by default as bold and italics in visual browsers.

A complete set of guidelines exists for developers who are interested in making their sites more accessible for users with disabilities. The Web Content Accessibility Guidelines 1.0[1] (WCAG) is recommended reading for all Web developers, with Guideline 3[2] treating the idea of avoiding presentational markup in favor of semantic markup.

Standards Compliance

The WCAG is not the only specification that advocates the use of CSS for the presentation properties of HTML documents. In fact, the latest HTML standards[3] themselves are written with this in mind!

---

[1] http://www.w3.org/TR/WCAG10/
[2] http://www.w3.org/TR/WCAG10/#gl-structure-presentation
[3] http://www.w3.org/MarkUp/#recommendations

The World Wide Web Consortium[4] (W3C) is the body responsible for publishing Recommendations (*de facto* standards) relating to the Web. Here are some of the W3C Recommendations that relate to using semantic markup and CSS:

HTML 4 (http://www.w3.org/TR/html4)

The latest (and last) major revision of the HTML Recommendation marks all non-semantic elements and attributes as **deprecated**[2]. The `<font>` tag[6], for example, is clearly marked as deprecated in this standard. Under the description of deprecated elements[7], the Recommendation has this to say:

> In general, authors should use style sheets to achieve stylistic and formatting effects rather than HTML presentational attributes.

XHTML 1.0 (http://www.w3.org/TR/xhtml1/)

A reformulation of HTML 4 as an XML document type, XHTML lets you use HTML tags and attributes, while also benefiting from the features of XML (mixing tag languages, custom tags, etc.).

This Recommendation includes the same tags and deprecations as HTML 4.

Web Content Accessibility Guidelines 1.0 (http://www.w3.org/TR/WCAG10/)

As described in the section called "Accessibility", the WCAG Recommendation strongly recommends using CSS and semantic markup in Web design to improve accessibility. I'll let the Recommendation speak for itself:

> Misusing markup for a presentation effect (e.g., using a table for layout or a header to change the font size) makes it difficult for users with specialized software to understand the organization of the page or to navigate through it. Furthermore, using presentation markup, rather than structural markup, to convey structure (e.g., constructing what looks like a table of data with an HTML PRE element) makes it difficult to render a page intelligibly to other devices

According to many Web developers, strict standards compliance is an idealistic goal that is rarely practical. One of the primary goals of this book is to demonstrate that this is no longer true. Today's browsers provide strong support for CSS and

---

[4] http://www.w3.org/

[2] A deprecated element or attribute is one that has been tagged for removal from the specification, and which therefore should not be used. For a document to strictly comply with the specification, it should not use any deprecated tags or attributes.

[6] http://www.w3.org/TR/html4/present/graphics.html#h-15.2.2

[7] http://www.w3.org/TR/html4/conform.html#deprecated

produce more consistent results when they are fed standards-compliant code. While bugs and compatibility issues still exist, they are no more insurmountable than the bugs that face designers who rely on noncompliant code.

CSS Success Stories

The following sites serve as great examples of what can be accomplished with CSS page layout:

SitePoint (http://www.sitepoint.com/)
I know, I know... it's unseemly to use my own publisher as an example of why CSS works, but you've got to hand it to these guys. They've not only taken a tired, table-laden layout and replaced it with a fresh, standards-compliant design, but they've also made the site vastly more usable in the process.

Though the flat colors in use on this site may look simplistic at first glance, this "low fat" approach to the design keeps the pages loading quickly, despite often lengthy content and a plethora of navigational options.

A List Apart (http://www.alistapart.com/)
Since its inception in 1998, this site, and the associated mailing list, has become one of the leading sources of information and advocacy for CSS design and layout. The site itself is a model of simplicity, but it demonstrates that simple doesn't have to mean boring or ugly.

Netscape DevEdge (http://devedge.netscape.com/)
DevEdge is Netscape's resource site for Web developers. With Netscape 6 and 7 having been based on a standards-compliant Web layout engine, it seemed only logical to redesign the site to take advantage of this technology. They've even published an article[13] that covers their approach to this redesign.

ESPN (http://www.espn.com/)
The first mainstream, commercial Website to be built with CSS page layout techniques, ESPN.com is the ice breaker that the Web design community has been waiting for!

When pitching a site design idea—especially when you propose to use "new" technologies like CSS layout—clients will often ask if you can show them another site that has implemented a similar solution successfully. Until now,

---

[13] http://devedge.netscape.com/viewsource/2003/devedge-redesign/

all the best examples of CSS site design were either sites written by Web developers, for Web developers, or personal sites that could afford to take risks because they weren't in it for the money.

For an in-depth interview with one of the designers behind this site, visit Netscape DevEdge[15].

Fast Company Magazine (http://www.fastcompany.com/)
The online presence for a popular business magazine, this site was redesigned to make use of CSS layout and semantic markup. The actual look and organization of the site hasn't changed drastically from its previous version, but thanks to CSS, its pages load much more quickly.

Our Sample Site: Footbag Freaks

For the rest of this book, I will relate each of the techniques we discuss, wherever possible, to a sample site that has been developed especially for this book. Called *Footbag Freaks*, this fictitious site can be found online at http://www.footbagfreaks.com/. The source code is also available for download from this book's Website[18]. You can see the front page of the *Footbag Freaks* site in Figure 4.2.

---

[15] http://devedge.netscape.com/viewsource/2003/espn-interview/01/
[18] http://www.sitepoint.com/books/

Figure 4.2. The Footbag Freaks Home Page

This site makes full use of CSS for both page layout, and the styling of text and other page elements. The HTML code is entirely semantic. The site has been designed and tested to work on the following browsers:

❏ Internet Explorer 5 or later for Macintosh and Windows

❏ Opera 6 or later

❏ Mozilla 1.0 or later and related browsers, including Netscape 6 or later and Camino

The site complies with the following W3C Recommendations:

❏ XHTML 1.0 (Strict)

❏ WCAG 1.0 (AAA Rating for Accessibility)

❏ CSS 2.0

Summary

In this chapter, I provided the justification for all that is to follow. I explained in detail the most important advantages that CSS has to offer for your Web design work. These advantages fell under the headings of:

❏ increased stylistic control

❏ centralized design information

❏ semantic content markup

❏ accessibility

❏ standards compliance

After presenting a few success stories—sites that have used CSS design techniques to good effect—I introduced our own, admittedly fictional, success story: *Footbag Freaks*. Throughout the rest of this book, we'll explore the wide range of CSS features and techniques that go into making a site like this one.

Chapter 5, begins this process by looking at how to build the skeleton of a page layout, and flesh out major pieces of design using, pure CSS techniques.

5

Building the Skeleton

Most books on CSS begin by teaching you how to deal with the bits and pieces of a Web page: fonts, colors, lists, and the like. Then, they move on to explaining the broader issues associated with CSS Positioning (CSS-P), which affect the *layout* of pages rather than the appearance of individual elements.

In this book, I take the opposite approach. I first look at the site-level and page-level issues involved with CSS design, so that we can understand the big picture perspective of page layout without tables (which is, after all, the primary thrust of this book). And later, in Part III, I'll discuss styling the content of the pages we'll be laying out in this and the next chapter.

This chapter focuses specifically on creating the basic structural layout of a Web page or site using CSS. In it, I'll discuss multi-column layouts—both in general and very specifically—as they relate to the *Foothag Freaks* site. I'll teach you about boxes, borders, and the famous box model of CSS design. I'll then apply these concepts to build the famed three-column layout that in many ways is the "holy grail" of CSS page layout.

Enumerating Design Types

One of the first decisions you have to make when you create any Website, but particularly one where you intend to put CSS to its most effective use, is how many different types of pages and elements you're going to need.

How Many Page Types?

Most sites use more than one basic page layout. The front, or index page, often has a different look and feel from the "inside" pages. In the *Footbag Freaks* site, for example, the specification tells us that bread-crumb navigation will appear on all but the front page. An inspection reveals that the large graphic that displays near the top of the front page does not appear on other pages of the site.

On a typically complex ecommerce site, you might run into far more page types. For example, such a site might include different layouts for its:

❑ front page (index)

❑ catalog pages

❑ secure ordering pages

❑ main content pages

❑ site map page

Some of these pages might display dynamic content that is stored in a database and generated in response to specific user requests. Others might be flat HTML pages that never change unless you redesign them.

The *Footbag Freaks* site appears to need only one *type* of page layout. The secondary page has fewer elements than the home page, but the relative positioning and layout of the common elements doesn't change from one page type to the other.

How Many Design Elements?

Figure 5.1. The Footbag Freaks Home Page

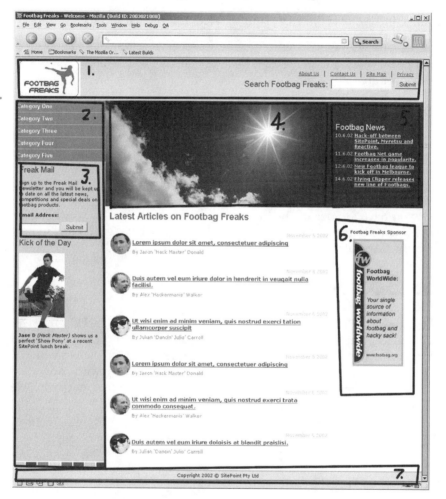

Looking at the *Footbag Freaks* home page, we can easily identify the following seven design elements, indicated in Figure 5.1:

1. the top of the page where the *Footbag Freaks* logo appears against a colored background

2. the left-hand column where the site's navigation is located

3. inside the navigation area, the text field for newsletter sign-up and related text

4. the large image area where the sun, the sky, and the hacky sack appear

5. the news area

6. the sponsor area

7. the footer where the copyright information appears

The second page of the site eliminates the fourth design element from this list and adds a submenu navigation element inside the main navigation. So, each page type has seven design elements, six of which are common, and one of which is unique to each page.

Now that you have an idea of the number of pieces of design for which you're going to define CSS rules, let's take a step back and get a basic grounding in how to use specific CSS rules to create these layouts and effects.

The CSS Box Model

From the perspective of a style sheet, everything you deal with in HTML pages can be viewed as living inside a box. This fact is generally far more obvious when you're formatting large chunks of content, like the seven design elements in the *Footbag Freaks* Website. But it's true even when you're dealing with individual components of those elements, like headings, lists, list elements, and even segments of text.

The basic CSS box model is shown in Figure 5.2.

Figure 5.2. Basic CSS Box Model

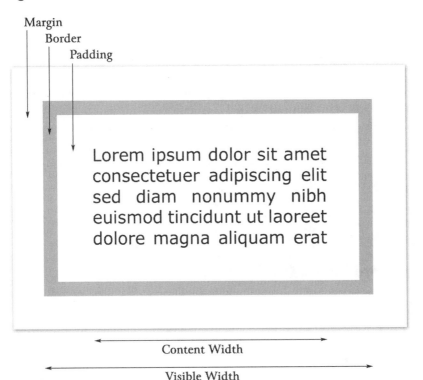

Margin
Border
Padding

Lorem ipsum dolor sit amet consectetuer adipiscing elit sed diam nonummy nibh euismod tincidunt ut laoreet dolore magna aliquam erat

Content Width

Visible Width

At the center of the CSS box model is the content itself. Don't think of this "content" as being the same as words or pictures that comprise the content of a news story or a set of links. The content is anything contained within the area of the box.

Notice from Figure 5.2 that the **visible width** of the box is determined by adding together the **content width**, the padding and the border. The margin determines the distance on each side between the visible box and adjacent elements. Similarly, the **visible height** of the box is determined by adding the content's height to the padding and border settings. Once again, the margin determines how far the box will be separated from adjacent objects vertically.

The width of each of these elements—margin, border, and padding—can be set using four CSS properties (one for each side of the box), or using a single **shorthand property**. Border behavior is slightly more complicated because a border can have not only a width but also visible characteristics such as line style and color.

I'll begin by explaining and demonstrating the use of padding in some detail. Then, I'll move on to a discussion of margins, which will be briefer, as it's so similar to padding. Finally, I'll discuss the border property and its variations.

For the next several sections, I'll use a basic, single-box layout to demonstrate CSS rule techniques. It starts out as in Figure 5.3 with no padding, border, or margin properties defined, so that the content is the same size as the box.

Figure 5.3. Starting Point for Box Model Demonstrations

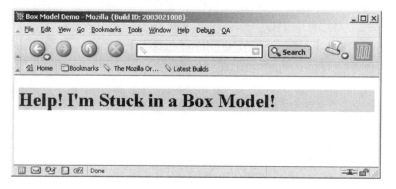

I've given the h1 element a gray background so you can see more easily the impact of the effects I'll be demonstrating. I'll describe the background-color property I've used here more fully in Chapter 7.

This HTML produces the page shown in Figure 5.3:

```
<!DOCTYPE html PUBLIC "-//W3C//DTD XHTML 1.0 Transitional//EN"
   "http://www.w3.org/TR/xhtml1/DTD/xhtml1-transitional.dtd">
<html xmlns="http://www.w3.org/1999/xhtml">
<head>
<title>Box Model Demo</title>
<meta http-equiv="Content-Type"
   content="text/html; charset=iso-8859-1" />
<style type="text/css">
<!--
h1 {
   background-color: #c0c0c0;
}
-->
```

```
</style>
</head>
<body>
<h1>Help! I'm Stuck in a Box Model!</h1>
</body>
</html>
```

Throughout the rest of this discussion, I'll be modifying only the style sheet information, so I'll reproduce only that section of the code, indicating any changes in bold.

Pixels Versus Percentages

Because the box model deals with the display of content on the screen, the pixel measurement (abbreviated px) is the most commonly used of the absolute measurement units in CSS. However, often we desire to create a "stretchy" layout, in which case it is necessary and appropriate to use the percentage model (with the % symbol), rather than pixels. I'll have more to say on this subject in Chapter 6.

Padding Properties

There are four properties that together define the padding around an object in a CSS rule: padding-left, padding-right, padding-top and padding-bottom.

Let's change just one of the padding settings to get a feel for how this works. Modify the style sheet in the sample file, so that it looks like the following fragment (remember that the new material is bold):

```
h1 {
   background-color: #c0c0c0;
   padding-left: 25px;
}
```

The result of this change is shown in Figure 5.4. Notice that the text now begins 25 pixels from the left side of the box, resulting in 25 pixels of blank, gray space to the left of the text.

Figure 5.4. `padding-left` Demonstration

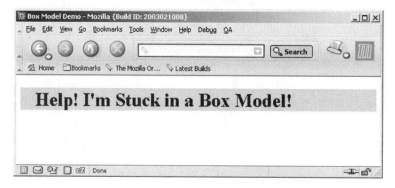

As you'd expect, you can set the other padding sizes the same way, as shown in this code fragment:

```
h1 {
  background-color: #c0c0c0;
  padding-left: 25px;
  padding-top: 15px;
  padding-bottom: 30px;
  padding-right: 20px;
}
```

You can see the effect of these changes in Figure 5.5.

Figure 5.5. All Four Padding Properties Defined

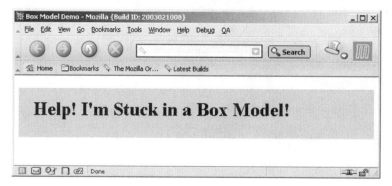

You may notice that the right side of the padding appears not to have worked. You asked for 20 pixels, but no matter how wide you stretch the window, the gray area defining the box that contains our h1 element just goes on and on.

This is because `padding-right` creates a space between the right edge of the text and the right edge of the heading, as represented by the gray box. This spacing is difficult to see in this case, because the heading automatically spans the width of the browser window, leaving plenty of room for the text to breathe on the right side. If you make the browser narrow enough, though, you can see the padding take effect.

Figure 5.6 demonstrates this principle. The first screenshot shows how the page in Figure 5.5 looks if you narrow the browser window so that there would be room on the first line for the word "in" if `padding-right` were not set as it is. The second screenshot reinforces this idea by showing the page resized so that one word only fits on each line. Notice that the right padding size looks, in several cases, large enough to accommodate the word on the next line. In fact, merely removing the `padding-right` property from the style sheet produces the result shown in the third screenshot.

Figure 5.6. Demonstration of Effect of `padding-right`

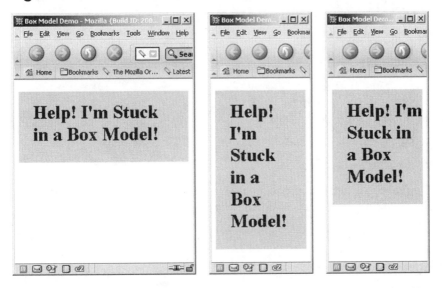

Because it's often necessary to adjust padding around objects in HTML, the CSS standards define a **shorthand property** simply called `padding`. You can give this property up to four values. Table 5.1 tells you how the properties will be assigned in each case.

Table 5.1. Effect of Multiple Values on `padding` Shorthand Property

No. of Values	Interpretation
1	Set all four padding values to this value.
2	Set the top and bottom padding to the first value, left and right padding to the second.
3	Set the top padding to the first value, right and left to the second value, bottom to the third value.
4	Set the top padding to the first value, right padding to the second, bottom padding to the third, and left padding to the fourth.[1]

[1]You can remember this as clockwise, starting from the top, or as TRBL (trouble), whichever you find easier to remember.

For example, the last code fragment above could be rewritten using the `padding` shorthand property as follows:

```
<style type="text/css">
<!--
h1 {
  background-color: #c0c0c0;
  padding: 15px 20px 30px 25px;
}
-->
</style>
```

To create equal top and bottom padding, and equal left and right padding, even though right padding is all but meaningless in this context, you could use:

```
<style type="text/css">
<!--
h1 {
  background-color: #c0c0c0;
  padding: 15px 25px;
}
-->
</style>
```

The result of this code fragment is shown in Figure 5.7.

Figure 5.7. Equal Top-Bottom and Left-Right Padding Using `padding` Shorthand

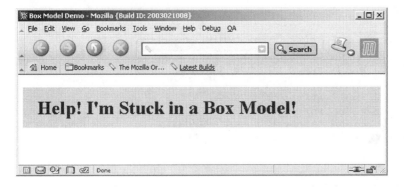

Finally, to create equal padding on all four sides of the h1 element, you could code this:

```
h1 {
  background-color: #c0c0c0;
  padding: 25px;
}
```

This code produces the result shown in Figure 5.8.

Figure 5.8. Equal Padding on All Sides Using `padding` Shorthand

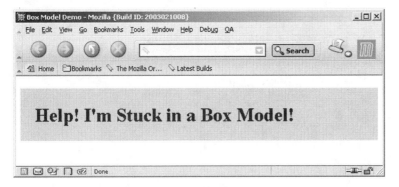

What if you use either ems or percentages for the padding values? The two have slightly different effects. The em unit scales the padding according to the size of the font of the content, while the percentage unit scales the padding according to the width of the block that contains the element. To demonstrate these effects, we'll work with a new HTML page that displays two headings against colored backgrounds on a page of a contrasting color.

Here's the HTML for that demo page.

```
<!DOCTYPE html PUBLIC "-//W3C//DTD XHTML 1.0 Transitional//EN"
   "http://www.w3.org/TR/xhtml1/DTD/xhtml1-transitional.dtd">
<html xmlns="http://www.w3.org/1999/xhtml">
<head>
<title>Box Model Demo</title>
<meta http-equiv="Content-Type"
   content="text/html; charset=iso-8859-1" />
<style type="text/css">
<!--
body {
   background-color: #808080;
}
h1, h4 {
   background-color: #c0c0c0;
}
-->
</style>
</head>
<body>
<h1>Help! I'm Stuck in a Box Model!</h1>
<h4>But it's not too crowded if you're just a little old h4
   heading like me! In fact, it's kind of cozy in here.</h4>
</body>
</html>
```

Notice that I've given the page a dark grey background and I've added an h4 element, which I've styled in the same CSS rule as the h1 element.

This HTML page displays as shown in Figure 5.9.

Figure 5.9. Proportional `padding` Page Starting Point

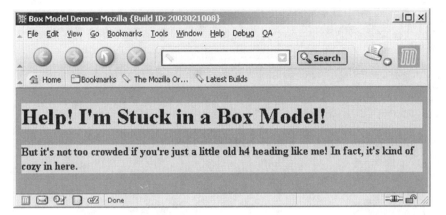

Now, let's change the style sheet in this page so that it uses the padding shorthand to create a 1em padding space around the objects. The code fragment below will do the trick:

```
body {
  background-color: #808080;
}
h1, h4 {
  background-color: #c0c0c0;
  padding: 1em;
}
```

As you can see in Figure 5.10, the amount of padding placed around the two heading elements is proportional to the size of the font in the elements themselves. Recall that 1em is equal to the height of the font in use. Consequently, much more space is placed around the h1 element than around the h4 element.

Figure 5.10. Using ems for Proportional Padding

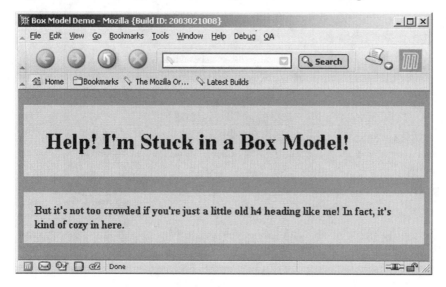

Now, let's see what happens if we use a percentage rather than an em for the proportional padding value. Change the HTML, so the style sheet looks like this:

```
body {
  background-color: #808080;
}
h1, h4 {
  background-color: #c0c0c0;
  padding: 10%;
}
```

The result of this change can be seen in Figure 5.11. Wow! There's a huge amount of space around those elements. The browser has applied 10% of the width of the page (the body is the containing block for heading elements) as the padding on all four sides.

Figure 5.11. Using Percentage for Proportional Spacing

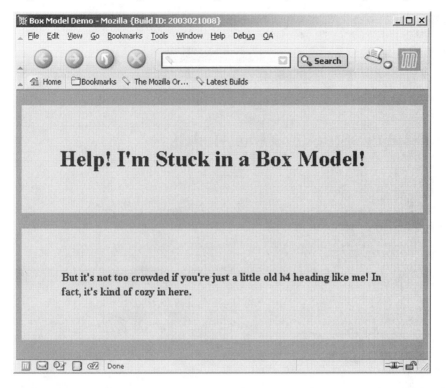

I've been using background color behind the text of the elements to make it easy for you to see the effect of these padding settings, but it's not necessary to have background colors behind those elements to position them. Figure 5.12 uses the same HTML code as Figure 5.11, the only difference being that I've removed the background colors of the body and the h1 and h4 elements. As you can see, they maintain their relative spacing.

Figure 5.12. Demonstration of `padding` Without Color Backgrounds

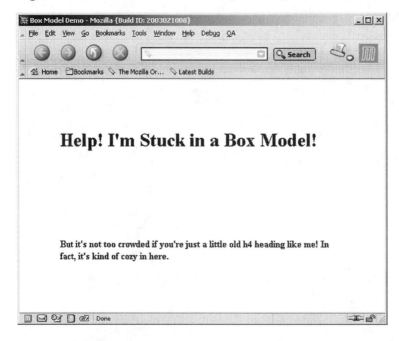

Margin Properties

The way we set margin properties is identical to the way we set padding properties. The property names substitute the word "margin" for the word "padding," including the shorthand property.

The difference between margins and padding is that margins exist *outside* the boundaries of the object, while padding exists *inside* those boundaries. Figure 5.13 illustrates this difference, based on the style sheet rules in the following code fragment.

```
body {
  background-color: #808080;
}
h1 {
  background-color: #c0c0c0;
}
h2 {
  background-color: #c0c0c0;
  margin-left: 5%;
```

```
}
p {
  background-color: #c0c0c0;
  margin-left: 20%;
}
```

Figure 5.13. `margin-left` Settings Push Content and Background Over

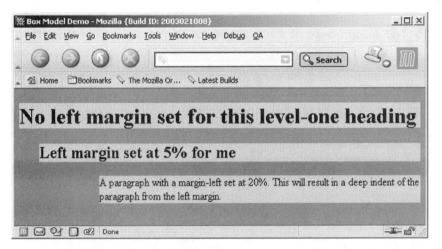

Notice that the second-level heading and the paragraph, for both of which we've set `margin-left` properties, are indented from the left edge of the browser. But here, unlike the example in which we set the `padding-left` property, the text *and* its background color block are indented. This is because the color block and the text are *inside* the content box and the margin is *outside* that box.

Let's next apply `padding-left` and `margin-left` settings to the code fragment.

```
body {
  background-color: #808080;
}
h1 {
  background-color: #c0c0c0;
}
h2 {
  background-color: #c0c0c0;
  margin-left: 5%;
  padding-left: 1em;
}
```

```
p {
  background: #c0c0c0;
  margin-left: 20%;
  padding-left: 10%;
}
```

As you can see in Figure 5.14, the margin has pushed the HTML elements and their surrounding background color blocks to the right, while the padding has moved the text to the right *within* the colored background blocks.

Figure 5.14. `margin-left` Combined with `padding-left` Setting

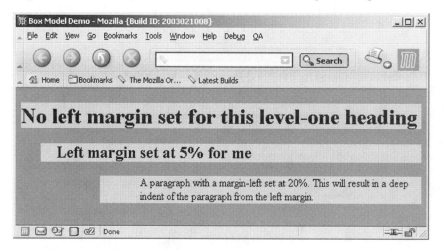

Horizontal margin effects are cumulative. Take a look at the following HTML code, and at Figure 5.15, which shows how it is rendered.

```
<!DOCTYPE html PUBLIC "-//W3C//DTD XHTML 1.0 Transitional//EN"
  "http://www.w3.org/TR/xhtml1/DTD/xhtml1-transitional.dtd">
<html xmlns="http://www.w3.org/1999/xhtml">
<head>
<title>Box Model Demo</title>
<meta http-equiv="Content-Type"
  content="text/html; charset=iso-8859-1" />
<style type="text/css">
<!--
body {
  background-color: #808080;
}
h1 {
  background-color: #c0c0c0;
```

```
}
h2 {
  background-color: #c0c0c0;
  margin-left: 5%;
  padding-left: 1em;
}
p {
  background-color: #c0c0c0;
  margin-left: 20%;
  padding-left: 10%;
}
li {
  background-color: #ffffff;
}
li p {
  margin-left: 10%;
}
-->
</style>
</head>
<body>
<h1>No left margin set for this level-one heading</h1>
<h2>Left margin set at 5% for me</h2>
<p>A paragraph with a margin-left set at 20%. This will result in
   a deep indent of the paragraph from the left margin.</p>
<ul>
<li>Item one</li>
<li><p>Paragraph item</p></li>
</ul>
</body>
</html>
```

Figure 5.15. Cumulative Effect of Horizontal Margin Settings

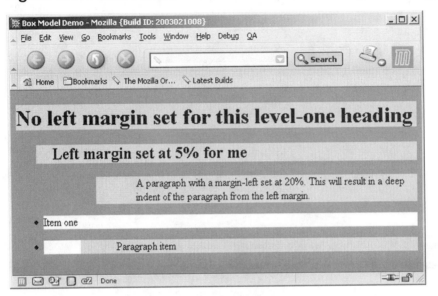

The big difference here is in the bulleted list. Notice that the first item in the list displays with no extra indentation. This is not surprising, as the style rules do not define any extra margin settings for an li element. Look at the second list element, however, which is a paragraph. The last style rule in the HTML above assigns a paragraph that is the descendant of an li element a margin-left setting of 10%. As you can see, this margin applies to the existing left margin of the bulleted list, which results in the paragraph item being pushed further to the right. Note also that this same element is a paragraph, so it retains the styling of all p elements, including their padding-left setting of 10%. This produces the additional indentation of the paragraph text within the gray box in the list.

If you load the above HTML (from the file boxmodel4.html included in the code archive for this book) and resize it, you'll notice that the indentation of the paragraph element inside the list changes as the width of the window changes. That's because I used a relative value of 20% for the margin and 10% for the padding. Both of these values are therefore calculated relative to the width of the containing block (the list item), which in turn takes its width from the browser window. The bigger the browser window, the bigger the margin and padding on the nested paragraph.

Margins, Padding, and Lists

All visual browsers by default will apply a 50 pixel margin to the left edge of a list. This allows room for the list item markers (bullets in the case of a bulleted list, numbers in the case of an ordered list). Unfortunately, the CSS Specification doesn't explicitly say whether this should be done with left margin or left padding. The description of the `marker-offset` property does imply that margin is the way to go, however.

Whatever the intention of the specification, Mozilla-based browsers (including Netscape 6 or later) have the dubious distinction of applying a default *padding* to the left side of lists, while most other browsers (including Internet Explorer and Opera) use a margin instead. You can easily see this by applying a `background-color` to a list element. On most browsers, the background will not cover the list item markers, whereas on Mozilla browsers they will.

For this reason, whenever you apply your own left margin or padding value to a list, you must be sure to specify both. If you applied only a margin, for example, the default list indentation would remain on Mozilla browsers while it was overridden on all others. If you applied only a padding, the default 50 pixel margin would remain on all browsers except Mozilla. Only by specifying both margin and padding (usually by setting the padding to 0 and using the margin to do the job) can you ensure consistent rendering across current browsers.

You can set vertical margins with the `margin-top` and `margin-bottom` properties. Here's another HTML page that demonstrates vertical margins:

```
<!DOCTYPE html PUBLIC "-//W3C//DTD XHTML 1.0 Transitional//EN"
  "http://www.w3.org/TR/xhtml1/DTD/xhtml1-transitional.dtd">
<html xmlns="http://www.w3.org/1999/xhtml">
<head>
<title>Box Model Demo</title>
<meta http-equiv="Content-Type"
  content="text/html; charset=iso-8859-1" />
<style type="text/css">
<!--
body {
  background-color: #808080;
}
h1 {
  background-color: #c0c0c0;
  margin-bottom: 5%;
}
h2 {
  background-color: #c0c0c0;
  margin-left: 5%;
```

```
  margin-top: 5%;
  margin-bottom: 5%;
  padding-left: 1em;
}
p {
  background: #c0c0c0;
  margin-left: 20%;
  padding-left: 10%;
  margin-top: 5%;
  margin-bottom: 5%;
}
-->
</style>
</head>
<body>
<h1>No top margin but 5% bottom margin</h1>
<h2>Top and bottom margins set 5% for me</h2>
<p>A paragraph with top and bottom margins set at 5%</p>
</body>
</html>
```

This page renders as shown in Figure 5.16. If you load this document (`boxmod-el5.html`) and resize the browser, you'll notice that vertical spacing increases and decreases accordingly, but stays proportional.

Figure 5.16. Demonstration of Vertical Margins

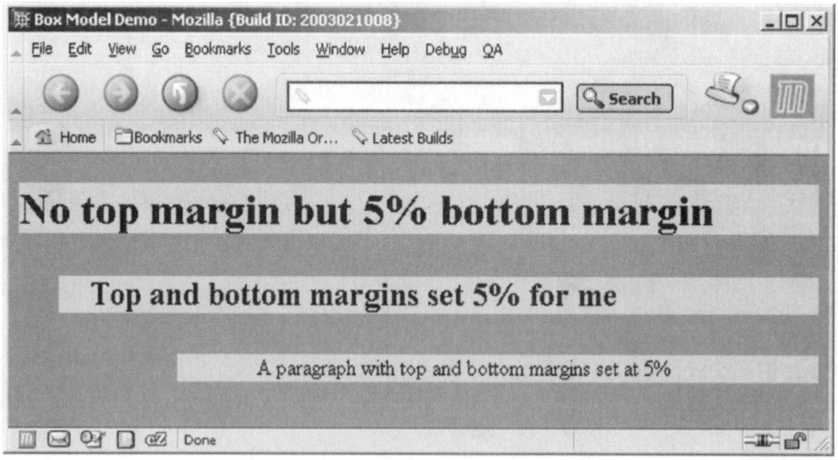

Vertical margins, unlike horizontal margins, are not cumulative. If you have two elements stacked on top of one another, like the h1 and h2 elements in Figure 5.16, the vertical spacing between them will be the greater of the margin-bottom setting of the top element, and the margin-top setting of the bottom element. In this case, they are both 5%, so the distance between the two elements is 5%, not 10% as you might have guessed. If I had defined the margin-bottom of the h1 as 10%, then the vertical distance separating the two elements would have been 10% of the height of the containing block. The containing block in this case is the body, which is, for all practical purposes, the same as the browser window's client area.

It is possible to use negative values for margin property settings. This comes in handy when you've set a margin-left property for the body of an HTML page, but you want to move an element closer to the left margin of the page. The following HTML results in the display shown in Figure 5.17.

```
<!DOCTYPE html PUBLIC "-//W3C//DTD XHTML 1.0 Transitional//EN"
  "http://www.w3.org/TR/xhtml1/DTD/xhtml1-transitional.dtd">
<html xmlns="http://www.w3.org/1999/xhtml">
<head>
<title>Box Model Demo</title>
<meta http-equiv="Content-Type"
  content="text/html; charset=iso-8859-1" />
<style type="text/css">
<!--
body {
  background-color: #808080;
  margin-left: 5%;
}
h1 {
  background-color: #c0c0c0;
  margin-left: -3%;
  margin-bottom: 5%;
}
h2 {
  background-color: #c0c0c0;
  margin-top: 5%;
  margin-bottom: 5%;
}
-->
</style>
</head>
<body>
<h1>Body margin is 5%, but I'm set to -3%</h1>
<h2>I have no margin-left setting, so I use the body 5%
  setting</h2>
```

```
</body>
</html>
```

Figure 5.17. Usefulness of Negative Margin Setting

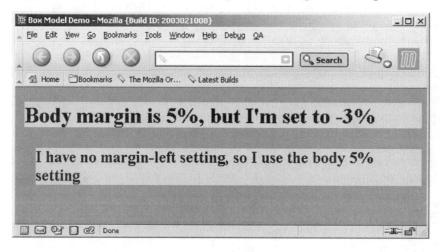

As with the `padding` property, the `margin` shorthand property lets you set all four margins with a single property declaration, and interprets multiple values using the rules shown in Table 5.1.

Border Properties

Border properties are more complex than padding and margin properties because they affect not only the spacing between objects, but also the *appearance* of that intervening space. A border can be, and usually is, visible. In most ways, managing border properties is similar to the process for managing margins and padding. But there are some key differences.

Borders have three types of properties: style, width, and color. By default, their style is set to `none`, their width to `medium`[2] and their color to the text color of the HTML element to which they are applied.

The `border-style` property can take any one of a range of constant values. The available values and the browsers that support them are shown in Table 5.2.

---

[2]Netscape 4 sets a default border width of **0**, so you can't rely on the default value if you wish to target that browser.

Table 5.2. CSS Border Style Constants

Constant	CSS Spec	Supporting Browsers	Sample
double	CSS1	All CSS Browsers	double
groove			groove
inset			inset
none			none
outset			outset
ridge			ridge
solid			solid
dashed		Netscape 6, Mozilla, IE 5.5/Win, IE 4/Mac	dashed
dotted			dotted
hidden	CSS2	Netscape 6, Mozilla, IE 5.5/Win, IE 4/Mac	hidden

The hidden value has the same effect as none, except when applied to table layouts. Refer to the border-style property in Appendix C, for further details.

W3C specifications leave the issue of the precise appearance of these borders largely up to the browsers, so don't be surprised if the results of using these characteristics vary a bit from browser to browser, and platform to platform. But, as is the case with default behaviors for other border settings, the browsers largely treat this issue predictably and satisfactorily within reason.

The width of a border around an object can be set either with four individual property-value pairs, or with the border-width shorthand syntax. The four property-value pairs are border-top-width, border-right-width, border-bottom-width, and border-left-width. Each of these values can be set with a pixel or em value setting, or with one of three descriptive settings: thin, medium, or thick.

If you use the descriptive settings of thin, medium, and thick, the results are browser-dependent. They are, however, fairly predictable and consistent across browsers and operating systems, within a pixel or so for each of the three descriptive settings.

Note that if you wish to use specific measurements for border widths, you should use pixels. This is the most meaningful unit of measurement for screen layouts, which is where border-width is an important property.

You can control the colors associated with all four borders using the border-color shorthand property. Alternatively, you can create different colors for all four borders by using the border-top-color, border-right-color, border-bottom-color, and border-left-color properties.

As I'll explain in greater detail in Chapter 7, you can supply a color argument in any of the standard ways: using a full RGB code as in #ff9900, using a three-digit RGB shortcut as in #f90, with the rgb method as in rgb(102,153,0), or using a standard color name as in red.

The shorthand properties border-style, border-width, and border-color all accept multiple values according to the rules in Table 5.1. Note, however, that Netscape Navigator 4.x does not recognize multiple arguments to these properties, nor does it support the side-specific style and color properties.

There is one additional shorthand property that is probably the most widely used approach to defining border properties. Using the border property, you can specify the style, width, and color of all four borders of an object in a compact form. Since a uniform border surrounding an object is most often your desire, this is an efficient way to set border property values.

This property declaration will produce a uniform 3-pixel, solid, green border around any element to which it is legally applied:

```
border: 3px solid green;
```

The display Property

Before we can move on to look at CSS positioning issues, there is one more CSS property we need to understand. It comes up infrequently, but when it does, it has a significant impact on page layout.

The `display` property determines how a browser displays an element—whether it treats it as a block, an inline text fragment, or something else. Although it can be assigned any of 17 legal values, browser support realities confine the list to six, only four of which are really important. For a full reference to `display`, see Appendix C.

The six possible values for the `display` property are:

- ❏ `block`

- ❏ `inline`

- ❏ `list-item`

- ❏ `none`

- ❏ `table-footer-group`

- ❏ `table-header-group`

The default value varies from element to element. Block elements such as `p`, `h1`, and `div` default to `block`, while inline elements such as `strong`, `code`, and `span` default to `inline`. List items, quite obviously, default to `list-item`. Assigning non-default settings to elements (such as setting a `div` to `display: inline`) can produce some interesting effects (imagine a paragraph containing two `div`s and a list being displayed in the middle of a line of text).

If you supply a value of `none`, the element to which it applies is not shown and the space it would normally occupy is collapsed. This differentiates the `display: none` property-value pair from the `visibility: hidden` setting commonly used to hide the element but preserve the space it would occupy if it were visible.

CSS Positioning Basics

The box model we've been examining so far in this chapter applies within groups of content. Generally, you use a `<div>` tag to group together collections of related content and to assign CSS styles to such a group.

But **CSS Positioning (CSS-P)** involves more than working with individual groups of related information. The connections *between* groups of content on an HTML page are equally important in determining the layout of the page. The primary CSS property involved in these connections is the `position` property.

The `position` property takes a single constant value. The value determines how the block is positioned on the page. The two most frequently used values for the `position` property are `absolute` and `relative`. Another value, `static`, is the default value, and is seldom used in CSS rules. A fourth value, `fixed`, is not supported by IE on Windows at all, which unfortunately means it's almost unusable in practical sites. Refer to Appendix C, for complete details on these more esoteric settings.

Absolute, Relative, and Positioning Contexts

Positioning can be confusing in CSS because the coordinate system within which a block is placed depends on the **positioning context** of the block. There's no universal set of coordinates to guide that placement, even when the `absolute` value is assigned to the `position` property. Each time a block is positioned on the page (with a `position` setting other than `static`), it creates a new positioning context for its descendants, in which the upper left corner of its content area has the coordinates (0,0). So, if you use CSS to position an element that is *within* the block, its position will be calculated relative to that new coordinate system—its positioning context.

The best way to understand this concept is to look at a few simple, interrelated examples. I'll start with a blank page. In this context, the upper left corner of the client area (also referred to in modern Web design parlance as the "document") is where the initial (0,0) coordinates are located. In that context, place a simple bit of text in a `div` (which uses a style sheet rule associated with the class `big-Title`, to make it more readable) as shown in Figure 5.18.

Figure 5.18. Initial Positioning of Element on Blank Page

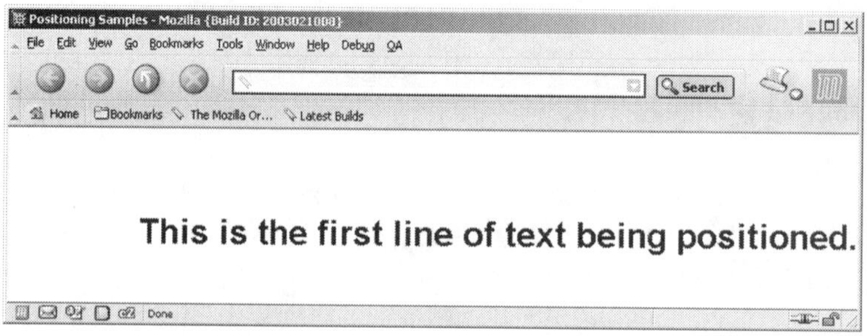

Here's the HTML fragment that produces the result shown in Figure 5.18. The CSS properties `top` and `left` are used to position the `div` on the page.

```
<div class="bigTitle"
  style="position:absolute; left:125px; top:75px;">
  This is the first line of text being positioned.
</div>
```

Now put a second `div` completely inside the first one, as shown here:

```
<div class="bigTitle"
  style="position:absolute; left:125px; top:75px;">
  This is the first line of text being positioned.
  <div class="bigTitle"
    style="position:absolute; left:25px; top:30px;">
    This is a second line.
  </div>
</div>
```

Figure 5.19. Positioning an Element Within a Pre-Positioned Block

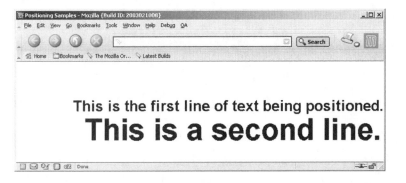

The result is shown in Figure 5.19. Notice that the second line of text is indented 25 pixels from the left of the first line of text, because that first line sets the **positioning context** for the second. Notice, too, that its font size is huge. Why? Take a look at the style rule for the `bigTitle` class and you'll understand:

```
.bigTitle {
  font-family: Arial, Verdana, sans-serif;
  font-size: 2em;
  font-weight: bold;
}
```

As the second `div` is a child of the first, its font size is calculated relative to that of the first `div`. The style rule defines the font as being of size 2 ems, which instructs the browser to render the text at twice the size it would otherwise be. When that 2 em rule is applied to the first line, its size is doubled. But when it is applied to the second line, the font size of the first line is doubled to calculate that of the second.

I can correct this by using an absolute font size constant:

```
.bigTitle {
  font-family: Arial, Verdana, sans-serif;
  font-size: large;
  font-weight: bold;
}
```

The two divs should now share the same font size.

The page now has two div elements, one nested inside the other. Both use absolute positioning. Now I'll add a third element, this time a span element that will be contained in the second div block. Using relative positioning, the HTML turns out to look like this:

```
<div class="bigTitle"
    style="position:absolute; left:125px; top:75px;">
  This is the first line of text being positioned.
  <div class="bigTitle"
      style="position:absolute; left:25px; top:30px;">
    This is<span style="position:relative; left:10px;
top:30px;">an example of</span> a second line.
  </div>
</div>
```

The result of this bit of HTML can be seen in Figure 5.20. Notice that the words "an example of," which are contained in the span, appear below, and slightly to the right of their original position. Relative positioning is always based on the positioned element's *original* position on the page. In other words, the positioning context of an element that uses relative positioning is provided by its default position. In this example, the span is positioned below and to the right of where it would appear in the line if the positioning were removed, as it is in Figure 5.21.

Figure 5.20. Relative Positioning an Element on a Page

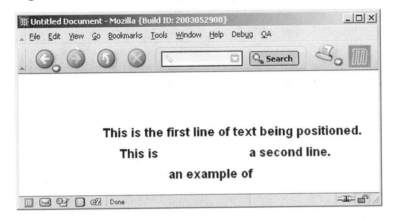

Figure 5.21. Original Location of Relatively Positioned Content

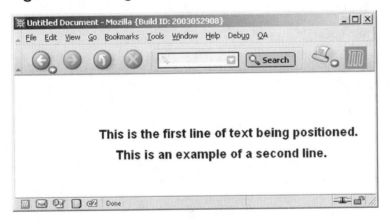

In summary, the basic rules that determine the positioning context for an element when we're using the CSS position property are:

1. Absolutely positioned elements are positioned relative to the positioning context in which they are located.

2. Relatively positioned elements create their own positioning context based on their static (original) location.

Basic Three-Column Layout

The sample site for this book, *Foothag Freaks*, uses a combination of a three-column layout with a header at the top and a footer at the bottom. This is a classic Web page design. Some have even called it "the Holy Grail" when it includes a fluid center column. The first place I saw this reference was on Eric Costello's Website, http://www.glish.com/.

To understand the CSS involved in creating this basic page layout, let's start by looking at the core code for building a three-column layout with a mixture of fixed and flexible column widths, commonly known as **fluid layout** (see the sidebar below for details). Then, we'll add the top-level header area, and a footer. In Chapter 6, we'll learn a few more advanced techniques for page layout, and take apart the *Foothag Freaks* home page to see how these basic techniques can be tweaked to produce a more creative design.

The Case for Fluid (or Stretchy) Page Layout

Ideally, all page designs should be **fluid**. That is, they should expand and contract as the user resizes the browser window. This is to some extent my personal opinion (there are many professionally designed sites on the Web that specify a fixed width), but I think it is an opinion founded on solid principles. Users select their browser window size because they are comfortable browsing Web sites at that width. You should strive never to take away a user's ability to express his or her preferences without a very good reason.

To create such a design is sometimes as easy as assigning percentage values to the widths of all elements that appear horizontally adjacent on the page. Each block will then occupy a set *relative* amount of horizontal space in the browser window. More complex fluid layouts (like the one discussed in this chapter) can be created by mixing absolute pixel widths with flexible widths that fill the remaining space.

Fluid layouts don't always look great in very narrow or very wide window sizes, but unfortunately that's a problem for which there's currently no good remedy. Your best bet is to simply trust your users to choose a reasonable browser window size.

A basic three-column layout begins with a CSS style sheet that contains separate rules for the layout and positioning of the left-hand column, the center column, and the right-hand column. We'll call these three blocks `left`, `center`, and `right` respectively.

Here is the CSS rule that defines the block whose identifier is `left`:

```
#left {
  position: absolute;
  left: 10px;
  top: 10px;
  width: 200px;
}
```

This is quite straightforward. Using absolute positioning, this column has its upper left corner placed 10 pixels below the top of the browser's document area and 10 pixels to the right of the left margin of that space. It sets a fixed `width` for the column, though as we'll see, you could supply a relative value (such as a percentage) to create a stretchy layout that would keep the left column's width proportional to the document area's width.

It is important to understand that when we talk about the `width` of a box, we're referring to its **content width**; we do not include margins, padding, or borders. IE5 for Windows (and IE6 for Windows, in compatibility mode) erroneously include the margins, padding, and borders in the width and height of the box. This is known as the **box model bug**, and a work-around is discussed in Appendix C under `width`.

The center column of the three-column layout uses this CSS rule:

```
#center {
  margin-left: 220px;
  margin-right: 220px;
}
```

Note that this column is not positioned. Its position will thus retain its natural place based on its location within the HTML file that generates the page (in technical CSS terms, this block is said to use **static positioning**). Margin settings of **220px** ensure that the left and right columns (each of which is 200 pixels wide, and displays 10 pixels from the document edge) will have enough room to display their content without overlapping either of the adjoining columns.

Finally, a basic right-hand column looks much like the left:

```
#right {
  position: absolute;
  right: 10px;
  top: 10px;
  width: 200px;
}
```

Here, the `right: 10px` property is used to ensure that the right hand side of this column is placed 10 pixels from the right hand side of the page. The impact of these style rules on a demonstration HTML page can be seen in Figure 5.22.

Figure 5.22. Demonstration of Basic Three-Column Layout

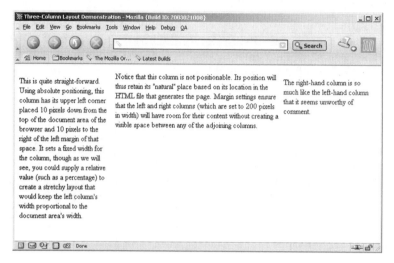

The only other CSS required for this page is a simple rule to remove the default spacing around the edges of the page. This is described in the following sidebar.

Page Margins and Padding

In this and other cases where you want to position elements relative to the edges of the browser window, you should always set the margins and padding of the page to zero. Failing to do this will produce different results in different browsers. In particular, standards-compliant browsers like Mozilla will apply a default page margin around your blocks unless you tell it otherwise, while Opera browsers apply a default padding.

Setting page margins and padding to zero is a simple matter of adding the following rule to your style sheet:

```
body {
  margin: 0;
  padding: 0;
}
```

Here's the HTML for the page in Figure 5.22. The `<link>` tag in the header points to the `threecoldemo.css` file, which contains the CSS rules described above.

```
<!DOCTYPE html PUBLIC "-//W3C//DTD XHTML 1.0 Transitional//EN"
  "http://www.w3.org/TR/xhtml1/DTD/xhtml1-transitional.dtd">
<html xmlns="http://www.w3.org/1999/xhtml">
<head>
<title>Three-Column Layout Demonstration</title>
<meta http-equiv="Content-Type"
  content="text/html; charset=iso-8859-1" />
<link rel="stylesheet" href="threecoldemo.css" type="text/css" />
</head>
<body>
  <div id="left">
    <p>
      This is quite straight-forward. Using absolute positioning,
      this column has its upper left corner placed 10 pixels down
      from the top of the document area of the browser and 10
      pixels to the right of the left margin of that space. It
      sets a fixed width for the column, though as we will see,
      you could supply a relative value (such as a percentage) to
      create a stretchy layout that would keep the left column's
      width proportional to the document area's width.
    </p>
  </div>
  <div id="center">
    <p>
      Notice that this column is not able to be positioned. Its
      position will thus retain its "natural" place based on its
      location in the HTML file that generates the page. Margin
      settings ensure that the left and right columns (which are
      set to 200 pixels in width) will have room for their content
      without creating a visible space between any of the
      adjoining columns.
    </p>
  </div>
  <div id="right">
    <p>
      The right-hand column is so much like the left-hand column
      that it seems unworthy of comment.
    </p>
  </div>
</body>
</html>
```

Adding a Top Header Area

Another common page layout modifies the basic three-column design by adding a top-level header area. As you can imagine, this is not difficult to achieve. Here are the style rules for the four content <div> blocks on such a page. The three holdovers are nearly identical; I've added a gray background to the center and top blocks to make it easier to see where these blocks start and end.

```
#top {
  margin: 20px;
  padding: 10px;
  background: #ccc;
  height: 100px;
}
#left {
  position: absolute;
  left: 10px;
  top: 170px;
  width: 200px;
}
#center {
  background: #ccc;
  margin-top: 0;
  margin-left: 220px;
  margin-right: 220px;
}
#right {
  position: absolute;
  right: 10px;
  top: 170px;
  width: 200px;
}
```

Figure 5.23 shows the result of applying those rules to a page that's nearly identical to the HTML that generated Figure 5.22. The only difference is that this HTML contains the following fragment, which defines the content of the top block on the page:

```
<div id="top">
  <h1>
    This is the header area of the three-column-plus-header
    layout
  </h1>
</div>
```

Figure 5.23. Basic Three-Column Layout With Top Header Block

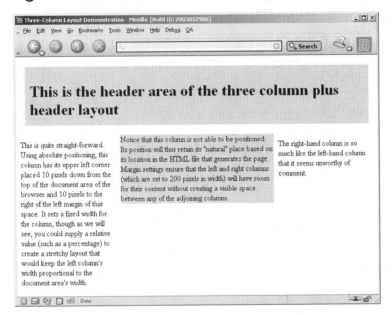

Adding a Footer

One final element is needed to apply these techniques to most practical page layouts: the **footer**. This additional block should span the width of the page just like the header, except it should appear at the bottom of the page, below the three columns. Figure 5.24 shows what a typical footer looks like.

Figure 5.24. Footer Block at the Bottom of the Center Column

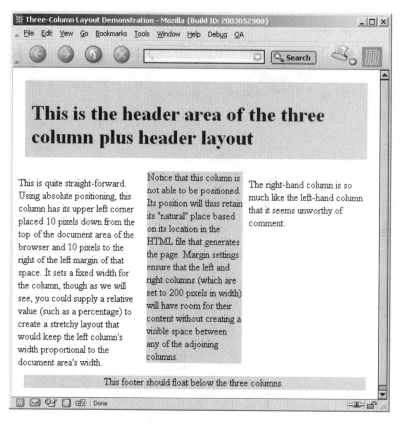

In theory, adding a footer is easy. Simply add another `div` to the bottom of the HTML:

```
<div id="footer">
  <p>
    This footer should float below the three columns.
  </p>
</div>
```

Since we're happy with the block's natural position below the center column block, we need not apply any special positioning to it. The CSS for the block is therefore purely decorative:

```
#footer {
  background: #ccc;
```

```
    margin: 20px;
    text-align: center;
}
```

Ah, but there's the rub! Since the absolute-positioned left and right columns float on top of the rest of the page, the position of the footer is determined solely by the height of the center column. As shown in Figure 5.25, this causes problems when the center column is shorter than the others.

Figure 5.25. Footer Block Position Determined by Center Column

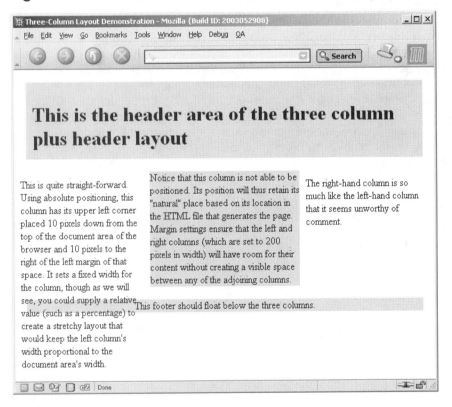

This is the biggest headache faced by new practitioners of CSS layout. This problem is a direct result of the lack of multi-column support in CSS2. As designers, we shouldn't have to resort to absolute positioning to create a multi-column layout, but CSS2 doesn't offer a better solution.

While padding out the center column with empty paragraphs is a possibility, it's an ugly one that violates the principle of semantic HTML markup, and doesn't work too well on database-driven sites where the content of the center column is usually generated on the fly.

But despair not, gentle reader! There are at least two ways to overcome these limitations, both of which we'll see in Chapter 6.

Summary

This chapter presented the important concepts involved in CSS layout and positioning, beginning with the box model and continuing through the multiple variations of the `position` property. We then drove a number of these points home by assembling an example of the "classic" three-column layout.

In Chapter 6, we'll look at a few more advanced CSS properties that affect the layout relationships of elements on the page. We'll then use these methods to address some of the limitations we ran into in this chapter. Finally, we'll dissect the *Footbag Freaks* Website to reveal how these techniques can be used in a more creative page layout.

6

Putting Things in Their Place

In this chapter, CSS Positioning (CSS-P) continues to be the focus of the discussion, but the emphasis shifts, from positioning individual elements, to the way positioning one object on a page affects other objects on the same page. Among the many applications we'll see for these techniques, we'll see how to overcome some of the limitations we identified with simple multi-column in Chapter 5.

Armed with a complete understanding of CSS layout techniques, we'll take a close look at the *Footbag Freaks* sample Web site to see how these techniques can be applied to a site with a more creative layout, breaking the familiar three-column mold.

More on Positioning Page Blocks

The `float` Property

One of the most interesting and often-used CSS properties is the `float` property. It takes a value of `left`, `right`, or `none` (though `none` is the default and is rarely used). This property, when set to `left` or `right`, forces the element to float outside of its natural position in the containing box, aligned either to the left or the right, respectively. Subsequent content wraps around the element. It can be used in any block element.

Two frequent uses of the `float` property are to create drop-cap designs, and flow text around images. To create a drop-cap effect using the `float` property, define a `<span>` element whose `float` property is set to `left`[1]. The `font-size` property is set to some multiple of the default, generally using the ems metric (e.g. a `font-size` of `2.5em` will make the drop-cap two-and-a-half lines high). For example, this HTML fragment will produce the output shown in Figure 6.1.

```
<p><span style="color: blue; font-size: 2.5em; float: left;
    padding-right: 2px;">M</span>aking the first letter much
    larger than the rest of the text in a paragraph and floating
    it left produces the drop-cap effect shown here. Text will
    wrap around the dropcap letter for as many lines as it takes
    to create a smooth flow. Try adjusting the width of your
    browser window and notice the effect it has on the amount of
    text that wraps under the big blue "M" at the beginning of
    this paragraph.</p>
```

Figure 6.1. Drop-cap Effect Using `float: left`

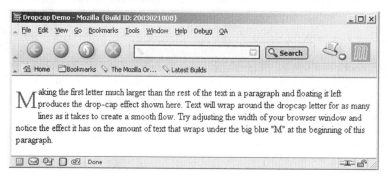

I could have achieved the same effect in a more repeatable way by defining a CSS class called `dropcap` as shown in this fragment:

```
.dropcap {
  color: blue;
  font-size: 2.5em;
  float: left;
  padding-right: 2px;
}
```

---

[1]CSS purists will prefer simply to assign the properties to the `:first-letter` pseudo-element of the paragraph; however, that pseudo-element is not supported by older browsers, so we use a more compatible method here.

Then I could redefine the span encompassing the drop-cap as shown here:

```
<p><span class="dropcap">M</span>aking the first letter much
   larger than the rest of the text in a paragraph and floating
   it left produces the drop-cap effect shown here. Text will
   wrap around the dropcap letter for as many lines as it takes
   to create a smooth flow. Try adjusting the width of your
   browser window and notice the effect it has on the amount of
   text that wraps under the big blue "M" at the beginning of
   this paragraph.</p>
```

The float property is designed to replace the align attribute associated with img tags in HTML, and has, for all practical purposes, precisely the same effect. The align attribute is deprecated in favor of the float property in recent releases of HTML recommendations from the W3C. The following HTML fragment uses the float property to produce the result shown in Figure 6.2.

```
<p><img src="images/logo.gif" alt="Footbag Freaks Logo"
   width="153" height="92" style="float: left;" />The Footbag
   Freaks logo appears to the left of this paragraph. Depending
   on whether I use the CSS float property, I will or will not
   see more than one line of text appearing next to the logo.
   The CSS float property replaces the deprecated align
   attribute of the HTML "img" tag and has essentially identical
   effect.</p>
```

Figure 6.2. Image-Text Alignment Using CSS float Property

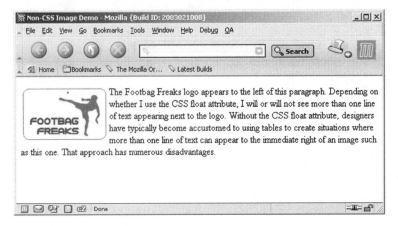

The float property has two key advantages over the align attribute in HTML. First is that float can be applied to other HTML elements than images (as demonstrated with the drop-cap example above). Secondly, using the `float` property allows you to create a CSS component to which you can then apply other property-value pairs. The `float` property is thus far more flexible than the old `align` attribute.

The `clear` Property

There are times when you want text or other objects to flow around an image up to a point, and then be placed so that the flowing content is guaranteed to appear below the image. For example, if you had a reference to "the above figure," it would confuse your readers if the text wrapped in such a way that this reference displayed to the right of the image.

Achieving this kind of controlled flow is the purpose of the `clear` property. In HTML, you can use the `clear` attribute in a `<br>` tag to achieve this, but as the use of that attribute is no longer considered "good practice", use the `clear` CSS property instead. One big advantage of `clear` in CSS is that it can be used in many more places than the confines of HTML's `<br>` tag.

The `clear` property can have any of four values: `left`, `right`, `both`, or `none`, Again, `none` is the rarely specified default. To demonstrate this property, first we'll create a slight variation on the HTML in the preceding section that flowed text around images. Divide the text into two paragraphs as shown below; the new tags are bolded in the following fragment.

```
<p><img src="images/logo.gif" alt="Footbag Freaks Logo"
   width="153" height="92" style="float: left;" />The Footbag
   Freaks logo appears to the left of this paragraph.
   Depending on whether I use the CSS float property, I will
   or will not see more than one line of text appearing next
   to the logo.</p>
<p>Without the CSS float property, designers have typically
   become accustomed to using tables to create situations
   where more than one line of text can appear to the
   immediate right of an image such as this one. That approach
   has numerous disadvantages.</p>
```

This fragment produces the layout shown in Figure 6.3. I've narrowed the width of the window a little, to dramatize the effect.

Figure 6.3. Awkward Text Flow with No `clear` Property

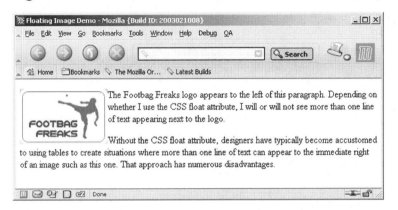

Modify the HTML one more time by adding a `clear` property to the second <p> tag as shown in bold below. This produces the result shown in Figure 6.4.

```
<p><img src="images/logo.gif" alt="Footbag Freaks Logo"
    width="153" height="92" style="float: left" />The Footbag
  Freaks logo appears to the left of this paragraph.
  Depending on whether I use the CSS float property, I will
  or will not see more than one line of text appearing next
  to the logo.</p>
<p style="clear: left;">Without the CSS float property,
  designers have typically become accustomed to using tables
  to create situations where more than one line of text can
  appear to the immediate right of an image such as this one.
  That approach has numerous disadvantages.</p>
```

Figure 6.4. Using the `clear` Property to Improve Text Wrap

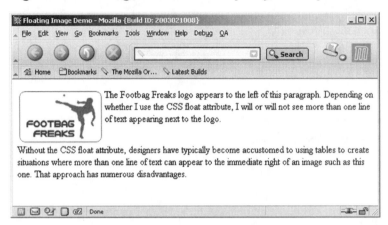

Notice that the text of the second paragraph does not wrap awkwardly back under the image on the left. `clear: left` forces the paragraph to appear after any elements floating in the left margin. Similarly, `clear: right` makes sure the right margin is clear of floating elements, and `clear: both` will clear both margins.

A convenient example of `float` and `clear` working together can be useful in laying out simple forms. Consider the following form code:

```
<form action="test.php" method="post">
<p>This is a form.</p>
<p><label for="name">Name:</label>
    <input type="text" id="name" name="name" size="30" /></p>
<p><label for="address">Address:</label>
    <textarea id="address" name="address" wrap="soft" cols="30"
      rows="5"></textarea></p>
<p><label for="country">Country:</label>
    <select id="country" name="country">
      <option>United States</option>
      <option>Canada</option>
      <option>Australia</option>
      <!-- More countries... -->
    </select></p>
<p><input type="submit" /></p>
</form>
```

Because of the simple code here, the fields are a bit of a jumble, as you can see in the first screenshot in Figure 6.5. Most form layouts rely heavily on tables to keep everything neatly lined up. But by applying a little CSS to this page, we can make even our simple form look great:

```
form p {
  width: 400px;
  clear: both;
}
form p label {
  float: left;
}
form p input, form p textarea, form p select {
  float: right;
}
```

We assign a comfortable width of 400 pixels to all paragraphs appearing within forms, and then float labels to the left, and form fields to the right of those paragraphs. The `clear` property we assigned to our paragraphs ensures that each appears below the form fields that float against the sides of the paragraph before it. The result is shown in the second screenshot in Figure 6.5.

Figure 6.5. Form Layout Without Tables, Thanks to `float` and `clear`

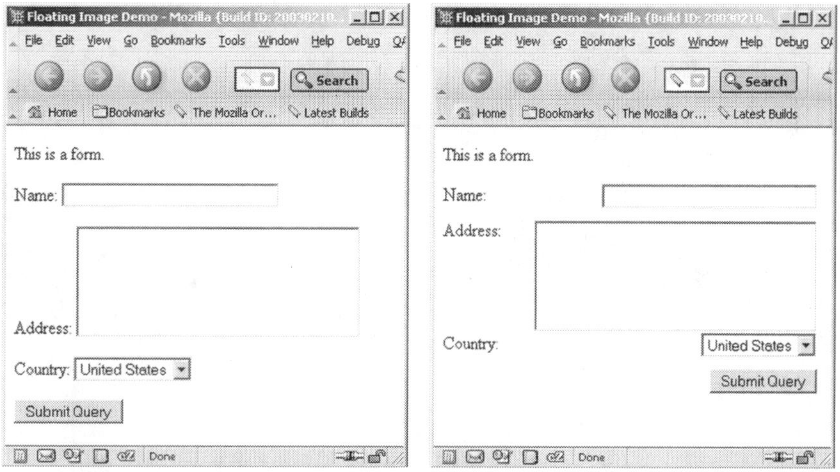

This is a powerful example of how tasks for which we've come to use tables out of habit can actually be more easily (and quickly!) achieved with CSS.

Perfecting Multi-Column Layout

In Chapter 5, I showed you the basics of multi-column layout with absolute positioning. Unfortunately, that technique seemed to run into a virtual dead end when it came to putting a footer beneath the columns. The uneven column heights, combined with the fact that the footer will always appear directly beneath the center column, meant that the left and right columns could overlap the footer in a most unattractive manner (see Figure 6.6).

Figure 6.6. The Problem with Absolute Positioning for Multi-Column Layout

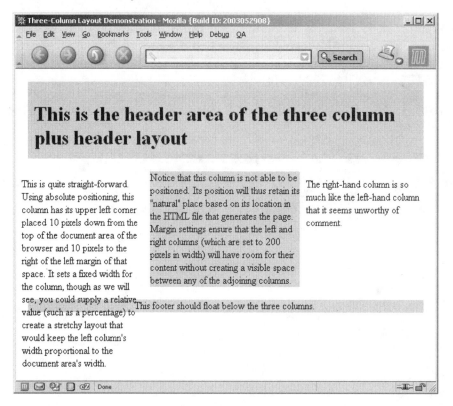

To solve this, we need to find a way to make the center column extend if needed to match the height of the longest column. In short, we need to equalize the column heights to match the one that contains the tallest content. And while absolute positioning alone cannot do this, there are at least two methods that can...

Equalizing Column Heights with DHTML

If absolute positioning with CSS alone can't achieve the desired layout, then one option is to use **Dynamic HTML**[2] (DHTML) to adjust the layout as needed. In this section, I'll show you how some simple JavaScript code can adjust the "broken footer" layout in Figure 6.6 so that the three columns are of equal heights and the footer rests neatly below them.

Instead of dealing with the differences between browsers ourselves, we'll leave it to the professionals and use the excellent X script from Cross-Browser.com[1]. Simply download `x_core.js` and `x_event.js` from that site and load them into the `<head>` tag of your page as follows:

```
<script src="x_core.js" type="text/javascript"></script>
<script src="x_event.js" type="text/javascript"></script>
```

Now, because the footer may well be covered by the left and right columns when the browser lays them out, we'll want to keep it invisible until we've adjusted the column heights. Make sure the footer `<div>` has `id="footer"` set, and add this style rule to the document:

```
#footer {
  visibility: hidden;
}
```

Now, when the browser has finished loading the page (and whenever the browser window is resized), we want to find out which of the columns is tallest and resize them all to that height. Then we can display the footer. Because this process may happen repeatedly as the user resizes the browser window, we need to wrap the content of each column in an additional `<div>`. The structure of the document becomes:

```
<div id="top">
  <!-- header content -->
</div>
<div id="left">
```

---

[2]Dynamic HTML is the technique of using JavaScript code to modify the CSS properties of HTML elements on the fly. As this is not a book about JavaScript, we will not delve any deeper into the subject here.

[1] http://cross-browser.com/

```
  <div id="leftcontent">
    <!-- left -->
  </div>
</div>
<div id="center">
  <div id="centercontent">
    <!-- content -->
  </div>
</div>
<div id="right">
  <div id="rightcontent">
    <!-- right -->
  </div>
</div>
<div id="footer">
  <!-- footer -->
</div>
```

It is these "inner" <div>s that we'll check for the natural height of each column before we set the height of the "outer" <div>s.

Here's the JavaScript function that adjusts the layout using the X library's xHeight and xShow functions, then shows the footer:

```
<script type="text/javascript">
function adjustLayout()
{
  // Get natural heights
  var cHeight = xHeight("centercontent");
  var lHeight = xHeight("leftcontent");
  var rHeight = xHeight("rightcontent");

  // Find the maximum height
  var maxHeight = Math.max(cHeight, Math.max(lHeight, rHeight));

  // Assign maximum height to all columns
  xHeight("center", maxHeight);
  xHeight("left", maxHeight);
  xHeight("right", maxHeight);

  // Show the footer
  xShow("footer");
}
```

All that's left is to make this function run when the page is loaded or resized. This is done with xAddEventListener:

```
window.onload = function()
{
  xAddEventListener(window, "resize", adjustLayout, false);
  adjustLayout();
}
</script>
```

And that does it! The result can be seen in Figure 6.7.

Figure 6.7. Perfected 3 Column Layout with JavaScript

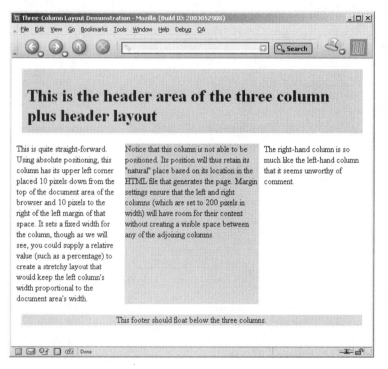

Try out the file 3col-dhtml.html in the code archive to see it in action for yourself!

The only real disadvantage of this method is that it relies on JavaScript. If JavaScript is disabled in the user's browser, none of the adjustments will occur, and the page will display with the three columns of unequal heights and the footer hidden. If that's not acceptable to you, then by all means read on!

Simulating Equal Column Heights with Floats

The layout method I provided in the previous section degraded quite gracefully in the absence of JavaScript, however, the three columns would no longer be of equal height, and the seamless layout would be spoiled. Fortunately, there is a non-JavaScript alternative.

Instead of absolute-positioning all but one of the columns on your page, you can use the `float` property we saw in the section called "The float Property" to float the left and right columns against the left and right sides of the page respectively.

```
#left {
  float: left;
  width: 200px;
}
#right {
  float: right;
  width: 200px;
}
```

In order to prevent the center column's content wrapping below the side columns, we simply assign it equivalent left and right margins (plus a little inter-column spacing, if desired):

```
#center {
  margin-left: 210px;
  margin-right: 210px;
  background-color: #ccc;
}
```

The neat side effect of using `float` to position the left and right columns is that it permits us to use `clear` to position content below them. To ensure that any content that follows the three columns is also pushed down, we wrap the columns in a single `<div>` (with `id="wrapper"`), then add a fourth, empty `<div>` (with `id="clear"`) following the three columns. Here's the structure in summary:

```
<div id="top">
  <!-- header content -->
</div>
<div id="wrapper">
  <div id="left">
    <!-- left content -->
  </div>
  <div id="right">
```

```
    <!-- right content -->
  </div>
  <div id="center">
    <!-- center content -->
  </div>
  <div id="clear"></div>
</div>
<div id="footer">
  <!-- footer -->
</div>
```

To the empty `<div id="clear">` we assign the CSS `clear` property, which ensures that it appears below the floated columns:

```
#clear {
  clear: both;
}
```

This stretches the `<div id="wrapper">`, ensuring that it encloses all three columns, whatever their lengths. Any content following `<div id="wrapper">` will perforce appear below all three columns.

The net result can be seen in Figure 6.8, or you can try it yourself by playing with `3col-float.html` in the code archive.

Figure 6.8. Perfected 3 Column Layout with Floats

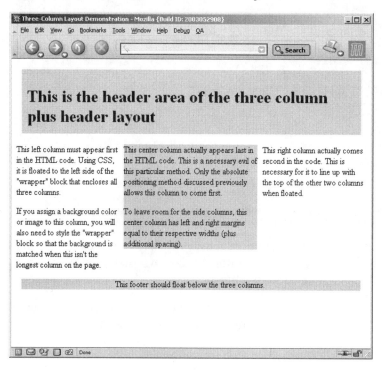

For the floats to work as intended, though, the three column `<div>`s must appear in the correct order in the document. As shown in the code above, we must have the left column first, then the right, then the center. This is the main disadvantage of this method: your two side columns (which usually contain secondary content or navigation) must come before the main content of the page.

Not only can this confuse visually impaired visitors using aural browsers (as the secondary content in your side columns is read before the main content in your center column), it also negatively impacts the search engine rank the page is likely to achieve. With the main content appearing later in the code, many search engines will lend less weight to—or even completely ignore—the critical content of the page. Only the method of absolute positioning can truly free you to put your three column blocks in whatever order you like.

The especially eagle-eyed reader will have noticed that, whereas the DHTML solution actually *did* equalize the heights of the three columns, this method merely makes the footer *behave* as if the three columns were of equal height. What's the difference? Well when you begin to add borders and backgrounds to the three columns, their actual heights become immediately apparent. As a case in point, note that the gray background of the center column in Figure 6.7 extends down to the footer, whereas in Figure 6.8 it only covers the height of the column's content.

Many intrepid members of the CSS community have pursued solutions to this issue, striving for the look of equal column heights without falling upon the crutch of JavaScript. As of this writing, at least thirty variations[2] upon the two solutions presented here can be found on the Web. The most flexible (in my opinion) has been developed by Petr Stanicek[3]. It wraps additional `<div>`s around the set of columns to allow each to have a background that extends all the way to the footer. Each of the wrapping `<div>`s contains an appropriately-aligned, vertically-tiled background (see the `background-position` and `background-repeat` properties in Appendix C) that matches the background of one of the columns.

A number of obscure bugs in Internet Explorer for Windows are related to backgrounds and floats, however, so these kinds of layouts can take a lot of tweaking before they'll display correctly in all browsers. If you want a solution that "just works", your best bet is the DHTML solution I presented above.

The `z-Index` Property and Overlapping Content

By default, HTML elements on a Web page will be placed by the browser so that they all sit neatly—or messily, depending on how good a designer you are—next to each other on the page. CSS positioning, as we have just seen, raises the possibility of overlapping content. Whenever elements overlap, there is a question of which element should be drawn "on top of" the other. You can think of overlapping elements as squares of paper glued to the user's screen. When these squares overlap, you need to decide in what order they should be stuck to the screen. The position of an element within this stacking (or sticking!) order is called it's **z-index**. An element with a higher z-index will be drawn on top of elements with lower z-indexes, partially—or even completely—obscuring overlapping elements. When combined with elements that can be positioned, the z-index can accomplish some layout effects that would be difficult, or even impossible with HTML alone.

---

[2] http://css-discuss.incutio.com/?page=ThreeColumnLayouts
[3] http://www.pixy.cz/blogg/clanky/css-3col-layout/

Left to their own devices, overlapping elements on a page arrange themselves in the order in which they appear in the HTML code. The last item listed appears at the "top" of the stack of elements (i.e. closest to the viewer). This is easier to show than describe, so let's take a quick look at an example.

Let's say we have two graphics and a headline we want to arrange to look like Figure 6.9.

Figure 6.9. Stacking Items on a Web Page

There are two ways to accomplish this effect. The first is to ensure that the three blocks are defined in the appropriate order. In the case of Figure 6.9, that would mean defining the image of the footbag player first, then the grey window frame graphic, then the headline. This works fine, but it isn't good design because it doesn't separate the HTML file from the display. One of the purposes of CSS is to break the connection between the relative order in which blocks and elements appear in the HTML file, and their position on the page. It's also easy to break this kind of layout if someone comes along later and inserts a new item in the mix.

The preferred way to accomplish this design goal is to use CSS' z-index property. You define a z-index for each object that will appear in the same area of the screen, and this determines their stacking order.

The higher an item's z-index value, the nearer it appears to the observer. A z-index of 3 appears to layer on top of an item with a z-index of 1 or 2, for example. This becomes particularly important when you're dealing with images that have transparency, as does the window image in Figure 6.9

Here's the HTML fragment that produces the display in Figure 6.9 using CSS positioning and the z-index property:

```
<div style="position: relative">
  <div style="position: absolute; z-index: 2;">
    <img src= "images/window.gif" />
  </div>
  <div style="position: absolute; top: 40px; margin-left: 70px;
    z-index: 1;">
    <img src="images/kod.jpg" />
  </div>
  <div style="position: absolute; margin-left: 15px;
    z-index: 3;">
    <h1>This is a test headline</h1>
  </div>
</div>
```

As you can see, the headline, which the design demands be at the "top" of the stack of overlapped content so that it's not obscured by the window, has a z-index setting of 3. As we want the window to overlay the footbag player, and show the player through the "panes" of the window (which are transparent), we define the player to have a z-index of 1 and the window a z-index of 2. Change the z-index settings of these objects and study the results. The use of the z-index property will become clear to you.

An important aspect to note about the z-index property is that the z-index of a block is always relative to its sibling elements. Consider this document structure:

```
<div id="outer1">
  <div id="inner1"> ... </div>
```

```
  <div id="inner2"> ... </div>
  <div id="inner3"> ... </div>
</div>
<div id="outer2">
  <div id="inner4"> ... </div>
</div>
```

Now, if we were to use absolute positioning to cause all these divs to overlap, the blocks would stack as shown in Figure 6.10.

Figure 6.10. Default Stacking Order

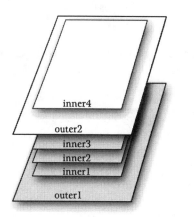

This shouldn't be surprising. As I've already explained, overlapping elements stack in the order in which they appear in the page. But consider what would happen if we assigned the following z-index values:

```
#outer1 { z-index: 4; }
#outer2 { z-index: 3; }
#inner1 { z-index: 6; }
#inner2 { z-index: 1; }
#inner3 { z-index: 5; }
#inner4 { z-index: 2; }
```

At a glance, you might expect them to stack as shown in Figure 6.11.

Figure 6.11. Stacking Irrespective of Document Structure (this is wrong!)

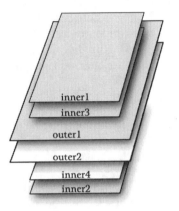

But as I said above, z-indexes are relative only to sibling elements. outer1 and outer2 are siblings, as are inner1, inner2, and inner3. inner4, which resides alone inside of outer2, has no sibling elements.

The actual effect of the z-index values assigned above is shown in Figure 6.12.

Figure 6.12. Actual Stacking Order

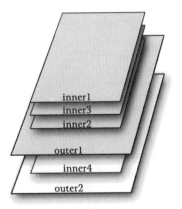

As you can see, a block's children are always drawn directly on top of any non-positioned content in the block, with their relative stacking order dictated by z-index (or document order, if no z-index is specified). Because inner1, inner2, and inner3 all reside within outer1, they will all be drawn directly on top of outer1, sharing outer1's relative z-index to outer2 and its contents. In other words, if outer1 is above outer2, then all of outer1's contents are also above all of outer2's contents. outer2's z-index of 3 doesn't make it higher than either inner2 (z-index: 1) or inner4 (z-index: 2), because neither of these is its sibling.

Again, if you need further reinforcement of these issues, I'd recommend having a play with the z-index values in this example to see exactly how z-index works.

CSS Layout in Practice: Footbag Freaks

Depending on how much past experience you've had with CSS, you may be feeling confident or bewildered after that whirlwind tour of CSS page layout techniques. However you came out of it, I'm certain you'll agree that most professional Web site layouts nowadays are significantly more complex than the three-column layouts that have been the focus of our attention thus far. In this section, we will dissect the page layout of the *Footbag Freaks* website[4] (Figure 6.13), which more closely approaches the level of complexity you'll face in your practical design work.

---

[4] http://www.footbagfreaks.com/

Figure 6.13. The Footbag Freaks Home Page

A glance at the layout in Figure 6.13 reveals that there is a top block. However, the presence of three columns is obscured by the fact that the large image of the sky near the top of the page straddles what might be seen as the center and right columns. Within that image, however, is another possible column, where "Footbag News" appears. If you look closely, you'll see that this embedded column lines up with the sponsor's ad that displays below the image area.

Reading the HTML for the `index.html` page of the site reveals that it relies on the `styles.css` style sheet rules, and that it is divided into the following major `div` blocks, listed in the order in which they appear in the HTML document:

☐ top

- [ ] `featureimg`

- [ ] `center`

- [ ] `left`

- [ ] `news`

- [ ] `sponsor`

- [ ] `footer`

There are two other `div` elements defined in the page: `otherleftstuff`, contained within the `div` called `left`, and `topcontent`, where the four small links to other locations on the site appear in the upper right corner of the page. Setting those aside for the moment, let's take a look at the CSS rules for the seven top-level `div` blocks that comprise the layout of the page, to see how they fit into—and differ from—basic multi-column layout.

Figure 6.14. The top Block

Here is the CSS rule for the `top` block (shown in Figure 6.14):

```
#top {
  padding: 4px;
  background: #BDC5CE url(images/bgtop.jpg) repeat-x;
  border-bottom: 1px solid #A5B5C6;
}
```

The `background` setting has nothing to do with CSS positioning, so we can safely ignore it for now. We'll discuss background styles in Chapter 7.

Notice that the `top` block has no `position` property defined, only padding of 4 pixels on all four sides and a thin border at the bottom. The absence of a `position` property makes this block assume its normal position in the document, while the absence of a `width` property allows it automatically to span the page width.

Figure 6.15. The `featureimg` Block

The CSS rule for the `featurimg` block (shown in Figure 6.15) looks like this:

```
#featureimg {
  margin: 0 25% 0 170px;
  height: 250px;
  background: #153976 url(images/sky.jpg) no-repeat right top;
  text-align: center;
  border-top: 1px solid #A5B5C6;
}
```

This block is not positioned, but it features a four-argument `margin` setting and a fixed `height` of 250 pixels. You can deduce from the `background` setting that this `featureimg` refers to the picture of the sky that dominates the top portion of the page.

It also defines a one-pixel top border that's the same color as the bottom border of the `top` block, creating a two-pixel border between the two elements. This rule is really included, however, to overcome some unexplained bad behavior on the part of Mozilla browsers. Otherwise, we could have just used a two-pixel border on the top `div` and been done with it. When, as is the case here with the flying hacky sack, you embed a child element into the `div`, Mozilla uses the child object's margin setting instead of that defined for the parent. This is obviously a bug, but this work-around makes its effect invisible.

As we haven't positioned the `featurimg` element, it displays in the position in which we'd expect it to display, based on its context within the HTML code. The lack of a `width` setting also makes this area fluid.

Figure 6.16. The center Block

Latest Articles on Footbag Freaks

November 8 2002
Lorem ipsum dolor sit amet, consectetuer adipiscing
By Jason 'Hack Master' Donald

November 9 2002
Ut wisi enim ad minim veniam, quis nostrud exerci tation ullamcorper suscipit
By Alex 'Hackermanis' Walker

November 10 2002
Duis autem vel eum iriure dolor in hendrerit in veuqait nulla facilisi.
By Julian 'Dancin' Julio' Carroll

November 11 2002
Lorem ipsum dolor sit amet, consectetuer adipiscing elit,e maqna aliquam erat volutpat.
By Jason 'Hack Master' Donald

November 12 2002
Ut wisi enim ad minim veniam, quis nostrud exerci trata commodo consequat.
By Alex 'Hackermanis' Walker

November 8 2002
Duis autem vel eum iriure doloisis at blandit praislisi.
By Julian 'Dancin' Julio' Carroll

Here is the CSS rule that defines the block whose identifier is `#center` (shown in Figure 6.16).

```
#center {
  margin: 0 25% 0 25%;
  padding: 1% 3%;
  background: #fff url(images/bgcenter.gif) no-repeat center;
  color: #000;
}
```

As you can see, this rule sets margins of 25% for the right and left edges of the column, but eliminates any top or bottom margin. Padding, in turn, is set to 1% for top and bottom, and 3% for left and right, to give the layout some "air." For the sake of example, we use the four-argument shorthand to specify the margin, and two-argument shorthand for the padding—feel free to use the two-argument version for both.

Figure 6.17. The `left` Block

The `left` column (shown in Figure 6.17) uses absolute positioning. Assuming that it is not contained within another positioned object (and as it turns out, it isn't), the top property positions the top of the column 101 pixels from the top of the document area of the browser. This leaves room for the header area, which is 100 pixels high with a 1 pixel bottom border.

```
#left {
  position: absolute;
  padding: 0;
  top: 101px;
  width: 25%;
  background: #A5B5C6 url(images/bgbotleft.gif) left bottom
repeat-x;
  color: #000;
}
```

Setting the left column's `width` to 25% ensures that its width remains proportional to the width of the browser window's document area as the user resizes it. This setting interacts with other width-related settings of the content that appears horizontally adjacent to the left column on the page, a factor that gets our attention in Chapter 7.

Figure 6.18. The news Block

The `news` block on the *Footbag Freaks* page (shown in Figure 6.18) appears on the right side of the `featureimg` block. Here is the CSS rule that defines its appearance and location:

```
#news {
  position: absolute;
  width: 21.9%;
  height: 250px;
  overflow: hidden;
  margin-left: 75%;
  padding: 0 1.5%;
  top: 101px;
  background-color: #153976;
  border-top: 1px solid #A5B5C6;
}
```

This rule sets the top of this block at 101 pixels, lining it up with the top of the `left` block. With a `margin-left` setting of 75%, and a `width` of 21.9%, this block of information will always appear three quarters of the way to the right from the left of the window, and will occupy a consistently proportional part of the horizontal space.

You might be wondering why we used 21.9% here, rather than 22%. After all, adding the 75% left margin and the 3% padding (1.5% each left and right), brings us to 78% of the space spoken for. It turns out that the fact that we have a decimal value for left and right padding can, at some window widths, generate a combined width of 101%. This, in turn, generates a horizontal scrollbar for the news block. To avoid that ugliness, we simply reduce the width by 0.1% so that the total never exceeds 100%. It may not be the ideal solution, but it works.

Figure 6.19. The sponsor Block

The CSS for the sponsor block (shown in Figure 6.19) is similar to that for the news block:

```
#sponsor {
  position: absolute;
  width: 21.9%;
  height: 251px;
  margin-left: 75%;
  padding: 10px 1.5%;
  top: 375px;
  text-align: center;
}
```

The two key differences between sponsor and news are the top value of 375 pixels and the top-bottom padding of 10 pixels. The height happens to be one pixel larger than the news block, but that's only an interesting coincidence.

Figure 6.20. The footer Block

Copyright 2002 © SitePoint Pty Ltd

Finally, here's the CSS for the footer block (shown in Figure 6.20):

```
#footer {
  clear: both;
  border-top: 1px solid #5C6F90;
  border-bottom: 1px solid #5C6F90;
  background-color: #D6D6D6;
  color: #000;
}
```

Summary

This chapter looked at some of the more esoteric aspects of CSS positioning techniques and strategies, focusing on how decisions you make about positioning one block can impact on the appearance of other blocks on the same page.

With this chapter, we conclude our top-level view of CSS as a page layout technique and standard. In Part III, beginning with Chapter 7, we'll shift our attention to the visual aspects of individual elements by first studying color in CSS.

Styling Text and other Content with CSS

Splashing Around a Bit of Color

This chapter begins Part III of the book. The focus will now shift from the block-level layout issues of CSS to the display of individual blocks and other elements.

Specifically, this chapter emphasizes colors applied to text and other objects, as well as page background colors. It will discuss how to describe colors, where to use them, how to make them work together to achieve specific effects, and other such techniques.

Backgrounds on Web pages can use far more intricate design techniques than simple colors. I'll defer discussion of those alternative ideas to Chapter 11, which includes a discussion of background tricks and techniques.

This chapter begins with a basic discussion about the possible collisions that arise between the way a designer believes a page should look, and the constraints put upon page appearance by the user.

Who's in Charge Here?

Under the rules of CSS2, user settings trump designer specifications every time. While it's important to keep this in mind, it's also important to realize that simple recognition of this fact doesn't provide any insight into *how* to design with the rule in mind. Simply put, you can't do so.

The user can set his or her preferences for colors particularly easily. All the modern browsers have simple color preference-setting panels, like that of Internet Explorer 5 for the Macintosh shown in Figure 7.1.

Figure 7.1. Typical Preference Setting Panel for User to Define Colors

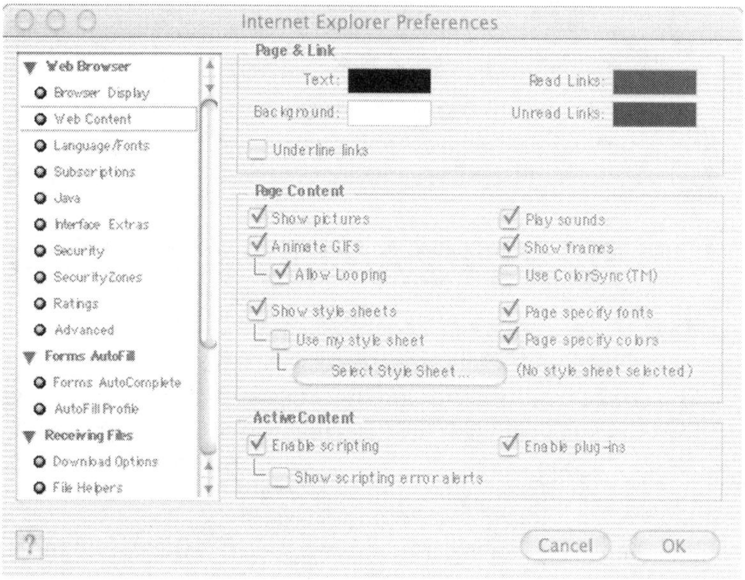

The top portion of the preference panel in Figure 7.1 allows the user to set colors for text, page background, links that have been read and links that have not yet been visited. In the section of the preference panel labeled "Page Content", you can see that the user can either allow your fonts and colors to override his or her preference, or not. If those two checkboxes are unchecked, the user preferences take precedence.

The preference panel in Figure 7.1 allows the user to choose a great many settings to express his or her preference for how pages look. Notice, too, that users can define their own style sheet, and tell the browser to use this to override any conflicting styles it finds on incoming pages. In such a situation, if the user defines a style for <h1> elements that defines a color but not a font, for example, your font setting will be used, but the user's color will be applied whether or not your style sheet defines one.

In all the information that follows in this part of the book, then, you need to keep in mind the caveat, "...unless the user overrides your settings." I won't bore you by reminding you of this rule repeatedly.

Color in CSS

Elements that can be displayed in colors defined through style rules are:

❑ backgrounds

❑ borders

❑ text

❑ links

❑ outlines

I've listed that last one for the sake of completeness. Outlines are not widely supported in any significant percentage of the browsers available today, so we won't spend time discussing them here. Refer to the `outline` property in Appendix C, if you're curious.

How to Specify Colors

When you specify a color for any CSS property that accepts color values, you have a choice of several methods:

❑ descriptive color names

❑ system color names

❑ RGB decimal values

❑ RGB hexadecimal values (including a three-character shorthand)

❑ RGB percentage values

The most human-readable way to specify colors in HTML is to use key words that are reserved to describe those colors. Although there are only 16 "official" descriptive color names that are supported in HTML and CSS[1], virtually all modern browsers support a range of 140 color names first suggested by Netscape in the early days of the Web.

These 140 colors, along with their RGB equivalents, can be found in Appendix B. The 16 "official" descriptive color names are:

- ❑ `black`

- ❑ `white`

- ❑ `aqua`

- ❑ `blue`

- ❑ `fuchsia`

- ❑ `gray`

- ❑ `green`

- ❑ `lime`

- ❑ `maroon`

- ❑ `navy`

- ❑ `olive`

- ❑ `purple`

- ❑ `red`

- ❑ `silver`

- ❑ `teal`

- ❑ `yellow`

---

[1]Although the HTML and CSS specifications define 16 standard color names, the Web Content Accessibility Guidelines 1.0 [http://www.w3.org/TR/WCAG10-CSS-TECHS/#style-colors] published by the W3C recommend always using numerical values, not names, for colors.

Whether you use the other 124 named colors or not is strictly up to you. Given that they are not officially supported in any W3C documentation, there is a potential element of risk that some future browser may not support them. Precisely how these colors render on some browsers and operating systems is not easily determined other than by personal, detailed testing. Frankly, I don't see much of a risk here and I use these names a great deal because their names are sufficiently descriptive that I get some idea what I'm likely to see, even before I view my page in a Web browser.

In addition to the descriptive color names, there is also a set of 28 **system color names**. These names, such as `AppWorkspace`, correspond to different parts of the graphical user interface (GUI) presented by the operating system. The actual color associated with each of these names is therefore operating system specific, and potentially subject to user preferences. Using these color names, you can create Web interfaces that match the user's operating system GUI. A complete list of system color names is presented in Appendix B.

Colors on computer monitors are rendered by combining three basic colors—red, green, and blue—in various intensities. There are two fundamental ways you can define other colors using these basic three:

❑ you can use the `rgb` function, and supply a set of three comma-separated values defining the mix of the three basic colors, or

❑ you can supply a hexadecimal value as a six-character string, which, in some cases, can be abbreviated to three characters. These strings are preceded by the pound sign or hash symbol (#) whether you use three or six characters.

For example, if you wanted to specify the color blue for a particular element in a CSS style rule, you could do it any of the following ways:

```
color: blue;
color: rgb(0, 0, 255);
color: rgb(0%, 0%, 100%);
color: #0000ff;
color: #00f;
```

You can use only the three-character hexadecimal approach when the six-character version consists of three matching pairs (i.e. `#abc` is equivalent to `#aabbcc`).

You've probably figured out that the decimal and hexadecimal values in the above represent the presence of no red, no green, and maximum amount of blue. Black is represented by the value #000000 (or, in shorthand, #000) and white is represented by the value #ffffff (or, again in shorthand, #fff). If you prefer the rgb function, black is rgb(0,0,0) and white is rgb(255,255,255) or rgb(100%,100%,100%).

Sometimes, by looking at a color value—or perhaps more easily, looking at two color values next to one another—you can figure out how to modify it to achieve a different effect. For example, if you've defined a color as #ff7f50 and you look at it and decide it needs to be a bit more blue, you can just increase the value of the last two digits to, say, #ff7f70.

This nearly infinite[2] control over the precise combination of red, green, and blue is the reason Web designers with artistic backgrounds tend to favor the hexadecimal approach. Those who, like me, are color-challenged, however, find the 140 names perfectly adequate, thank you very much!

Color Selection and Combining Colors

Part of the graphical design of a site is the selection of color combinations that work well. If you've ever put a chartreuse background next to an image with a dark blue background and then run screaming for the exit when the page displayed, you have some idea of the difficulty involved.

The selection of colors becomes an important issue primarily in two situations: where you have adjacent objects with colored backgrounds and you want to avoid clashing, and where you have colored text on colored backgrounds and you want to ensure readability.

There are some basic artistic principles involved in selecting colors that complement one another.

Everything starts with the color wheel. There are literally hundreds of places on the Web where color wheels are discussed, but the clearest and most concise I have found is by the makers of a program called Color Wheel Pro™, in their article called *Color Theory Basics*[2].

Essentially, you start with a color wheel that includes the range of colors from which you want to choose. Colors that are adjacent to one another on the color wheel are said to be "harmonious" colors that look good together. Choosing two

---

[2]Actually, "nearly infinite" is a bit of an overstatement. There are over 16.7 million possible combinations of red, green, and blue in CSS, and therefore over 16.7 million possible individual colors.
[2] http://www.color-wheel-pro.com/color-theory-basics.html

or three adjacent colors on a color wheel, and applying those colors to large areas, such as backgrounds and menus, can produce very pleasing aesthetic effects.

For greater vibrancy, you will want to select colors that are *opposite* one another on the color wheel.

To find great color combinations for Web design, move an equilateral triangle around the middle of a color wheel, and use the combinations of colors that lie at the triangle's corners.

Some graphics programs and Web design tools include palettes and other interfaces to allow you to select colors without knowing their rgb or hexadecimal codes. These aids make it much easier to experiment with color combinations, and determine what works and what doesn't. They also have ways of making sure you stay within the bounds of what are called "Web-safe colors," a palette of 216 colors that will render nearly identically across platforms and browsers.

Putting colored text on colored backgrounds can be problematic. Trial and error can be incredibly time-consuming, but often the specific effect you want won't be achievable without some effort. However, there is some help available on the Web, and one of the best places I know of is a site called ColorCombo[3]. Check out http://www.colorcombo.com/bgtxt.html, a sample of which is shown in Figure 7.2. As you roll the mouse over the colored squares in the right rectangle, the background color of the page changes. You can see instantly what different text colors will look like against the background.

[3] http://www.colorcombo.com/

Figure 7.2. Text-Background Color Combination Selector at colorcombo.com

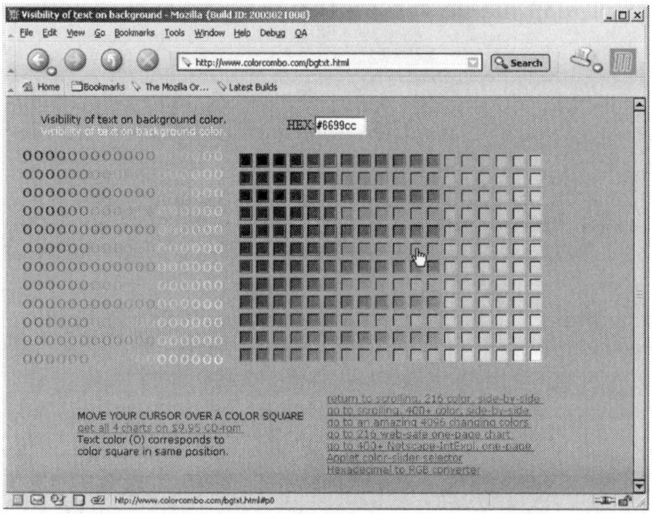

And, while we're on the subject of picking your own colors, keep in mind the special needs of people who may be red-green color-blind. While this condition affects a fairly small percentage of the population, it is easy to design your site so that it doesn't rely on red and green to distinguish important information.

Discovering new color combinations that may defy conventional wisdom, but work well together regardless, is one of the most interesting areas of creative exploration in Web design. So, don't limit yourself to the accepted combinations that everyone uses.

Setting body Color

A lot of the time, you will not define a `color` property for the `body` tag, either inline or in a style sheet rule. The default browser definition creates black text on a white or gray background (white on newer browsers, gray on older ones). For many layouts, that's fine.

But, if the need arises to define a different color combination, then you can define the text color for all the text that appears on a page, using a style sheet entry like this:

```
body {
  color: red;
}
```

I don't recommend you use this approach exactly as shown above, even when you wish to declare all the fonts on a page (or site) to be a specific color. Why? Because there's a fundamental rule in CSS, from which you should never deviate: *if you set a foreground color, always set a background color, and vice versa.* You never know if the user has set a specific background color, against which your carefully chosen text color will look like mud. Or worse yet, the user may have defined a background color that matches your foreground color and will see only what appears to be a blank page.

So if you decide to define a foreground color using the color property, combine it with a background-color definition as in this example:

```
body{
  color: white;
  background-color: maroon;
}
```

Note, too, that if you set a color property for the body element, it applies to all elements nested inside that tag (including headings, paragraphs and lists, among other things), unless you override it (or the user's preferences trump you).

Transparency, Color, and User Overrides

You can ensure that the background color of any HTML element is identical to that of the body of the page. To do this, we define its background-color as transparent:

```
#transbox {
  color: white;
  background-color: transparent;
}
```

In fact, the background-color property is transparent by default; it is not inherited from the parent element. This ensures that an image background assigned to an element will display continuously through child elements, rather than being displayed again in alignment with each child.

So why would you explicitly declare a background color of transparent? The most common use for this approach occurs when you have defined a background-color property for a particular type of HTML element (such as divs), but you have one or more specific types of div tags for which you wish to display transparent backgrounds.

This issue of "default" background color gets sticky when users muck about with their settings. For example, if a user defines a local style sheet, settings in that style sheet—including background colors—may override yours.[3]

Fortunately, very few users change their browsers' default settings, so your page settings will usually win out, with browser defaults taking over where you don't specify anything. For example, the default background color for the body of a page is white or gray. If, however, you define the background color of the body to be transparent, then all bets are off. As the W3C puts it in its CSS specification, in such cases, "the rendering is undefined."

Interesting Uses of Color

Coloring text, backgrounds and borders is all well and good—and not terribly complicated—but of what use other than aesthetics can it be? In this section, I'll outline three specific examples of using color combinations to produce useful results.

Warnings and Cautions

In online documentation, it is frequently useful to call specific attention to pieces of information that are of particular importance to the reader. Printed manuals, generally produced in black-and-white, rely on typographic techniques to accomplish this attention-getting: boxes, bold or italic type, special fonts, and the like.

On a Web page, where color is more freely usable, we can use these typographic techniques as well, but we can combine them with colored text against a colored background to create notices that grab the reader's attention more certainly and effectively than is usually possible in print. Table-based layouts are often used to create these kinds of effects. Let's see how we can take advantage of CSS rules to accomplish the same result, which is shown in Figure 7.3.

---

[3]On IE5 for the Macintosh, for example, local style sheet settings declared by the user override your page settings. But, on IE6 for Windows, this happens only if the user defines a local style sheet *and* tells the browser to override the designer's settings. Netscape Navigator, on the other hand, doesn't allow the user to define a style sheet, but the Windows version does pay attention to the settings in a predefined style sheet named ua.css, which is editable. It appears that on the Macintosh, Netscape Navigator has no equivalent file.

Figure 7.3. Using Color to Create Attention-Getting Cautions and Notes

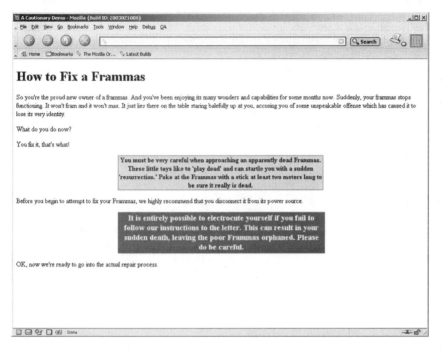

The HTML for the page shown in Figure 7.3 looks like this. I've used bold to indicate where the style sheet for this page is invoked.

```
<!DOCTYPE html PUBLIC "-//W3C//DTD XHTML 1.0 Transitional//EN"
  "http://www.w3.org/TR/xhtml1/DTD/xhtml1-transitional.dtd">
<html xmlns="http://www.w3.org/1999/xhtml">
<head>
  <title>A Cautionary Demo</title>
  <link rel="stylesheet" href="frammas.css" type="text/css"
    media="All" />
</head>
<body>
  <h1>How to Fix a Frammas</h1>
  <p>So you're the proud new owner of a frammas. And you've been
    enjoying its many wonders and capabilities for some months
    now. Suddenly, your frammas stops functioning. It won't fram
    and it won't mas. It just lies there on the table staring
    balefully up at you, accusing you of some unspeakable offense
    which has caused it to lose its very identity.</p>
```

```
<p>What do you do now?</p>
<p>You fix it, that's what!</p>
<div class="caution">You must be very careful when approaching
    an apparently dead Frammas. These little toys like to 'play
    dead' and can startle you with a sudden 'resurrection.' Poke
    at the Frammas with a stick at least two meters long to be
    sure it really is dead.</div>
<p>Before you begin to attempt to fix your Frammas, we highly
    recommend that you disconnect it from its power source.</p>
<div class="danger">It is entirely possible to electrocute
    yourself if you fail to follow our instructions to the
    letter. This can result in your sudden death, leaving the
    poor Frammas orphaned. Please do be careful.</div>
<p>OK, now we're ready to go into the actual repair
    process.</p>
</body>
</html>
```

As you can see, I've identified two classes called caution and danger. I used
classes here, rather than identifiers, because it's quite likely that I'll have more
than one instance of each of these kinds of notes in a document, and identifiers
are limited to one usage per page.

Here are the CSS style sheet definitions of the two classes:

```
.caution {
    text-align: center;
    font-weight: bold;
    background-color: gray;
    color: black;
    margin-left: 25%;
    margin-right: 25%;
    border: 1px solid red;
}

.danger {
    text-align: center;
    font-size: 1.2em;
    font-weight: bold;
    background-color: red;
    color: white;
    margin-left: 25%;
    margin-right: 25%;
    border: 3px solid red;
}
```

There is nothing new and startling here. Each of these classes defines a background color and text color combination designed to bring the eye's attention to it. Each is also positioned so that it stands out from the page. As you can see from the example, using CSS makes the HTML code much easier to read and maintain than if we were using nested tables to accomplish the same purpose.

Coloring Alternate Rows of Data Tables

While we are learning how to avoid the use of tables for page layout, we must remain appreciative of the situations in which tables are a perfectly legitimate tool. Principally, displaying tabular data is a task that should still be entrusted to HTML tables.

We can, however, make what are otherwise fairly ordinary tables into more readable and attractive page elements by applying a little CSS to them.

Figure 7.4 shows an admittedly stark example of a table presented in HTML. Obviously, you'd never release a Web page with such a sparse table design, but it serves as a good starting point for this discussion.

Figure 7.4. A Starkly Ordinary Table Design

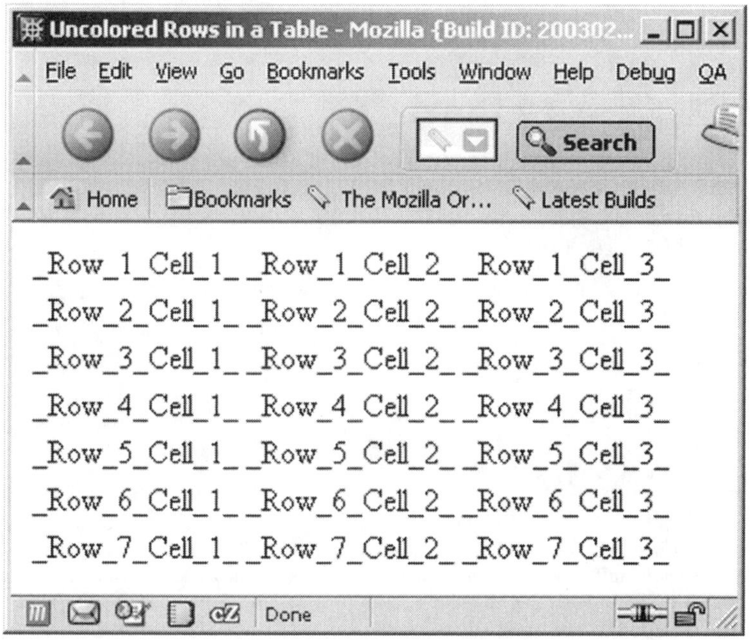

Among the other problems this table has are its lack of borders, and the fact that it's hard to tell one cell from another as you read across the table. We can address both of those issues with a bit of simple CSS magic[4].

Below is the HTML for a modified version of this table page, in which I've defined a couple of trivial CSS rules. This is a case where an external style sheet is probably overkill, though it may still be good design practice.

```
<!DOCTYPE html PUBLIC "-//W3C//DTD XHTML 1.0 Transitional//EN"
  "http://www.w3.org/TR/xhtml1/DTD/xhtml1-transitional.dtd">
<html xmlns="http://www.w3.org/1999/xhtml">
<head>
  <title>Coloring Rows in a Table</title>
  <meta http-equiv="Content-Type"
    content="text/html; charset=iso-8859-1" />
  <style type="text/css">
  <!--
  .odd {
    background-color: lightgrey;
  }

  .even {
    background-color: yellow;
  }

  table {
    border: 1px solid black;
    border-spacing: 0;
  }

  td {
    padding: 4px 6px;
    border: 1px solid black;
  }
  -->
  </style>
</head>
<body>
  <table>
    <tr class="odd">
      <td>_Row_1_Cell_1_</td>
```

---

[4]Actually, this example is somewhat contrived. For historical reasons, Web browsers will display tables with a 1-pixel border by default, so Figure 7.4 actually represents a table that has had its default borders removed, either with CSS or with the now-deprecated (but common) practice of setting the `border` attribute of the table to `0`.

```
      <td>_Row_1_Cell_2_</td>
      <td>_Row_1_Cell_3_</td>
    </tr>
    <tr class="even">
      <td>_Row_2_Cell_1_</td>
      <td>_Row_2_Cell_2_</td>
      <td>_Row_2_Cell_3_</td>
    </tr>
    <tr class="odd">
      <td>_Row_3_Cell_1_</td>
      <td>_Row_3_Cell_2_</td>
      <td>_Row_3_Cell_3_</td>
    </tr>
    <tr class="even">
      <td>_Row_4_Cell_1_</td>
      <td>_Row_4_Cell_2_</td>
      <td>_Row_4_Cell_3_</td>
    </tr>
    <tr class="odd">
      <td>_Row_5_Cell_1_</td>
      <td>_Row_5_Cell_2_</td>
      <td>_Row_5_Cell_3_</td>
    </tr>
    <tr class="even">
      <td>_Row_6_Cell_1_</td>
      <td>_Row_6_Cell_2_</td>
      <td>_Row_6_Cell_3_</td>
    </tr>
    <tr class="odd">
      <td>_Row_7_Cell_1_</td>
      <td>_Row_7_Cell_2_</td>
      <td>_Row_7_Cell_3_</td>
    </tr>
  </table>
</body>
</html>
```

I simply define two classes, odd and even in an embedded style sheet, then label alternate rows of the table to correspond to those styles. I've also defined a basic style rule for the table to surround it in a 1-pixel-wide black border. Because table cells inherit their default border from the parent table, each cell is also surrounded by a 1-pixel border; the net result is a 2-pixel line between and around every table cell. This is shown in Figure 7.5.

Obviously, this is much more readable, and while it isn't a final solution, it gives us a much more pleasing starting point from which to begin additional work on the table.

With some of the less frequently used aspects of table definitions in HTML, such as header (`<th>` and `<thead>`) and grouped columns (`<colgroup>`), you can create some professional-looking and eminently readable tables of data.

Figure 7.5. Coloring Alternate Rows of Table with CSS Rules

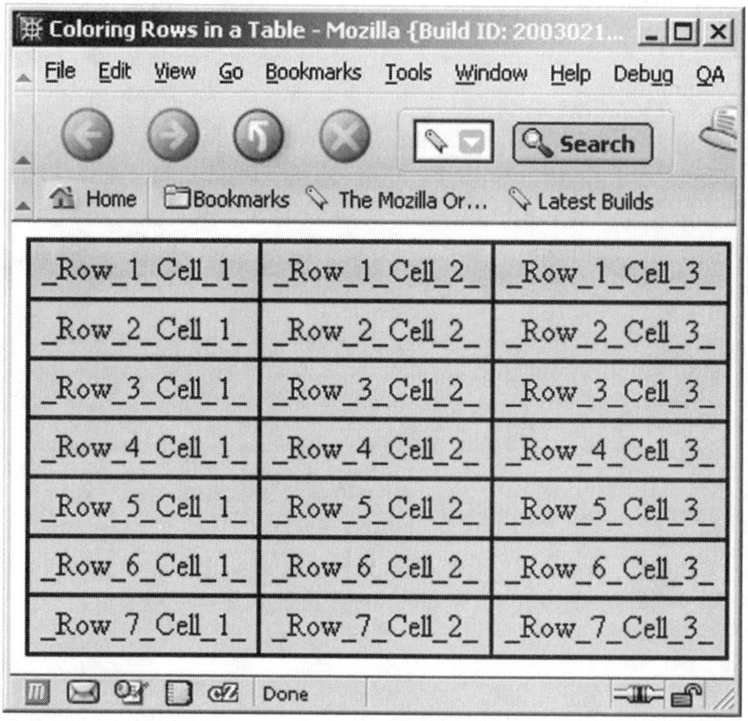

Summary

This chapter discussed how to use color in CSS rules to spruce up your Web pages, and how to move away from deprecated HTML tags and attributes, into the modern CSS era of design.

Chapter 8, provides a similar perspective on text in a broader context, including standard versus nonstandard fonts.

Making Fonts Consistent

This chapter examines the question of how to use fonts properly in CSS-based Web page design. After an explanation of how CSS deals with fonts at the most abstract level, I'll look at the use of "standard" and nonstandard fonts in delivering Web pages. Finally, I'll offer some guidelines on choosing font families and sizes for your page designs.

How CSS Deals With Fonts

With the emergence of CSS, the HTML `<font>` tag is deprecated in favor of using styles to achieve the same or better results.

Using CSS gives you great flexibility in working with fonts. While HTML limits you to working with only seven standard font sizes, CSS allows you to specify font sizes in a number of different ways, providing a nearly unlimited range of sizes. In addition, CSS formalizes the ability to define a fallback, or default, font to be used in case none of the fonts you specify in a style rule is available on the user's machine when your page is rendered. This capability existed with the deprecated `<font>` tag in HTML, but the list of defaults was never officially standardized.

With CSS, you also get the ability to change the **weight** of fonts (e.g. bold or normal), their **style** (e.g. italic or oblique), and even to declare a font to display in small caps.

The CSS properties you'll work with in this chapter include:

❏ `font-family`

❏ `font-size`

❏ `font-style`

❏ `font-variant`

❏ `font-weight`

❏ `font` (shorthand property)

Together, these properties give you considerable flexibility to control the appearance of text on your Web pages.

The `font-family` Property

The issue of font families gets tangled up with questions of standard versus nonstandard, and supported versus unsupported fonts, which are deserving of an entire section of this chapter. Here, I'll cover them briefly, but later in this chapter I'll cover the subject in much greater detail.

You can use the `font-family` property to assign a specific family, a list of specific families, and/or a generic family to any HTML block or element.

Most of the time, to achieve the result you want in the way the page looks, you'll supply a list of specific fonts, separated from one another by commas, and end the list with the **generic font** that is to be used if none of your specified fonts is available. Here's how that looks:

```
font-family: Arial, Helvetica, sans-serif;
```

Fonts are used in the order in which they are listed in the rule. In the above example, the browser will look to see if the user has Arial installed. If so, the text affected by this style rule will be shown in Arial. If Arial isn't present on the user's system, then the browser looks for the next font, Helvetica. If it finds Helvetica, it uses it. If it doesn't find Helvetica either, the browser uses whatever is defined as the default sans-serif font for the browser.

Generic Fonts

It's worth pausing just a moment here to discuss how the browser gets its default sans-serif and other generic font settings. The browser has preset defaults for the following generic font families:

- ❏ `serif`

- ❏ `sans-serif`

- ❏ `monospace`

- ❏ `cursive`

- ❏ `fantasy`

The user may, however, be able to change these default fonts through preference settings in the browser. If that's the case, then all bets are off. In such cases, the generic specification of `sans-serif` doesn't even guarantee a sans-serif font will be used. If the user has overridden the default value for `sans-serif`[1] to display a serif or monospaced font, for example, the user's settings trump your CSS rules.

Regardless of how the browser arrives at its default setting for a generic font, that font will be used as the last resort in any case where a comma-separated list of font choices is defined, and none of the specific families of fonts is available.

If the name of a specific family of font you wish to specify in a `font-family` property value list contains embedded spaces, you'll need to enclose that family name in quotation marks, as shown here:

```
font-family: "New Century Schoolbook", Baskerville, serif;
```

Note that while you will generally want to include only fonts of the same type (serif, sans-serif, monospaced, etc.) in your list, it is not mandatory that you do so. You can legally specify, for example, a list of specific font families that includes a sans-serif family, a serif family, and uses `monospaced` as the default. I'm not sure why you'd want to do this, but it is possible.

---

[1]No current browsers expose this setting to the average user, if they support changing it at all.

The `font-size` Property

Font size is one of the most troublesome aspects of Web design. This is because browsers vary widely in the ways they understand and apply some of the key concepts that determine how fonts will be sized for display. Before we explore this any further, let's take a look at the official definition of the ways in which you can define the size of a font on a Web page. You can specify the font size you wish to use by selecting from a collection of seven constants:

- ☐ xx-small

- ☐ x-small

- ☐ small

- ☐ medium

- ☐ large

- ☐ x-large

- ☐ xx-large

These define what are referred to as *absolute* sizes, but as we'll see, in reality, there's nothing terribly absolute about them in the usual sense of that word. You can also define absolute font sizes by specifying a length value in units, such as pixels or points.

You can also use two constants that define *relative* sizes: `larger` and `smaller`. In addition, you can use the relative measurement of ems. Finally, you can set the font size using a percentage value, an alternative to the ems approach to relative font sizing.

HTML Sizes Versus CSS Sizes

In the days before CSS, designers often assigned font sizes using absolute or relative values from 1 to 7. You could specify a size of +1 (meaning you wanted the font to be one "level" higher than the default font size for that element), -1 (to create a font one "level" smaller than the default font size for that element), or 1 (one of seven absolute values, with no sign).

The fact that there were seven such values in HTML and now there are seven absolute size constants in CSS has led some people to conclude that there must be a one-to-one correspondence between those two scales. In fact, there is no real connection between the two. You cannot count on the idea that `<font size="7">` in HTML produces the same result as `font-size: xx-large` in a CSS rule.

Variability Across Browsers and Platforms

Beyond that almost-understandable discrepancy lies a deeper issue, which is demonstrated in Figure 8.1. There, the same Web page's contents are shown as rendered by a number of different browsers, browser versions, and platforms.

Figure 8.1. Discrepancies Between Browsers Displaying Text Using Absolute Size Constants

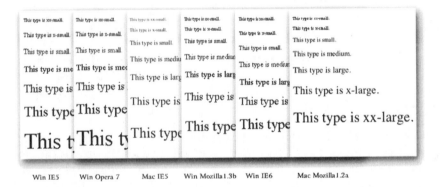

Given such variability between browsers, platforms, and even versions of the same browser, how in the world can you achieve anything like a predictable design of the fonts on your Web pages?

The short answer is that there is no way to accomplish this, short of using graphics or Adobe Acrobat PDF files to render and display your pages[2]. It's inevitable that your pages will look somewhat different across these variable platform-browser-version combinations.

---

[2]It is true, however, that if you use pixels for your font sizes, you can get very close to pixel-perfect matches between browsers. Actual sizes will still vary with screen resolution in that situation (smaller pixels mean smaller fonts), but using pixels is the current best practice for obtaining close to perfect consistency. This comes at the significant expense of reduced accessibility.

What's a designer to do?

As a first step, use CSS rules rather than the deprecated <font> tag to define the fonts in your designs. The W3C is always working on ways to overcome the limitations in Web page rendering, and with CSS support in current browsers, you're already much closer to the ideal of accessible, yet predictable font sizes.

Relative to What?

When you use relative font sizes, such as ems or percentages, and even the relative constants larger and smaller, you need to understand the base measurement to which they relate. Recall from Chapter 3, that ems tell the browser to render text in a size that is some multiple or fraction of that base measurement. Thus, a font-size setting of 1.5em tells the browser to blow up the font size to 1.5 times the base measurement, and a font size of 0.5em tells the browser to shrink the font size to half the base measurement.

So what is the base measurement?

In the case of text contained directly in the body of a document, the base measurement is the default font size for the browser. If the default setting for text in a browser is, for example, 12 points, then a font-size setting of 1.5em produces 18 point type.

For text inside other elements, the base measurement used by relative font sizing is the font-size of the element's *parent container*, rather than the size of the element's default font, as you might have expected. You might, for example, expect that if you define a particular class or instance of an h1 tag to have a font-size of 1.5em, you'd end up with a heading that was one and a half times the size of all other h1 headings. In reality, the font size will be 1.5 times that of the parent element of the h1 in question. Figure 8.2 demonstrates this by showing two headings, both of which have the document body as their parent element. The top heading is a standard h1. The second is an h1 that's been defined as having a font-size of 1.5em. Not quite what you might expect, is it?

Figure 8.2. Relative Font Size Produces Unexpected Result if You Make a Wrong Assumption

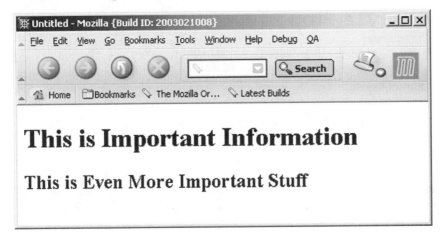

Figure 8.3 shows how defining a font-size of 1.5em in a span of text within an h1 heading affects that span's size. The word "Important" is 1.5 times as large as the other words in the heading because the heading is the span's parent element.

Figure 8.3. Using Relative Font Size Inside <h1> Tag Produces Predictable Result

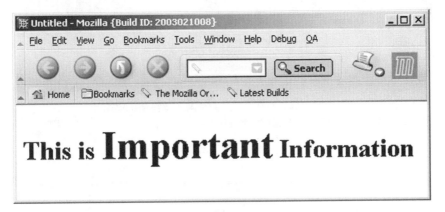

Other Font Properties

The `font-style` Property

The `font-style` property determines whether the element is rendered in `normal` (Roman), `italic`, or `oblique` font style. For all practical purposes, `italic` and `oblique` are identical.

The `font-variant` Property

In its current incarnation, the `font-variant` property has only one effect: it determines whether text should be displayed in small-caps format. In an ideal world, if the current font has a small-caps variant defined, the browser would use that font. Unfortunately, no current browser is smart enough to do that. Rather, current browsers render lowercase letters as capital letters with a smaller size than that used for the main font.

Figure 8.4 demonstrates the `font-variant` property set to a value of `small-caps`. The only other value this variant can take is `normal`.

Figure 8.4. Using the `font-variant` Property With Setting of `small-caps`

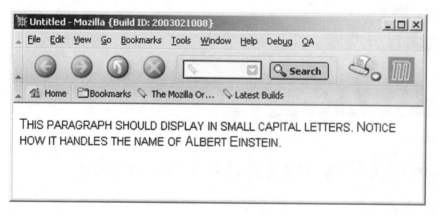

Note that in IE for Windows prior to Version 6, small-caps type is rendered as all-caps, with no difference in sizes.

The `font-weight` Property

"Weight" in the context of CSS font control refers to the boldness of the characters. The `font-weight` property can take two types of values: relative and absolute. Relative values are `bolder` and `lighter`. Absolute values range from 100 (lightest) to 900 (boldest) in 100-unit increments, and also include the shortcut names `normal` (equivalent to 400) and `bold` (700). This set of values is actually more fine-grained than any current browser supports. The Adobe OpenType™ font standard does allow for nine levels of boldness in a font family; however, I have yet to see a practical application of all these levels.

As is the case with other relative measurements in CSS properties, the relative settings here are based on the setting of the parent of the element affected.

Because neither browsers nor fonts support the full range of nine different settings for the `font-weight` property, you will usually find that two or more adjacent values produce identical output on the screen.

The `font` Shorthand Property

This shorthand property allows you to set multiple font-related properties in one CSS style rule.

As with other CSS shorthand properties we've seen, values are separated from one another by spaces, with commas used in multiple-property situations such as the `font-family`. Here's an example of a reasonably complex font description in CSS:

```
h3 {
  font: bolder small-caps 22px Arial, "Lucida Console", sans-serif;
}
```

Notice that the font size (`22px`) and the `font-family` list are included in the definition of the style in sequence at the end of the list of properties. You must always include at least the `font-size` and the `font-family` property values, in that order, as the final or only values in the `font` shorthand property.

The above CSS rule produces the output shown in Figure 8.5.

Figure 8.5. Heading Produced by Style Rule Calling for 22-Pixel Bolder Small-Caps Font

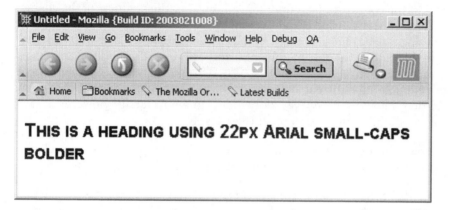

There are a couple of intriguing subtleties in the use of the font shorthand property that are worth noting. First, you can add a line-height property to the font declaration by placing a forward slash (/) after the setting for the font size, followed by an additional valid size or number. We'll cover line-height in greater detail in Chapter 9. Here's an example:

```
p {
    font: small-caps 12px/2em Arial, "Lucida Console", sans-serif;
}
```

The bold type in the above code fragment instructs the browser to render paragraph text in a 12 pixel high font and to set the line height to double the height of the font. Figure 8.6 shows what a paragraph looks like without the added line-height value. Figure 8.7 shows what it looks like when I add the 2 ems of line height.

Figure 8.6. Font Without Line Spacing Addition

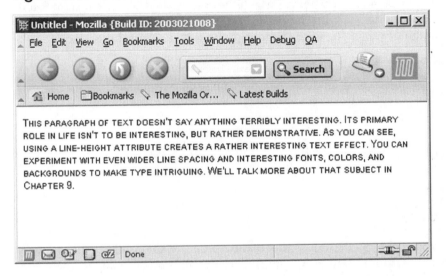

Figure 8.7. Same Text as Figure 8.6 with 2em Line Height Property Value

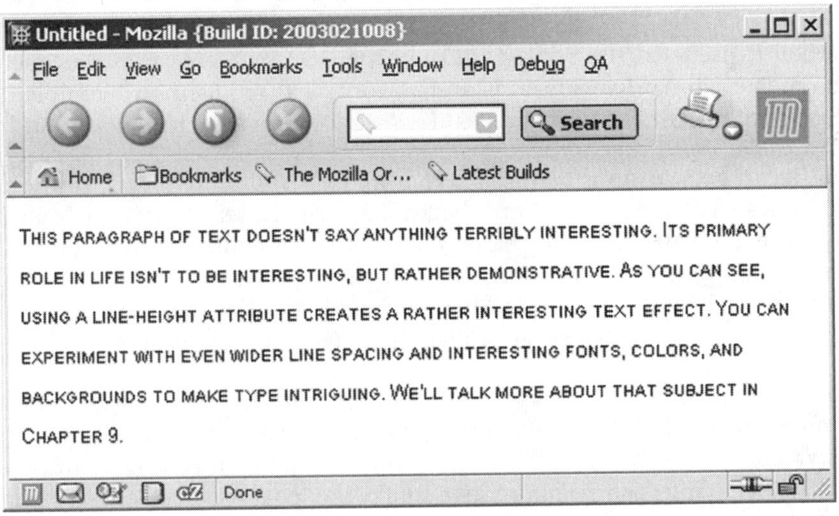

CSS2 introduces the concept of a font constant that you can use when you're creating user interfaces and want to match user expectations based on their browser and operating system. Theoretically, these constants will use the font defined by the browser and/or operating system as the base font from which to create the appearance of the text to which they are applied. These constant values may be assigned to the `font` shorthand property, as they represent a particular combination of values for all of the font properties. The constants are:

- [ ] `caption`

- [ ] `icon`

- [ ] `menu`

- [ ] `message-box`

- [ ] `small-caption`

- [ ] `status-bar`

Before you make heavy use of this feature, you'll want to check the browser compatibility information in Appendix C, as not all browsers support these constants.

Standard and Nonstandard Font Families

Earlier, when I discussed the `font-family` property, I indicated that a deeper discussion of the standard versus nonstandard fonts was requisite to a complete understanding of the issue of font families. This section provides that background.

What do I mean by **standard fonts**? There is no CSS standard or specification that determines what fonts will always be available on a user's system. It's also impossible to make any real assumptions about font availability on user systems that won't encounter some exceptions. In fact, there is not one font that is installed in common by default on both Macintosh and Windows operating system based computers. Not one. Can you believe that, after all these years?

There are, however, some fonts that are sufficiently similar across those platforms, that specifying them is both safe and mostly predictable. Table 8.1 lists the default fonts for Windows and Macintosh systems that are sufficiently similar to one another that specifying them as alternative fonts in a `font-family` property will produce fairly consistent results. If the user of a Windows or Macintosh computer installs any of several popular software products (including Internet Explorer and Microsoft Office), there is another set of fonts that are similar or identical; these are also listed in Table 8.1, but are not shown as installed by default.

Table 8.1. Font Commonality Across Windows and Macintosh Platforms

Font Name - Windows	Font Name - Macintosh	Default Install?
Courier New	Courier	Yes
Arial	Helvetica (or Geneva)	Yes
Times New Roman	Times (or New York)	Yes
Arial Black	Arial Black	No
Comic Sans MS	Comic Sans MS	No
Trebuchet MS	Trebuchet MS	No
Verdana	Verdana	No

While I've indicated that Helvetica is a reasonable substitute for Arial, the match is not clean. Geneva comes a bit closer to matching the look of Arial. A bigger concern with respect to Helvetica, though, is that it's an Adobe PostScript font. Most Macintoshes have no problem supporting Adobe PostScript fonts, and all the recent-vintage Macs that run the new OS X versions support these fonts natively. But few Windows and Linux systems include the Adobe software necessary to render Postscript fonts correctly, resulting in jagged-looking displays.

In addition to the fonts in Table 8.1, Microsoft at one time offered a free collection of downloadable TrueType fonts from its Websites. Due to licensing issues, Microsoft discontinued their availability, but thanks to a quirk in the original licensing, it was determined that anyone who had legally downloaded these fonts earlier could redistribute them. As a result, they are now available at http://corefonts.sourceforge.net. Additionally, these fonts are available in a form that works on Unix and Linux machines. They are:

❑ Andale Mono

❑ Arial

❑ Comic Sans

❑ Courier New

❑ Georgia

❑ Impact

- ❑ Times Roman

- ❑ Trebuchet MS

- ❑ Verdana

- ❑ Webdings

A significant percentage of systems in use today have these fonts installed, so they can be used, if not with absolute certainty, at least with some confidence.

Specifying Font Lists

As you know, when you define a `font-family` style rule, you generally supply not one font, but rather, a list of fonts separated by commas. Fonts that contain spaces must be enclosed in quotation marks.

But, what exactly does the browser do with this list of font families? Essentially, it begins with the first font family on your list and looks for it on the user's system. If it finds the first font, it uses it to display the text that is associated with the `font-family` property. Failing to find the first font, it moves to the second, then to the third, and so on.

To be just a bit more precise, the browser looks for the font families you specify in the places it has been told to look for fonts on the user's system. The font must be stored in a directory that the operating system or the browser normally searches for fonts. Some applications come with their own fonts and store them in nonstandard places; those fonts will remain invisible to the browser.

This left-to-right sequential font family searching technique produces two basic rules about the order in which you list font families in your styles.

First, you want to arrange the fonts in order from the most desirable to the least desirable appearance of the text.

Second, you want the last font on the list to be the generic name for the style of font family you're using (generally, `serif`, `sans-serif`, or `monospace`). This ensures that even if none of the fonts you specify is found on the user's system, at least the appearance won't be completely wrong.

Serif fonts such as Times New Roman have a small decoration or tail added to the ends of many of the lines in each letter. This helps to define the ends of the stalks of the font. Sans-serif fonts such as Arial have no such decorations on the end of lines. Typically, the stalks of a sans-serif font are straight and of uniform width. A monospace font is a font where each letter of the font occupies the same width, like a typewriter. A cursive font is intended to mimic the connected character style of handwriting. A fantasy font is a more decorative or fancy style of font.

Artistic views about which fonts look better on a Web page differ. Many people believe that serif fonts are easier to read because the small extenders along the bottoms of the letters give the eye something to track across a line. I'm not going to get into those issues here; there are many people more expert on the subject.

Figure 8.8 shows you a sample of each of the three most popular generic `font-family` types. As you can see, they are quite different from one another.

Figure 8.8. Samples of Sans-Serif, Serif, and Monospace Fonts

As a rule, then, you won't want to mix `serif`, `sans-serif`, `monospace`, `cursive`, and/or `fantasy` fonts in a single CSS style rule. You'll decide which type of font family you want to use, then list one or more font families in order of preference. Always end with the name of the generic font family that describes your choice of generic style.

The following three CSS style rules are typical of the usual sequencing you'd probably define:

```
p {
    font-family: "Courier New", Courier, monospace;
}
```

```
p {
    font-family: "Times New Roman", Times, serif;
}
```

```
p {
    font-family: Arial, Geneva, sans-serif;
}
```

The specific font families you specify need not be those shown in the examples, and the sequence isn't locked in concrete, either. The point is that in each case I've used font family names that specify common style, and then appended the generic family style name to the end of the list of specific fonts.

Using Nonstandard and Downloadable Fonts

As the user's browser will always display the text you present, no matter how you might mangle the font-family property's settings, it follows that you can certainly supply font family names that you have no way of knowing are installed on the user's system within reach of the browser. The worst-case scenario is that text displays in a way you would not have specified, and may not appreciate all that much, for that matter.

So, if you have an affinity for a particular font that is not normally installed on Windows machines, for example, and for which there isn't really a good Windows equivalent, you can specify it, and then design a sort of gradual degradation of the appearance of the content when the font isn't available.

Here, for example, is a situation where I've specified the Chicago font that Apple uses extensively on the Macintosh, but isn't supplied with Windows, and is almost never installed there.

```
h1 {
    font-family: Chicago, sans-serif;
}
```

Figure 8.9 shows what the display looks like in IE on a Macintosh where the Chicago font is available. On a Windows machine, this would display as the default sans-serif font, which might not be quite as aesthetic (or ugly, depending on your opinion of the stark Chicago font), but it will be as close as you're likely to come to matching the font cross-platform.

Figure 8.9. Specifying Nonstandard Chicago Font Works on Macintosh

The Chicago Font is used when available.

When the Chicago Font is unavailable, the default Sans-Serif Font Family is used.

You can gain even greater control over the font family situation if you want to implement a solution that works only on IE[3]. I never recommend such solutions, but you may find yourself on an intranet, for example, where the company dictates the browser to be used. In that case, special fonts such as corporate identity kit-

---

[3]This technique is documented as part of the CSS2 recommendation, so even though it's only supported by IE at the moment, you can expect other browsers to add support as new versions are released.

standard fonts could be stored on a central server and dynamically downloaded by the browser as needed.

To make this work, you have to take the following steps:

1. Use the Microsoft Web Embedding Font Tool (WEFT)[2] to create a font definition file by converting a standard font definition file. This program can scan your hard drive, find font definition files, and more or less automatically create the font definition files you need to upload.

2. Store the font definition file in one or more central locations.

3. Insert a @font-face rule in style sheets that need to access the font.

For example, let's say your company has a font it likes everyone to use on internal memos. You have been asked to place this font on the intranet so that people who wish to use their browsers to create memos in HTML format can do so while complying with the rules. The font is stored in a file called gigantico.eot[4]. Assuming you've created the font definition file and stored it on the central corporate intranet server, you can associate the font with an arbitrarily chosen name using the following @font-face rule:

```
@font-face {
  font-family: "Corporate Memo";
  src: url(http://mainserver.com/fonts/gigantico.eot);
}
```

With that definition in place, you can specify the font as you would any other font:

```
p {
  font-family: "Corporate Memo", sans-serif;
}
```

If the font in question has yet to be downloaded to the user's system when the page is ordered up, the browser will display the text in an alternative font taken from your font list, or from the system or browser default, while it downloads the font. After the font is downloaded, the page will be redrawn using the specified font where appropriate.

---

[2] http://www.microsoft.com/typography/web/embedding/weft3/

[4]The .eot extension stands for Embedded Open Type, the standard format for such fonts.

@font-face is just one of a number of special **at-rules**, so-named because they all start with a @ (at) symbol. In general, at-rules are supported only by recent browsers. The full range of at-rules is documented in Appendix A.

Summary

This chapter explained how to use several font-related properties in your CSS rules to control the display of text on your pages. It also provided you with useful background on font selection and description.

Chapter 9, moves beyond the issue of which fonts are used to display text, and offers some additional CSS styles and other capabilities to make your text more engaging and lively.

9

Text Effects and the Cascade

This chapter builds on the last, where we looked at those characteristics of text associated with font and its related style properties. Here, we'll explore a range of other characteristics, including:

❏ alignment

❏ first-line indentation

❏ horizontal and vertical spacing

❏ text "decorations" such as underline, overline, and strike-out

❏ shadowed, or 3-D text

The browser treats hyperlinks differently from other text, and, as such, they're subject to special appearance techniques. Lists also present a particular set of opportunities for the styling and presentation of text. We'll be looking closely at both hyperlinks and lists here.

The chapter concludes with a discussion of an important concept in CSS, namely, cascading. I've largely ignored the "C" in CSS until now, principally because its primary application is in controlling the display of textual elements on the page.

We begin by delving into the `<span>` element, which I've touched on briefly in previous chapters. As you'll see, this element is most useful when dealing with segments of text within larger text blocks.

Using the span Element

Sometimes, you want to treat some text in a paragraph, or even a headline, differently from the rest of the text of which it is a part. For example, you might want to change the font, or some font characteristic, such as size or color, of one or two words in the midst of a paragraph. Obviously, you can't create a new paragraph within the existing paragraph without completely messing up the formatting of the page.

That's where the `<span>` tag comes in. A `<span>` tag creates an inline collection of text to which styles can be applied. A `<span>` tag is similar to a `<div>` tag, but is treated as an inline element by default instead of a block element.

As you might expect, a span element can be connected to an ID or class where its style properties are defined, or it can be assigned inline styles.

The span element is most useful for assigning special font properties, and some of the more esoteric text decorations and effects discussed later in this chapter.

For example, Figure 9.1 shows a case where the designer wanted to emphasize two words by increasing their size relative to the type around them.

Figure 9.1. Using the span Element to Oversize Two Words

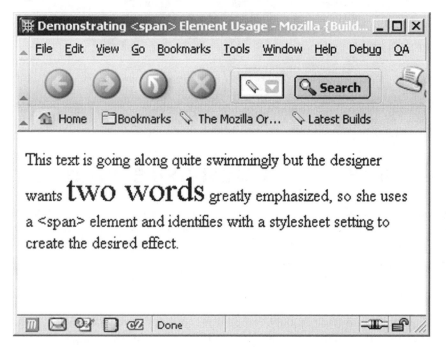

Here's the HTML for the page that produces that result. The style rule and span element are shown in bold, so you can easily spot the important point in this code.

```
<!DOCTYPE html PUBLIC "-//W3C//DTD XHTML 1.0 Transitional//EN"
  "http://www.w3.org/TR/xhtml1/DTD/xhtml1-transitional.dtd">
<html xmlns="http://www.w3.org/1999/xhtml">
<head>
  <title>Demonstrating &lt;span&gt; Element Usage</title>
  <meta http-equiv="Content-Type"
    content="text/html; charset=iso-8859-1" />
  <style type="text/css">
  <!--
  .bigtype {
    font-size: 2em;
  }
  -->
  </style>
</head>
<body>
```

```
<p>This text is going along quite swimmingly but the designer
   wants <span class="bigtype">two words</span> greatly
   emphasized, so she uses a &lt;span&gt; element and
   identifies with a stylesheet setting to create the desired
   effect.</p>
</body>
</html>
```

As you'll see, as we move through this chapter, the span element comes in quite handy when you want to do any kind of special formatting on substrings within other text elements.

Text Alignment as a Design Technique

Professional artists and designers know that any design, whether it's a Web page, a print ad, or a painting, comprises negative and positive space. Positive space consists of places in the design that are occupied by some object. On a Web page, text, graphics, forms, and other content and user interface elements make up positive space. Negative space, on the other hand, is space that is empty, or not occupied by any object.

Good design dictates a balance between positive and negative space. We're not about to get into this subject in detail, but suffice it to say that pages that are "designed" as a lot of closely packed text content, with few (if any) "breaks" for negative space, are pretty ugly and hard to use.

But, even text-only pages can be made more inviting by the application of negative space. And one of the best ways to create negative space on a Web page is through the judicious use of text alignment.

Examples of text alignment have appeared in numerous places in this book. Viewed at its most basic level, text alignment is hardly rocket science, so explanations of those examples has not been necessary. Now, however, it's time to understand precisely how text alignment works in CSS.

Text Alignment in CSS Versus HTML

In HTML, text alignment was typically handled using the `<center>` tag and the `align` attribute. Both of these are deprecated in HTML 4.0 as part of the move toward CSS becoming the preferred presentation mode[1].

As we adopt CSS, we instead use the `text-align` property to describe the alignment of text.

The `text-align` property can take any of the following values:

☐ `left`

☐ `center`

☐ `right`

☐ `justify`

The default value is `left`. Support for the `justify` value is not required in the W3C's CSS recommendations, and support for it is spotty. But you can use it with impunity, if not always with the intended effect, because browsers that don't support it generally resort to left alignment.

Moving from Crowded to Airy Design with Alignment

To see how you can use `text-align` to create more pleasing effects on your pages, let's start with the simple page shown in Figure 9.2, in which no alignment styles are included.

Here's the HTML that produced Figure 9.2.

```
<!DOCTYPE html PUBLIC "-//W3C//DTD XHTML 1.0 Transitional//EN"
  "http://www.w3.org/TR/xhtml1/DTD/xhtml1-transitional.dtd">
<html xmlns="http://www.w3.org/1999/xhtml">
<head>
  <title>Text Layout Sample 1</title>
  <meta http-equiv="Content-Type"
```

---

[1]Actually, the **align** attribute is still permitted in HTML 4.0, but only within the context of table cells.

```
     content="text/html; charset=iso-8859-1" />
</head>
<body>
  <h1>Ten Keys to Optimum Performance</h1>
  <p>A careful study and analysis of more than 35,000 pages of
     self-improvement materials published in the past 100 years
     leads to the conclusion that there are really only 10
     basic keys to optimum performance and success.</p>
  <h2>Energy - Committing to Peak Power</h2>
  <p>There are no dead optimum performers, are there? To achieve
     even minimal performance, you have to be, act, and feel
     alive. If you don't have the energy to do whatever it takes,
     you'll never perform up to your true potential.</p>
  <h2>Mission - Living What's Most Important</h2>
  <p>Until you know what's important, you're spending the only
     life you have on things that simply don't matter. Lacking
     direction and purpose, you're powerless to make a real
     difference in your life. However, all self-imposed
     limitations are removed when you tap into the infinite power
     generated by 'working from your heart,' fulfilling a clearly
     defined mission.</p>
  <h2>Attitude - Transform Passion Into Action</h2>
  <p>Even though you may have a passion for what's most important,
     until you also believe that you can make a real difference
     in your life and those around you, nothing's going to happen.
     Nothing is produced, nor even attempted, until you believe
     in yourself enough to transform your passion into
     action.</p>
  <h3>From "The Power of TQ" by Nine to Five Screen Gems Software,
     Inc. Reprinted by permission</h3>
</body>
</html>
```

Figure 9.2. Simple Text Page Layout with No Alignment Styles

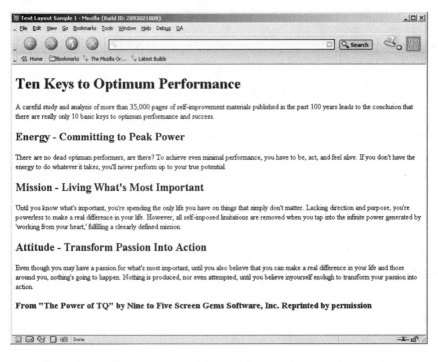

There's nothing too complicated here. Nor is there anything very interesting to look at, even though the content itself might interest someone.

Now, let's see what happens when we center the top headline, and move the subheadings so they're aligned to the right side of the page rather than the left. The result is shown in Figure 9.3.

Figure 9.3. Applying Headline Alignment to Basic Text Layout

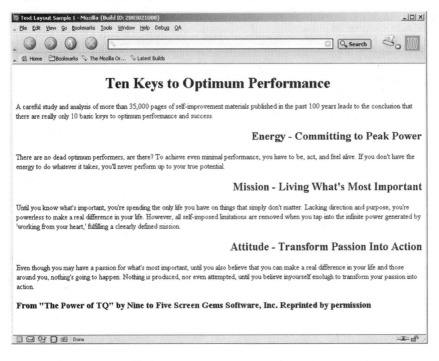

The style sheet rules that produce the effect in Figure 9.3 are pretty simple:

```
h1 {
  text-align: center;
}
h2 {
  text-align: right;
}
```

While the layout of the page is admittedly unorthodox, you have to admit that it's more interesting than what we started with. The "air", or negative space, created to the left of the subheadings is attention-getting.

This page consists of headlines, followed by associated paragraphs of pithy advice. The whole scheme seems to lend itself to something more closely resembling a promotional design. So, let's try centering the text of the paragraphs. Now, we have a page that looks like Figure 9.4.

Figure 9.4. Centering Text in Paragraphs Creates Different Effect

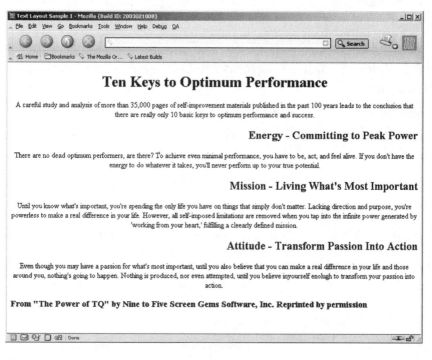

The style sheet that generates Figure 9.4 is shown here:

```
h1 {
   text-align: center;
}
h2 {
   text-align: right;
}
p {
   text-align: center;
}
```

Whether or not you like your paragraphs centered, you can probably see where I'm heading with this concept. By altering the `text-align` property of text elements on your page, you can create more negative space and more pleasing page layouts—even if you don't do anything else.

But, I couldn't resist making one last change that involves color, not alignment. Figure 9.5 shows you what putting a background color behind the heading text does for the additional negative space. I've used a yellow background, although you can't tell, but the fact that it's a solid color produces the same effect as negative space, while providing yet another way for us to guide the reader's eye where we want it to go: to the main subheadings.

Figure 9.5. Adding Color Background to Subheadings to Emphasize Negative Space

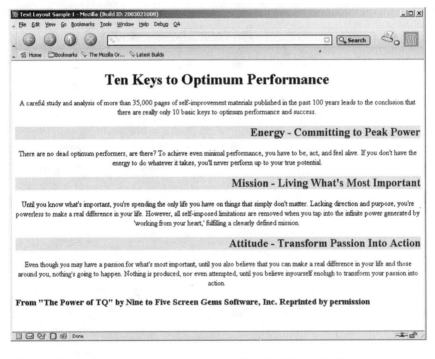

Here's the style sheet that creates the effect in Figure 9.5.

```
h1 {
  text-align: center;
}
h2 {
  text-align: right;
  background-color: yellow;
}
p {
  text-align: center;
}
```

First-Line Indentation

In the example in the previous section, I centered the text in the explanatory paragraphs under each subheading. That was not, as I said at the time, necessarily a great design, but it did demonstrate how alignment can produce "air" or negative space.

Another, perhaps more conventional, way to accomplish this objective with blocks of text is to **indent** the first line of each paragraph.

The `text-indent` property controls the amount of extra left padding that's applied to the first line of a block of text. The property requires a measurement or percentage of the element width as a value.

Replace the style rule for paragraphs in the above CSS with a new one like this:

```
p {
  text-indent: 2em;
}
```

The result will look like Figure 9.6.

Figure 9.6. Indenting the First Line of Text in Each Paragraph

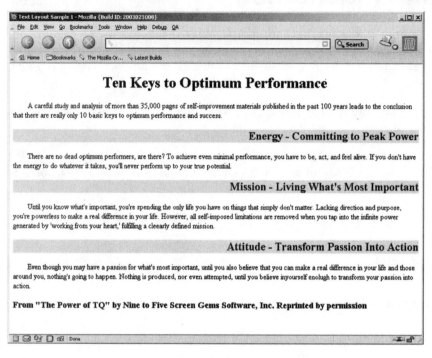

A variation on first-line indent is **first-line outdent**, also called a **hanging indent**, where the first line is closer to the left margin than the rest of the paragraph. You can see this effect in the first paragraph of Figure 9.7.

Figure 9.7. Outdenting the First Line of Text in a Paragraph

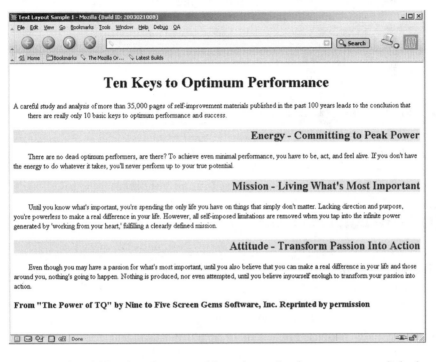

Here are the CSS rules that we add to the style sheet to accomplish the styling shown in Figure 9.7.

```
p.outdent {
  padding-left: 2em;
  text-indent: -2em;
}
```

What I've done here is assigned a left padding of 2 ems to the entire paragraph, and then removed that padding from the first line by setting a negative text-indent of the same amount.

In the HTML, I've simply assigned the outdent class to the first paragraph of the document:

```
<h1>Ten Keys to Optimum Performance</h1>
<p class="outdent">A careful study and analysis of more than
  35,000 pages of self-improvement materials published in the
```

```
past 100 years leads to the conclusion that there are really
only 10 basic keys to optimum performance and success.</p>
```

When you use a negative value for the `text-indent` property, you have to be careful that the first line of text doesn't end up falling outside the boundaries of the browser window. In general, this means you need to assign a `padding-left` of at least the same size as the negative indent you choose.

Horizontal and Vertical Spacing

CSS rules allow you to control spacing between lines, letters, and words. You can use these properties to create interesting visual effects, or merely to improve readability of text, or sometimes, to fit text into a tight spot.

The `line-height` Property

All elements in a Web page have a `line-height` property. This property refers to the total distance from the top of the tallest element in one line to the top of the tallest element in a line immediately below or above the line[2]. By default, browsers create a `line-height` that ensures readability of vertically adjacent lines or elements. For example, if the text in a paragraph is set in a 12-point font, the browser will usually provide one point of spacing above and another point of spacing below the line to create a total `line-height` of 14 points.

When you explicitly set the `line-height` for an element such as a heading or paragraph, you effectively tell the browser to increase or decrease the amount of space between that line and those that are vertically adjacent to it. This space is called "leading" (pronounced like "bedding", not like "reading"), a term left over from the days when type was set using molten lead formed into bars of type, one for each line. Spacing was created by placing thin blank "slugs" between lines.

Leading can create additional negative space in a Web page layout. Figure 9.8 shows you what the page we've been working with looks like if the following style rule is applied:

```
p {
  text-indent: 2em;
  line-height: 1.5em;
}
```

---

[2]Technically, line-height refers to the distance between the two lines' "baselines", but in practice this turns out to be the same as I've described it here.

This effectively creates text that is one and one-half line spaced.

Figure 9.8. Using the `line-height` Property to Create 1.5-line Spaced Text

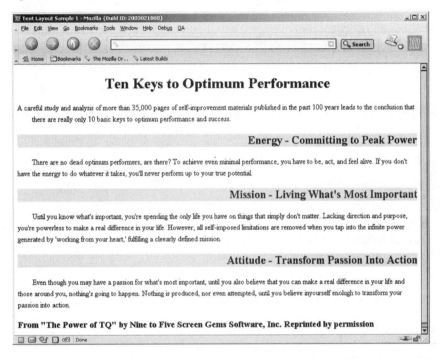

It's important to realize that when you set the `line-height` property using a relative measurement (such as an em value or percentage), the value is applied based on the current element's font settings, not, as is the case with most other font control properties, on those of the parent. Thus, if you have a 12-pixel font assigned to a paragraph that's contained in a `<div>` with an 18-pixel font, for example, a `line-height` value of 2 ems for the paragraph would produce an actual line height of 24 pixels, not 36.

The `line-height` property is the first CSS property we've encountered that can take a pure numerical argument, as in this example:

```
p {
  line-height: 2.0;
}
```

This has the same visual effect as supplying a value of 2 ems, or a value of 200%. The difference between a numeric value and a CSS measurement is that a numeric value is inherited directly by child elements, which will apply it to their own font sizes, while relative values cause the actual line height to be inherited by children. This is easier to demonstrate than explain.

Figure 9.9 shows two different paragraphs, set in large type, to dramatize the different effects of numeric and relative `line-height` properties. The text in the figure explains how each paragraph was formatted relative to the `<div>` container of which it is part.

Figure 9.9. Relative Versus Numeric `line-height` Property Values

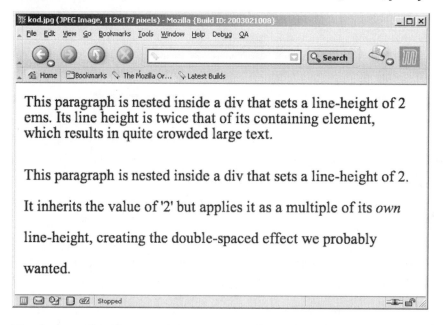

The first paragraph is contained in a `div` with a `line-height` of 2em. The paragraph therefore inherits the line height that results when you double the default line height produced by the `div` element's font (in this case, the basic font size of 12 points, as defined by the browser). As the paragraph uses a larger font than the `div`, the line spacing looks very crowded.

The second paragraph is contained in a `div` with a `line-height` of 2. Instead of passing on the exact line height, the inherited value of 2 is used by the paragraph to determine a `line-height` based on its own, larger font. This produces the double-spaced effect we probably intended.

For this reason, it is generally best to stick to numeric values for the `line-height` property, unless you know you're striving for a really different vertical spacing effect, and understand the consequences of using CSS measurement values.

The `letter-spacing` and `word-spacing` Properties

The `letter-spacing` property defines the amount of space between the letters in the text element to which it is applied. It can take an absolute or relative value, and its default setting is `normal`.

Figure 9.10 shows an extreme example of `letter-spacing` so you can see the effect.

Figure 9.10. Using `letter-spacing` to Define Distance Between Letters

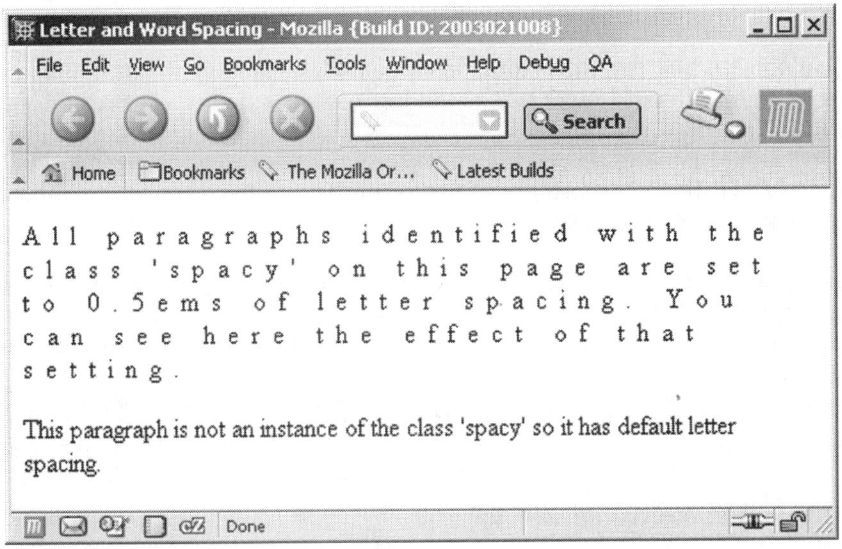

Here's the HTML page that generates Figure 9.10.

```
<!DOCTYPE html PUBLIC "-//W3C//DTD XHTML 1.0 Transitional//EN"
  "http://www.w3.org/TR/xhtml1/DTD/xhtml1-transitional.dtd">
<html xmlns="http://www.w3.org/1999/xhtml">
<head>
  <title>Letter and Word Spacing</title>
  <meta http-equiv="Content-Type"
    content="text/html; charset=iso-8859-1" />
  <style type="text/css">
  <!--
  .spacy {
    letter-spacing: 0.5em;
  }
  -->
  </style>
</head>
<body>
  <p class="spacy">All paragraphs identified with the class
    'spacy' on this page are set to 0.5ems of letter spacing.
    You can see here the effect of that setting.</p>
  <p>This paragraph is not an instance of the class 'spacy'
    so it has default letter spacing.
  </p>
</body>
</html>
```

Notice that the spacing between words is elongated as well, so words continue to appear as a grouping of letters that are closer together than the words are to one another.

You can apply negative values to the letter-spacing property to cause letters to appear closer to one another.

One situation in which letter-spacing comes in particularly handy occurs where a headline appears to have a bit too much inter-letter spacing. This often happens with monospaced fonts, but it can be annoying or distracting with sans-serif fonts as well. Figure 9.11 demonstrates this effect put to good use. The top headline on the page does not use any letter-spacing. Notice how the words containing the letters "i" and "l" and "t", in particular, look a little too "airy." This is a characteristic of monospaced fonts, but with CSS letter-spacing property settings you can overcome this problem and continue to use this type of font where it's most appropriate.

Figure 9.11. Negative `letter-spacing` Tightens Up Monospace Fonts

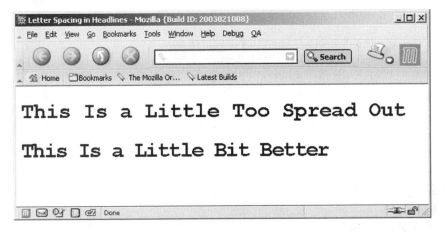

Here's the HTML that produces the page in Figure 9.11. Notice I've defined a class called "compress" and then applied it to one of the <h1> heading elements.

```
<!DOCTYPE html PUBLIC "-//W3C//DTD XHTML 1.0 Transitional//EN"
  "http://www.w3.org/TR/xhtml1/DTD/xhtml1-transitional.dtd">
<html xmlns="http://www.w3.org/1999/xhtml">
<head>
  <title>Letter Spacing in Headlines</title>
  <meta http-equiv="Content-Type"
    content="text/html; charset=iso-8859-1" />
  <style type="text/css">
<!--
h1 {
    font-family: Courier, "Courier New", monospace;
}
.compress {
    letter-spacing: -0.05em;
}
-->
  </style>
</head>
<body>
  <h1>This Is a Little Too Spread Out</h1>
  <h1 class="compress">This Is a Little Bit Better</h1>
</body>
</html>
```

As you can see, I decreased letter spacing by only a small amount (5% of the width of a character) to achieve the desired result. You'll need to experiment with the effect the `letter-spacing` property has with various fonts and sizes to know what will work best in any given situation.

Another case in which `letter-spacing` is particularly effective is in creating a different visual effect for a page heading. Figure 9.12 shows a heading that makes effective use of letter spacing to create a graphically interesting effect, without requiring us to use graphic tools.

Figure 9.12. Using `letter-spacing` to Create an Interesting Visual Effect

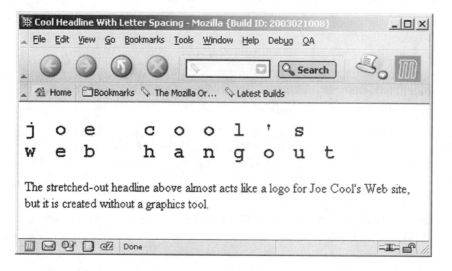

The HTML that creates the effect shown in Figure 9.12 is simplicity itself.

```
<!DOCTYPE html PUBLIC "-//W3C//DTD XHTML 1.0 Transitional//EN"
  "http://www.w3.org/TR/xhtml1/DTD/xhtml1-transitional.dtd">
<html xmlns="http://www.w3.org/1999/xhtml">
<head>
  <title>Cool Headline With Letter Spacing</title>
  <meta http-equiv="Content-Type"
    content="text/html; charset=iso-8859-1" />
</head>
<body>
  <h2 style="letter-spacing: 1em;
    font-family: Courier, 'Courier New', monospace;">joe cool's
    web hangout</h2>
```

```
<p>
  The stretched-out headline above almost acts like a logo for
  Joe Cool's Web site, but it is created without a graphics
  tool.
</p>
</body>
</html>
```

The word-spacing property determines the spacing between words. It seems to me to be of less practical utility than the letter-spacing property for a couple of reasons.

First, versions of Internet Explorer earlier than 6 on Windows and 5 on the Macintosh do not support this property, nor do Netscape Navigator versions earlier than 6. In fact, the IE5 Macintosh support is buggy, resulting in word overlap in some circumstances. Even though this property was defined in CSS Level 1, the main browsers have only recently made the move to support it.

Secondly, if you use word-spacing in conjunction with text that has a text-align: justify property set, results are often unpredictable, and seldom what you intended.

As a result, I recommend that you avoid using this property unless it creates a specific result you really want or need, and you've tested it and know what it looks like on all the browsers you're required to support.

That said, Figure 9.13 depicts the effect a word-spacing setting of 1em has on an oversized sentence of text in a browser that supports the word-spacing property.

Figure 9.13. Demonstration of `word-spacing` Property

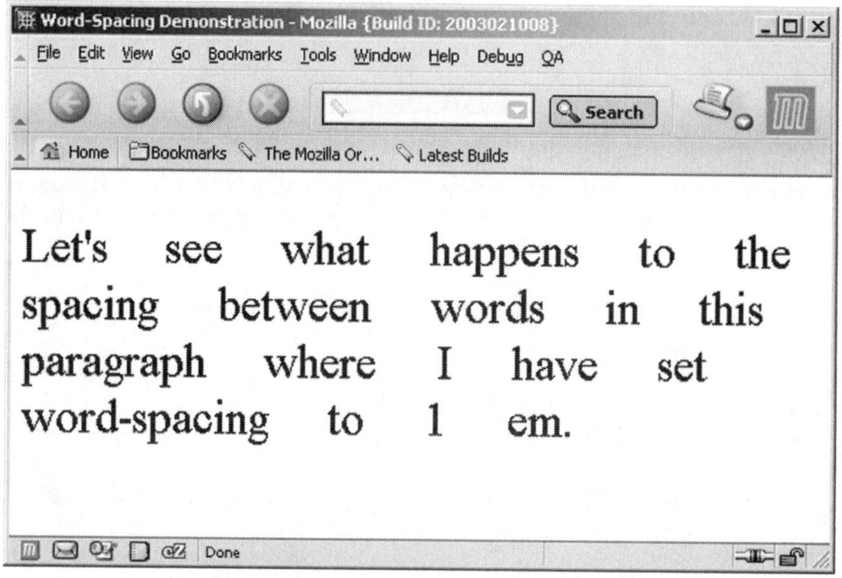

Here's the HTML that produces the page shown in Figure 9.13.

```
<!DOCTYPE html PUBLIC "-//W3C//DTD XHTML 1.0 Transitional//EN"
  "http://www.w3.org/TR/xhtml1/DTD/xhtml1-transitional.dtd">
<html xmlns="http://www.w3.org/1999/xhtml">
<head>
  <title>Word-Spacing Demonstration</title>
  <meta http-equiv="Content-Type"
    content="text/html; charset=iso-8859-1" />
</head>
<body>
  <p style="word-spacing: 1em; font-size: 2em;">
    Let's see what happens to the spacing between words in this
    paragraph where I have set word-spacing to 1 em.
  </p>
</body>
</html>
```

Text Decorations

The `text-decoration` property allows you to add any of four specific effects to text:

❏ underline

❏ overline

❏ blink

❏ line-through

In addition, the `text-decoration` property can take a value of none, which has utility in one specific situation I'll discuss in a moment.

I'm going to ignore blinking as a text decoration. Many mainstream browsers ignore it, because it fell into almost immediate disrepute when Netscape first introduced it as a nonstandard HTML tag. Blinking text is widely considered amateurish and bad design.

I also believe that using underlining is a bad idea, but I have less company in that position than with the blinking text issue. Users are accustomed to seeing hyperlinks underlined. My view is that deliberately underlining text that is not a hyperlink creates only confusion for the user.

Overlining can be used to create an interesting and potentially useful effect, in which a border appears above the text and extends only the width of the text itself. This makes it different from using the top border line we learned about in Chapter 3. Figure 9.14 shows the effect, and the HTML that produces the effect follows.

Figure 9.14. Overlining Delineates a Headline

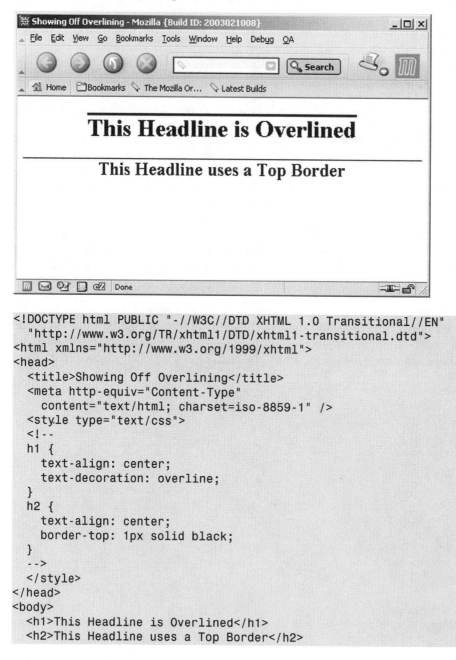

```
<!DOCTYPE html PUBLIC "-//W3C//DTD XHTML 1.0 Transitional//EN"
  "http://www.w3.org/TR/xhtml1/DTD/xhtml1-transitional.dtd">
<html xmlns="http://www.w3.org/1999/xhtml">
<head>
  <title>Showing Off Overlining</title>
  <meta http-equiv="Content-Type"
    content="text/html; charset=iso-8859-1" />
  <style type="text/css">
<!--
h1 {
   text-align: center;
   text-decoration: overline;
}
h2 {
   text-align: center;
   border-top: 1px solid black;
}
-->
  </style>
</head>
<body>
  <h1>This Headline is Overlined</h1>
  <h2>This Headline uses a Top Border</h2>
```

```
</body>
</html>
```

The border over the second headline extends the full width of the page because that marks the top of the box containing the headline. The top heading on the page uses a text-decoration property with a value of overline to create a decidedly different result.

Another way to place a separator line between two text elements is to use the <hr> tag. However, even though you can control the width and alignment of a horizontal rule, you still can't reliably specify such an element to behave like the overline decoration, extending precisely from the start to the end of the text.

Another value the text-decoration property can take is line-through. This has the same effect as defining an HTML element with the <del> tag, and that tag has not been deprecated. I recommend, however, using the line-through CSS style, unless the semantic meaning of the <del> tag (to mark content for deletion during editing) is appropriate.

Figure 9.15 demonstrates the line-through value of the text-decoration property.

Figure 9.15. Using the `line-through` Value of the `text-decoration` Property

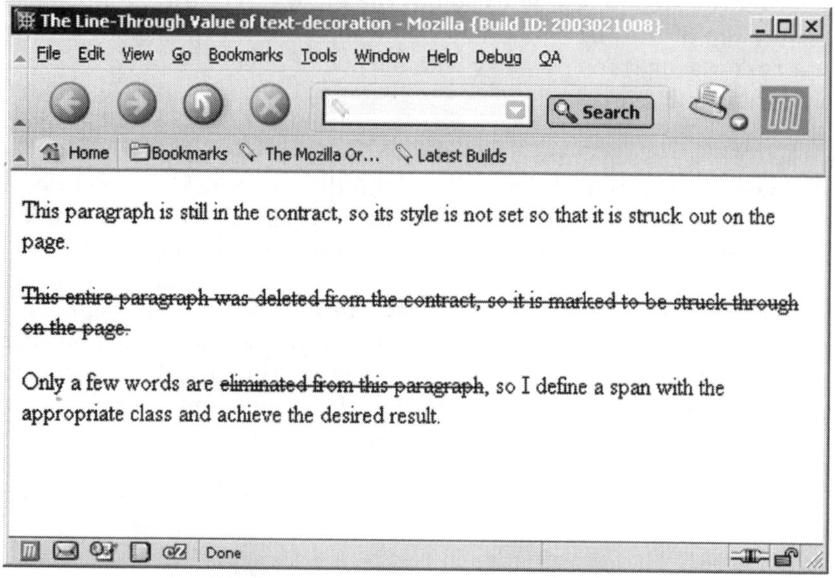

```
<!DOCTYPE html PUBLIC "-//W3C//DTD XHTML 1.0 Transitional//EN"
  "http://www.w3.org/TR/xhtml1/DTD/xhtml1-transitional.dtd">
<html xmlns="http://www.w3.org/1999/xhtml">
<head>
  <title>The Line-Through Value of text-decoration</title>
  <meta http-equiv="Content-Type"
    content="text/html; charset=iso-8859-1" />
  <style type="text/css">
  <!--
  .deleted {
    text-decoration: line-through;
  }
  -->
  </style>
</head>
<body>
  <p>This paragraph is still in the contract, so its style is
    not set so that it is struck out on the page.
  </p>
  <p class="deleted">This entire paragraph was deleted from
    the contract, so it is marked to be struck through on the
    page.
```

```
    </p>
    <p>Only a few words are <span class="deleted">eliminated from
      this paragraph</span>, so I define a span with the appropriate
      class and achieve the desired result.
    </p>
  </body>
</html>
```

The last `text-decoration` value I'll describe is `none`. Given that text, without being told otherwise, doesn't display any decoration, you might wonder why you'd ever want to use this value. You can assign the `none` value to the `text-decoration` property to turn off underlining of hyperlinks. This usage can be more or less effective depending on whether the user has already turned off underlining of hyperlinks as a browser preference. Most modern browsers offer this option and many users take advantage of it.

Shadowed Text Without Graphics

One of the most effective ways of setting off a headline and giving a Web page a professional look and feel, is to use shadowed text, or text that looks like it's standing off the page with a shadow behind it. All graphics tools make the creation of such text effects trivial, but they all suffer from one drawback: the text they draw is not true string text that can be searched, indexed, or translated into other languages. And, as graphics, they'll always tend to load more slowly than pure text.

Using CSS positioning[3], you can create shadowed text effects that are as good as any graphics program, without giving up the advantages of pure text on your Web page.

Figure 9.16 shows a line of shadowed headline text. You can't tell here, but the text is red and the background shadow is gray.

---

[3]In fact, CSS2 has a `text-shadow` property that is intended to achieve this effect. Unfortunately, no currently-available browser supports it. See Appendix C, for details on this property if you're curious.

Figure 9.16. Creating Shadowed Text Effect Without Graphics

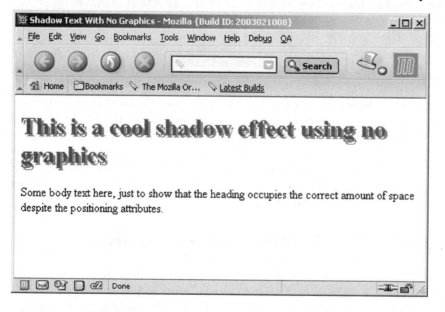

Here's the HTML that generates the page in Figure 9.16.

```
<!DOCTYPE html PUBLIC "-//W3C//DTD XHTML 1.0 Transitional//EN"
  "http://www.w3.org/TR/xhtml1/DTD/xhtml1-transitional.dtd">
<html xmlns="http://www.w3.org/1999/xhtml">
<head>
  <title>Shadow Text With No Graphics</title>
</head>
<body>
  <div style="position:relative;">
    <h1 style="color:red; position:relative; z-index:2">
      This is a cool shadow effect using no graphics
    </h1>
    <h1 style="color:gray; position:absolute; left:3px;
      top:3px; z-index:1; margin:0;">
      This is a cool shadow effect using no graphics
    </h1>
  </div>
  <p>Some body text here, just to show that the heading
    occupies the correct amount of space despite the
    positioning properties.</p>
</body>
</html>
```

I create a `div` element to contain the two pieces of text I want to position to create the shadowed effect. The `div`'s `position` property is set to `relative` so that I can position the elements inside it (the two `h1` tags) relative to the position of the `div`, rather than that of the page (i.e. it creates a positioning context for its children). I use `relative` positioning on the 'real' heading, so that it can float above the shadow (you can't assign a `z-index` value to statically-positioned elements), while occupying the correct amount of space. And, I use `absolute` positioning on the shadow (so that it can float behind the heading without occupying space on the page), indenting it slightly to the right, and down from the position of the 'real' heading.

The `margin: 0` on the shadow `div` is there prevent some browsers (most notably, Mozilla) from adding a margin to the top of the shadow `h1`.

Styling Hyperlinks

Hyperlinks are a special category of text used on a Web page. They are active elements that create navigational points for users to change their viewpoint to elsewhere on the same page, another page on the same site, or another site. They can, in fact, be used for many tasks if you call on the capabilities of JavaScript, but those uses are beyond the scope of this book.

There are two ways to control the style of hyperlinks. You can treat links like any other text for the purposes of styling their initial static appearance. Or you can take advantage of four anchor pseudo-classes to style the appearance of text in any of the four interactive states in which it can exist. These four states and their corresponding pseudo-classes are shown in Table 9.1.[4]

---

[4]While I'm discussing these pseudo-classes in conjunction with anchors here, the CSS recommendation allows `:hover` and `:active` to be applied to other types of HTML elements, as well as links. A fifth pseudo-class, `:focus`, also exists, but is not supported by Internet Explorer for Windows, and is therefore not commonly used.

Table 9.1. Anchor Pseudo-Classes

Anchor Pseudo-Class	Corresponding Hyperlink State
`a:link`	Not yet visited
`a:visited`	Visited
`a:hover`	Cursor positioned over link but mouse not being clicked
`a:active`	Being clicked on at the moment

Although most links appear inline with text and take on the same basic characteristics (font family and size, for example) as the text in which they are embedded, hyperlinks by default are blue and underlined. Sometimes, you want to apply a different font family, or size, or background color combination to links. In addition, links that appear as lists or pseudo-lists on pages—that is, not surrounded by other text—can sometimes be more effectively presented if you deliberately style them differently from normal text on the page. You can use all the normal text identification schemes to alter the appearance of links. For example, you can define a class called, say, `majorlink`, which creates a specialized font family and color combination, and then define a link as belonging to that class. This is how you'd do it:

```
<a class="majorlink" href="somelocation">Click here</a>
```

Figure 9.17 shows two separate hyperlinks. The top one is a normal link, where either the user or the style sheet has turned off underlining, and the second is an instance of the class `majorlink`, where I've identified a different font family, size, background color, and text color.

Figure 9.17. Two Hyperlinks With Different Formatting

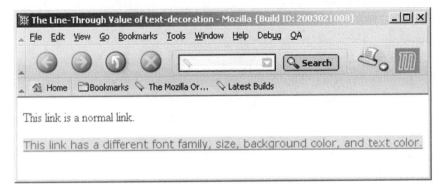

The anchor pseudo-classes can be used in style sheets to create specific designs associated with each condition in which a hyperlink can be found. Here's a typical style sheet providing for the special treatment of hyperlinks:

```
a:link {
  color: darkgreen;
  background-color: transparent;
}
a:visited {
  color: lightgreen;
  background-color: transparent;
}
a:hover {
  color: green;
  background-color: black;
}
a:active {
  color: black;
  background-color: green;
}
```

The order in which you declare each of these pseudo-classes is important because, given the rules of cascading (discussed in the final section of this chapter), each of these sets of rules will be overridden by an earlier rule of the same importance. Thus, if you declare a rule for a :hover pseudo-class before you define a rule for the :link or :visited pseudo-classes, the color you choose for :hover links will never appear, as all links are either visited or unvisited. In the above code fragment, if you relocated the a:hover rule to the first position in the list, it would never be used, because the subsequent :link or :visited rule (whichever applied to the specific link in question), would override it.

It is possible to specify two pseudo-classes in one rule (though not mutually exclusive ones like :link and :visited, of course). For example, you can apply a special "hover" color to visited links with this rule:

```
a:visited:hover {
  color: blue;
  background-color: transparent;
}
```

You can turn off the underlining of all hyperlinks in a document with a single style rule:

```
a {
  text-decoration: none;
}
```

Styling Lists with CSS

Lists in HTML begin with one of two tags: `<ul>` for an unnumbered or bulleted list, or `<ol>` for a numbered or ordered list[5]. These are both container tags, so they end with the respective closing tags, `</ul>` and `</ol>`. The items within a list are marked with the `<li>` tag in both types of lists.

Apart from headings and paragraphs, lists are probably the most commonly used of those elements defined to present textual content to the Web user.

Because lists are block elements, all the techniques we've covered with respect to positioning, margins, borders, and related subjects apply equally well to them. I won't go through all that information again here. Instead, I'll focus on three specific styling properties in CSS that apply only to lists:

❑ `list-style-type`

❑ `list-style-position`

❑ `list-style-image`

There is also a `list-style` shorthand property with which you can set multiple properties of a list.

---

[5]There are other types of lists for glossary items or definitions, directories, and menus, but they are seldom used, so I've omitted them from this discussion. For the most part, they're styled identically to the two major kinds of lists I'll discuss here.

The `list-style-type` Property

The `list-style-type` property defines the kind of item marker to be associated with each item in the list. The property takes a constant value chosen from the options shown in Table 9.2 and Table 9.3.

Table 9.2. Values for `list-style-type` Property and Unordered Lists

Constant Value	Meaning
circle	open circle
disc	filled circle (bullet)
square	filled square[6]

[6] The filled square is not supported on Version 4 browsers on the Macintosh.

Table 9.3. Values for `list-style-type` Property and Ordered Lists

Constant Value	Meaning
decimal	1, 2, 3, 4 ,5...
decimal-leading-zero	01, 02, 03, 04, 05....
lower-alpha	a, b, c, d, e...
lower-roman	i, ii, iii, iv, v...
upper-alpha	A, B, C, D, E...
upper-roman	I, II, III, IV, V...

There are a number of other possible values for the `list-style-type` property, including those that define item markers in non-English languages such as Hebrew, Armenian, Japanese, and Chinese.

An unordered list displays by default with an item marker of a filled circle, or bullet. Nested unordered lists then change their item marker to an open circle for the first level of indentation, and a square for the second level, as shown in Figure 9.18.

Figure 9.18. Nesting Lists Without CSS Styling

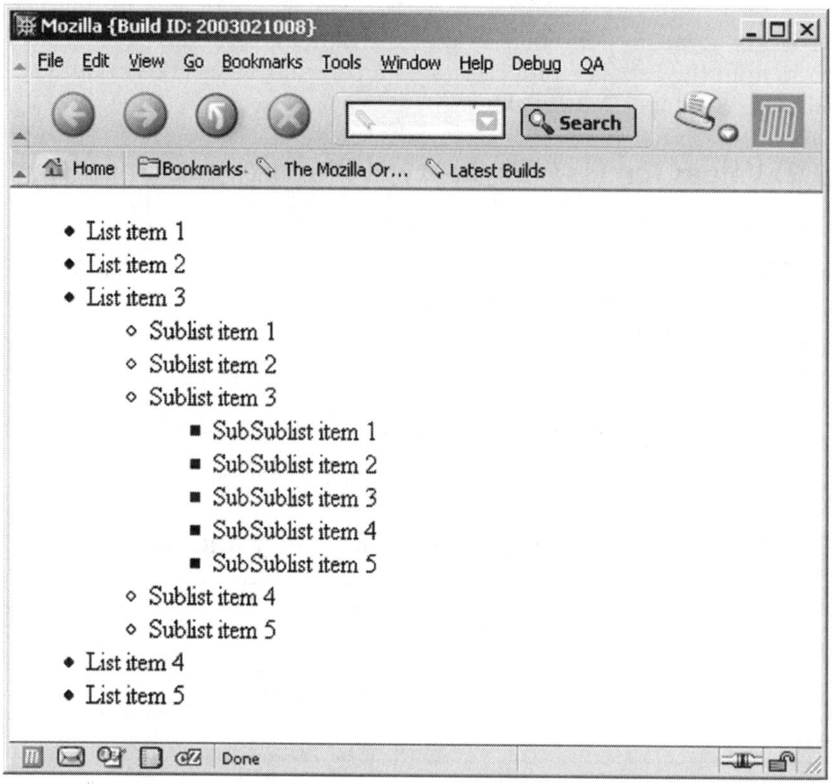

What if you prefer to have the item marker be a square for the outermost list, a bullet for the next one, and an open circle for the third? Apply a set of style sheet rules like the ones below, and you can accomplish this objective quite easily.

```
ul {
  list-style-type: square;
}
ul ul {
  list-style-type: disc;
}
ul ul ul {
  list-style-type: circle;
}
```

Notice that I've used contextual selectors to define the three nesting levels of lists and their associated styles. Figure 9.19 shows the result.

Figure 9.19. Applying `list-style-type` Property to Nested Unordered Lists

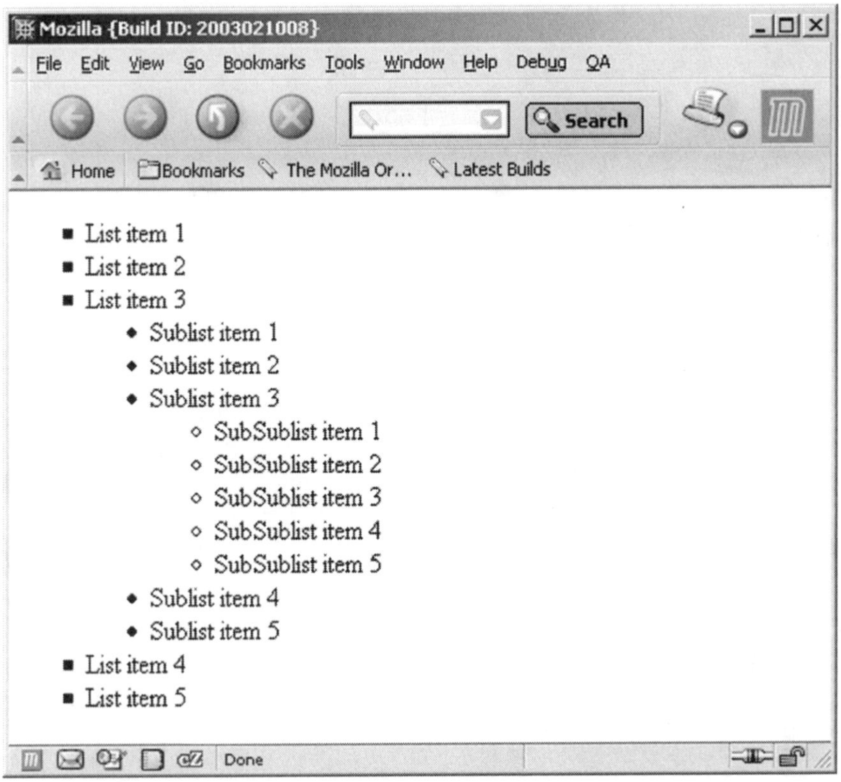

Ordered lists appear more complex because of their wide variety of markers, but they are essentially the same as unordered lists. If you use CSS to set the type of list item markers for a given kind of list, that same type will be used for nested lists. For example, Figure 9.20 shows the effect of assigning upper-case Roman numerals as the `list-style-type` on a set of nested ordered lists.

Figure 9.20. Nested Ordered Lists with a Single CSS list-style-type

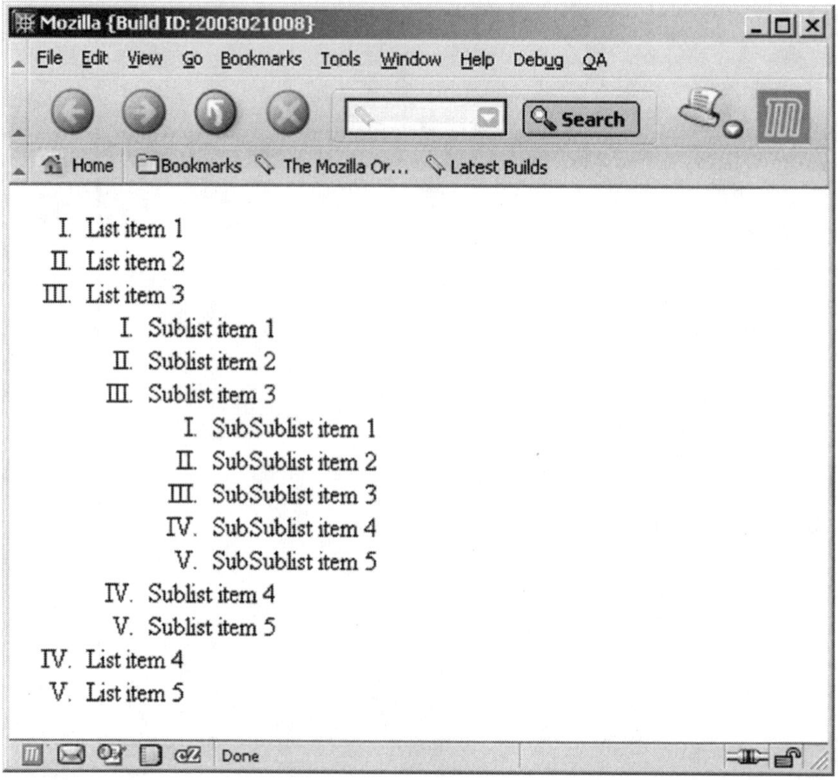

Not very attractive or helpful, is it? Let's fix it by applying some different list-style-type values to nested lists with the CSS rules shown here:

```
ol {
  list-style-type: upper-roman;
}
ol ol {
  list-style-type: upper-alpha;
}
ol ol ol {
  list-style-type: decimal;
}
```

This results in the much-improved output shown in Figure 9.21.

Figure 9.21. Nested Ordered Lists with CSS Styling Applied

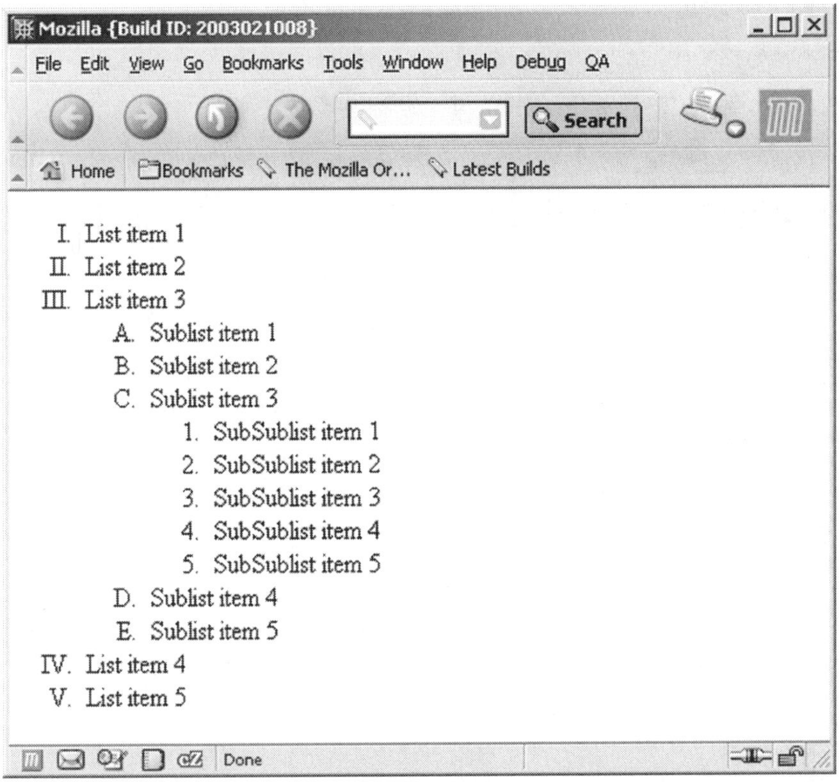

The `list-style-position` Property

Both ordered and unordered lists are displayed so that their item markers align vertically and the text associated with each item is indented from the marker. This gives a neat, orderly appearance and is almost always the right design choice.

CSS permits you to define a list in such a way that the item markers line up vertically, but text in the line items wraps under each item marker as it returns to the left margin. To create this effect, use the `list-style-position` property and give it a value of `inside`. Figure 9.22 shows two lists, one using the default `list-style-position` value of `outside`, and the second with a value of `inside`.

Figure 9.22. Two Different Settings for the `list-style-position` Property

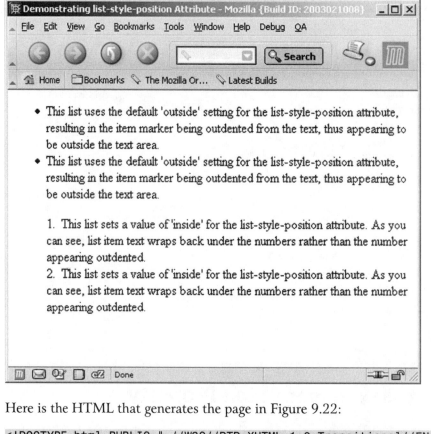

Here is the HTML that generates the page in Figure 9.22:

```
<!DOCTYPE html PUBLIC "-//W3C//DTD XHTML 1.0 Transitional//EN"
  "http://www.w3.org/TR/xhtml1/DTD/xhtml1-transitional.dtd">
<html xmlns="http://www.w3.org/1999/xhtml">
<head>
  <title>Demonstrating list-style-position property</title>
  <meta http-equiv="Content-Type"
    content="text/html; charset=iso-8859-1" />
  <style type="text/css">
<!--
ol {
  list-style-position: inside;
}
-->
```

```
    </style>
  </head>
  <body>
    <ul>
      <li>This list uses the default 'outside' setting for the
          list-style-position property, resulting in the item
          marker being outdented from the text, thus appearing to
          be outside the text area.</li>
      <li>This list uses the default 'outside' setting for the
          list-style-position property, resulting in the item
          marker being outdented from the text, thus appearing to
          be outside the text area.</li>
    </ul>
    <ol>
      <li>This list sets a value of 'inside' for the
          list-style-position property. As you can see, list
          item text wraps back under the numbers rather than the
          number appearing outdented.</li>
      <li>This list sets a value of 'inside' for the
          list-style-position property. As you can see, list item
          text wraps back under the numbers rather than the number
          appearing outdented.</li>
    </ol>
  </body>
</html>
```

The `list-style-image` Property

You can replace the bullets in front of items in unordered lists with any graphic image for which you have a URL, and which the browser is capable of rendering. This includes GIF, JPEG, and PNG images at a minimum.

The `list-style-image` property takes as a value a full or relative URL pointing to the image you wish to use. Figure 9.23 shows the use of the footbag image from the *Footbag Freaks* page as an item marker in a list.

Figure 9.23. Using an Image as an Item Marker With `list-style-image` Property Setting

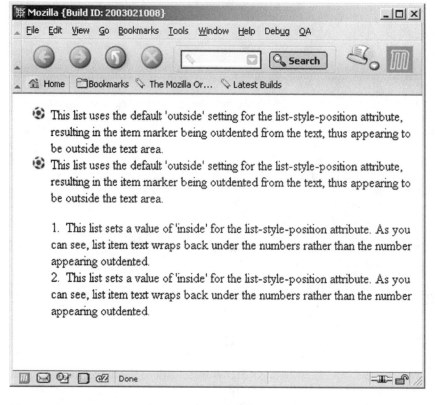

Here's the style sheet that creates the effect:

```
<style type="text/css">
<!--
ol {
  list-style-position: inside;
}
ul {
  list-style-image: url(images/footbag.gif);
}
-->
</style>
```

Notice that you must supply the URL in CSS format, which requires that you use the `url` operator and provide the location in parentheses, without using quotation marks.

Cascading and Inheritance

The "C" in CSS stands for "cascading". Until now, we haven't dealt with any aspect of CSS that required an understanding of that term. Now that we're dealing with relatively complex display-related issues, however, the time has come to spend some serious time with this topic.

Cascading is not confined to text components, objects, and elements. It applies across the board to CSS usage on a Web page. The reason it is often discussed in conjunction with textual elements is because its impact is most apparent and most easily demonstrable in this context.

Inheritance is related to cascading in terms of its impact, but the two terms have quite different meanings.

Cascading addresses the question of how any given element will be displayed if there are multiple style rules that *could* be applied to it. Inheritance addresses the question of how any given element will be displayed if one or more of its properties is defined in a style rule that applies to an ancestor element, but is omitted in the element itself.

This sounds much more complicated than it generally is in practice. I'm going to start by providing a couple of simple examples that will clearly demonstrate the difference. Then, I'll drill down more deeply into both of these subjects

Basic Principles of Cascading

If you keep your use of CSS simple, you will seldom encounter a need to understand cascading at a deep level. For example, if you always use external style sheets and only override the settings in those style sheets with embedded style rules for specific situations, you will probably not need to spend a great deal of time ferreting out the nuances in the cascading process.

But, when you begin to design pages of any complexity—and to use style sheets across multiple pages and sites in the interest of efficiency and ease of maintenance—you will almost certainly run into situations where what you see isn't what you intended. Additionally, if you're designing complex pages and sites, you can take advantage of the basic rules of cascading to apply CSS rules logically, consistently, and effectively.

There are four basic factors involved in creating what is called the "cascade" in CSS:

❑ weight

❑ origin

❑ specificity

❑ sort order

These factors are taken into account in the order in which I've listed them.

To sort out possible conflicts in style rules that could be applied to any element in an HTML page, think of the browser as going through a set of decisions about each element. This decision-making process follows this path, in precisely this order:

1. Scan through the style rules that apply to the element and look for those that contain the key symbol `!important`. Assign each of those rules a greater weight than those without the symbol. This is the "weight" factor referred to above.

2. Within the style rules marked as `!important`, assign a greater weight to those that come from the user's style sheet (if there is one) than to those that come from the author's style sheet. This is the "origin" factor referred to above.

3. Within the style rules that are *not* marked `!important`, assign a greater weight to those that come from the author's style sheet than to those have come from the user's style sheet. This is also the "origin" factor at work.

4. To resolve any remaining ties, examine each rule to see how narrowly it applies to the specific element in question. If, for example, you have a paragraph element of class `warning`, a style rule that applies to paragraphs in general will be given less weight than one that applies to paragraphs of the class `warning`. Rules declared inline (with the `style` attribute in HTML) apply only to one element, and therefore always win out at this stage. This is the "specificity" factor at work.

5. Finally, if any ties still remain after all the above steps, sort things out based on the order in which the rules are defined in the document, with rules declared later taking precedence over those declared earlier. This is the "sort order" factor referred to above.

At the end of all this processing, all applicable rules are applied in the order established above, with the property values that are assigned in rules of greater weight overriding those assigned in rules of lesser weight.

Generally, you think about this process in the reverse order from that which the browser uses. Most often, you have only to deal with the sort order issue on pages of relatively low complexity. As designs and sites become more complex and your use of style sheets becomes more involved, specificity will become the next major concern for you. You'll typically use !important very rarely, if ever. I'll discuss the cascading rules in the order in which you are most likely to think of them, rather than in the order in which the browser uses them.

Sort Order

As you know, styles can be defined in three different places: an external style sheet, an embedded style sheet, or an inline style attribute as part of a markup tag for a particular HTML element. The sort order factor in the cascade ensures that, no matter if a style sheet is embedded in the head of the document or if it's loaded with a <link> tag, it's the *order* in which it appears that determines its relative precedence.

For example, let's say that you have an external style sheet called mylayout.css. Among other rules, it has this entry:

```
h2 {
    color: green;
}
```

Within a particular document, you decide that you don't want to use the normal site-wide style of green second-level headings. So, you embed a style sheet (with a <style> tag in the document header) with the following rule *after* the <link> tag that loads mylayout.css:

```
h2 {
    color: blue;
}
```

In this case, where I've defined only one property-value pair, it's pretty easy to see how cascading works. The external style sheet rule is overruled by the embedded rule—h2 elements within the document will appear in blue.

It's important to realize that the second rule doesn't overrule the first because it's declared in an embedded style sheet—it overrules it because the embedded style sheet comes *after* the linked style sheet. Move the <style> tag above the <link> tag, and h2 elements will turn green again.

But things are generally not quite so clean and obvious. Going back to the external (green) style sheet rule above, let's add a couple of property-value pairs so we have something like this:

```
h2 {
  color: green;
  background-color: transparent;
  margin-left: 10px;
  font-family: Arial, Helvetica, sans-serif;
  text-decoration: overline;
}
```

In an embedded style sheet in another document, assume we have a rule that looks like this:

```
h2 {
  margin-left: 20px;
  text-decoration: none;
}
```

Once again, let's assume the embedded style sheet is declared *after* the linked style sheet. In this case, any second-level heading in this specific document will be displayed in green on a transparent background, offset from the left margin by 20 pixels, using the font set identified in the external style sheet, with no decoration.

One way of thinking about this process is that a style rule is like a waterfall. It starts out with certain property-value pairs (for color, background-color, left-margin, font-family, and text-decoration in the example). Then, that style sheet's rules fall like a waterfall cascading over rocks. When it encounters rocks with property-value pairs that have different values from those in the waterfall, the cascade effect substitutes the new value for the old.

In resolving any conflict between two or more style rules that *could* apply to a given element, and which are tied on the specificity, origin, and weight factors, the rule declared last will be applied.

Specificity

Specificity refers to the issue of how closely a style rule's selector describes a particular element in your document. On one level, this is pretty easy to understand. As I mentioned earlier, when I listed the factors involved in the cascade decision-making process, a style that applies to paragraph elements is less specific to a paragraph of class warning, than is a rule that specifically applies to paragraphs of that class. In other words, given the following code fragment, the paragraph will be displayed in red type on a white background rather than white type on a blue background, despite the order of the rules. Remember, specificity has greater impact in the cascade than sort order:

```
<!DOCTYPE html PUBLIC "-//W3C//DTD XHTML 1.0 Transitional//EN"
  "http://www.w3.org/TR/xhtml1/DTD/xhtml1-transitional.dtd">
<html xmlns="http://www.w3.org/1999/xhtml">
<head>
  <title>Untitled</title>
</head>
<style type="text/css">
<!--
p.warning {
  color: red;
  background-color: white;
}
p {
  color: white;
  background-color: blue;
}
-->
</style>
<body>
<p class="warning">This is a warning paragraph.</p>
</body>
</html>
```

The more closely the rule's selector matches the element, the more specific it is, and the more likely it is to be applied to that element.

But the CSS recommendation that describes specificity does so in a generic way that you may find useful to understand if you get into something really tricky, with potentially conflicting style rules. Every selector in your style sheet is given a specificity rating that is calculated by the browser using a strict formula. That formula can be expressed as follows:

`(100 * IDCount) + (10 * OtherTypeCount) + NamedElements`

In other words, the CSS-compliant browser looks at a rule selector and processes it like this:

1. If it has one or more ID selectors (e.g. `#critical`), count those selectors and multiply the count by 100.

2. If it has any other types of selectors (e.g. class name or pseudo-class), count those selectors and multiply that count by 10. Do not count pseudo-elements.

3. If it has any named elements (e.g. `p` or `div`), count those selectors.

4. Now add all the values together.

Table 9.4 provides examples of different types of selectors, and what their specificity ratings would be.

Table 9.4. Sample Specificity Ratings for CSS Rule Selectors

Selector	IDs	Others	Names	Specificity
em	0	0	1	1
p em	0	0	2	2
.critical	0	1	0	10
a:hover	0	1	1	11
div p span.critical	0	1	3	13
#critical	1	0	0	100
p#critical	1	0	1	101

Style properties declared inline (with the `style` HTML attribute) have the highest specificity, since they apply to one element and one element only. No property declared elsewhere can overrule an inline style property based on specificity.

In resolving any conflict between two or more style rules that *could* apply to a given element, and which are tied on the origin and weight factors, the rule with higher specificity will be applied.

Origin

The origin factor in the cascade resolves conflicts between rules declared by the page author and rules declared by the user of the browser (e.g. in a user style sheet). In general, any property setting assigned by the page author takes precedence over a conflicting property setting assigned by the user of the browser.

The exception to this occurs when the two conflicting property settings are assigned greater weight with the !important modifier, as described below. In such cases, the origin factor is reversed, and the user's property setting takes precedence over the page author's. In effect, style properties that the user considers important are *more* important than style rules that the page author considers important.

In resolving any conflict between two or more property settings that *could* apply to a given element, and which are tied on the weight factor (i.e. they're all marked !important or none are), then the origin of the property decides which is applied.

Weight (!important)

If you declare a property's value to be of greater than usual weight by following it with the key word !important, it will always override a contradictory setting in the cascade that is not marked !important. For example, you might decide that it is really essential for all level-three headings to be blue and indented 20 pixels, so you'd code a rule like this:

```
h3 {
  color: blue !important;
  margin-left: 20px !important;
}
```

If, in rendering your page, the browser encounters a situation where a specific level-three heading has a different color setting (for example, because of the way a grouped selector defines the layout), it will ignore that setting and make the heading blue.

Recall that if you increase a rule's weight with the !important symbol, and the user specifies a conflicting style to which he also applies an !important symbol, the user's rule will trump yours, according to the origin factor described above.

However, this doesn't mean that you won't find uses for !important. In the vast majority of cases, the user doesn't define or use a style sheet. In that case, your use of !important will ensure that if there are conflicts among style rules you have declared in various external style sheets, and perhaps also in an embedded style sheet, the one that is most crucial to your design will prevail.

Summary

This chapter demonstrated a number of techniques for using CSS styles to spruce up the otherwise ordinary text on a Web page. From the basic use of alignment, indentation and other techniques, the chapter demonstrated the use of positioning to create shadowed text effects, and described how to manipulate the display of lists as well.

This chapter also provided a detailed description of the role of the cascade in CSS. You now understand how to control the impact of style rules in complex page designs, where display rules may be coming from multiple sources.

Chapter 10, will take a look at how to use CSS in relationship to graphics on a Web page.

10 Adding Graphics to the Design

While CSS focuses a great deal on the positioning of all kinds of elements on the page, and on the display and behavior of text, it has relatively little to say on the specific subject of graphics. That's probably because graphics are... well... graphics. Once they're designed and placed on a page, there's not much else you can expect of them. They can be used as hyperlink anchors, but it's not as if there's much you can do to change their style or appearance; those are under the control of the artist or designer who created them.

Still, the way graphics interact with text elements on a page is a subject of interest to all designers. And graphics *effects*, based principally on the use of color blocks with or without text, are also of consequence.

This chapter takes a brief look at the connections between graphics and CSS by discussing:

❏ alignment issues, including runaround text and placing text on top of images

❏ the clipping of images and other HTML elements

Alignment of Images and Text

As we learned in Chapter 7, CSS defines the `float` property to aid in the alignment of images and text. `float` corresponds to the deprecated `align` attribute associated with the HTML `<img>` tag.

Figure 10.1 is a reminder of the way we can make text under an image wrap to the left margin, simply by defining a `float` property for that image. In this case, the image has its `float` property set to `left`, which is precisely equivalent to the effect of the old HTML tag `<img align="left">`.

Figure 10.1. Using CSS `float` Property to Flow Text Smoothly Around an Image

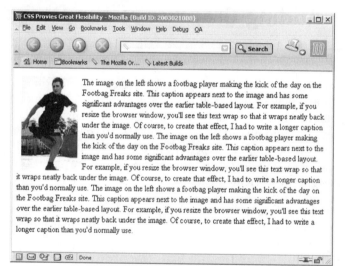

Here's the HTML that produces Figure 10.1.

```
<!DOCTYPE html PUBLIC "-//W3C//DTD XHTML 1.0 Transitional//EN"
  "http://www.w3.org/TR/xhtml1/DTD/xhtml1-transitional.dtd">
<html xmlns="http://www.w3.org/1999/xhtml">
<head>
  <title>CSS Provides Great Flexibility</title>
</head>
<body>
  <img src="/images/kod.jpg" style="float: left; width: 112px;
    height: 177px; margin: 0 1.5% 0;" />
```

```
<p>The image on the left shows a footbag player making the kick
   of the day on the Footbag Freaks site. This caption appears
   next to the image and has some significant advantages over
   the earlier table-based layout. For example, if you resize
   the browser window, you'll see this text wrap so that it
   wraps neatly back under the image. Of course, to create that
   effect, I had to write a longer caption than you'd normally
   use. The image on the left shows a footbag player making the
   kick of the day on the Footbag Freaks site. This caption
   appears next to the image and has some significant advantages
   over the earlier table-based layout. For example, if you
   resize the browser window, you'll see this text wrap so that
   it wraps neatly back under the image. Of course, to create
   that effect, I had to write a longer caption than you'd
   normally use. The image on the left shows a footbag player
   making the kick of the day on the Footbag Freaks site. This
   caption appears next to the image and has some significant
   advantages over the earlier table-based layout. For example,
   if you resize the browser window, you'll see this text wrap
   so that it wraps neatly back under the image. Of course, to
   create that effect, I had to write a longer caption than
   you'd normally use.</p>
</body>
</html>
```

Recall also from Chapter 6, that you can use the `clear` property to force a new paragraph (or any other HTML block element, for that matter) to drop below any floating elements with which it would otherwise share the width of the page.

For example, imagine we wanted to break the text in Figure 10.1 into two paragraphs, and guarantee that the second would never appear to the right of the image, no matter how wide the user opened the browser. We could achieve this by applying to our code the minor modifications that appear in bold below. The product of this HTML is shown in Figure 10.2.

```
<!DOCTYPE html PUBLIC "-//W3C//DTD XHTML 1.0 Transitional//EN"
  "http://www.w3.org/TR/xhtml1/DTD/xhtml1-transitional.dtd">
<html xmlns="http://www.w3.org/1999/xhtml">
<head>
  <title>Using clear to Force Paragraphs to Left Edge of
    the Window</title>
  <meta http-equiv="Content-Type"
    content="text/html; charset=iso-8859-1" />
</head>
<body>
  <img src="/images/kod.jpg" style="float: left; width: 112px;
```

```
    height: 177px; margin: 0 1.5% 0;" />
  <p>The image on the left shows a footbag player making the kick
    of the day on the Footbag Freaks site. This caption appears
    next to the image and has some significant advantages over the
    earlier table-based layout. For example, if you resize the
    browser window, you'll see this text wrap so that it wraps
    neatly back under the image. Of course, to create that effect,
    I had to write a longer caption than you'd normally use. The
    image on the left shows a footbag player making the kick of
    the day on the Footbag Freaks site.</p>
  <p style="clear: left;">This caption appears next to the image
    and has some significant advantages over the earlier
    table-based layout. For example, if you resize the browser
    window, you'll see this text wrap so that it wraps neatly back
    under the image. Of course, to create that effect, I had to
    write a longer caption than you'd normally use. The image on
    the left shows a footbag player making the kick of the day on
    the Footbag Freaks site. This caption appears next to the
    image and has some significant advantages over the earlier
    table-based layout. For example, if you resize the browser
    window, you'll see this text wrap so that it wraps neatly
    back under the image. Of course, to create that effect, I
    had to write a longer caption than you'd normally use.</p>
</body>
</html>
```

Figure 10.2. Using the `clear` Property to Force Paragraph to Left Edge of Browser Window

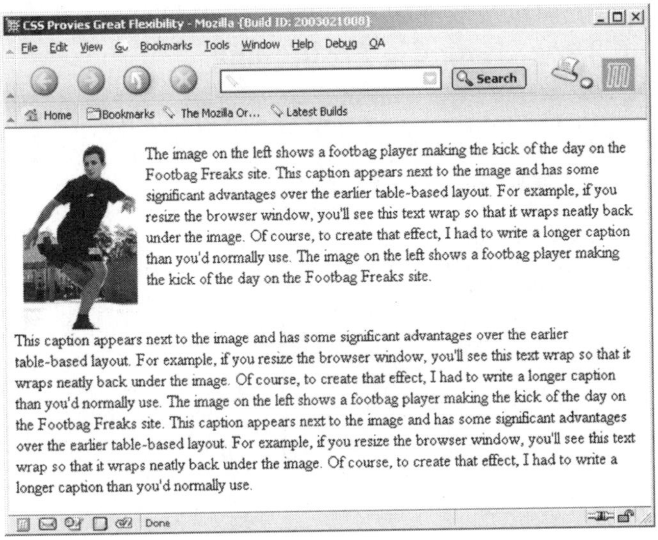

Placing Text On Top of Images

A final technique for the arrangement of text relative to images allows the placement of text on top of a graphic. In print circles, this is sometimes referred to as **knockout type**, as it "knocks out" part of the image and replaces it with text. However, I'll also show you how to use a screen to avoid the complete knockout of the image.

There's actually nothing terribly tricky about this technique. You just position both the graphic and the text so that they overlap, and make sure that the z-index of the text is higher than that of the graphic. You can handle this second requirement either by specifying the text after the image is defined, or explicitly assigning `z-index` values as described in Chapter 6.

In fact, the hardest part about this technique is getting the type's size and position just right, so that it creates the desired effect over the graphic. It's usually best to use pixel font sizes in these cases. Since images are made of pixels, and therefore have fixed pixel dimensions, any text that you need to line up with an image should use the same units for its dimensions.

Figure 10.3 shows a simple example of the use of knockout type. Here, we had a nice, neutral background, so any dark color would do. I used black, though red or dark blue would do equally well.

Figure 10.3. Knockout Type Using CSS Positioning

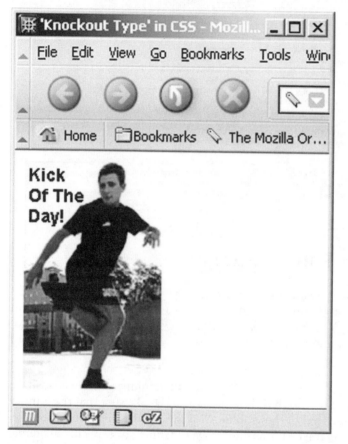

Here's the HTML that produces the page in Figure 10.3.

```
<!DOCTYPE html PUBLIC "-//W3C//DTD XHTML 1.0 Transitional//EN"
  "http://www.w3.org/TR/xhtml1/DTD/xhtml1-transitional.dtd">
<html xmlns="http://www.w3.org/1999/xhtml">
<head>
  <title>'Knockout Type' in CSS</title>
  <meta http-equiv="Content-Type"
    content="text/html; charset=iso-8859-1" />
```

```
</head>
<body>
  <div style="position: relative;">
    <img src="/images/kod.jpg" width="112" height="177"
      alt="Jase D performs a perfect Show Pony" />
    <h3 style="position: absolute; left: 3px; top: 3px;
      font: bold 14px Arial, Helvetica, sans-serif;">Kick<br />
      Of The<br />
      Day!</h3>
  </div>
</body>
</html>
```

That works quite well, but what if you really wanted the knockout type to appear over the body of the footbagger? Figure 10.4 shows a first attempt at this, which involves simply repositioning the text in Figure 10.3 onto a single line.

Figure 10.4. Knockout Type Over Non-Neutral Background

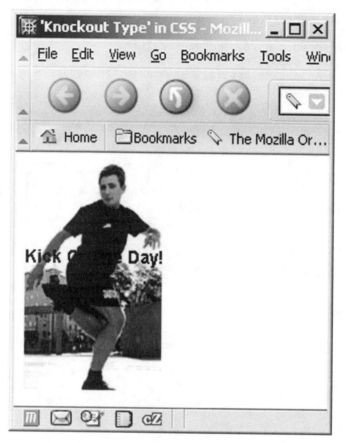

The result isn't very satisfactory, is it? Some of the type is illegible. Some of it is readable. And, clearly, changing to, say, a white font will fix part of the problem, but make other aspects of it worse. We could fiddle around with color combinations and come up with one that shows reasonably well across the entire non-neutral background, but the result is always likely to feel a little artificial.

There is a way to fix this. It involves using a background image behind the knockout type, a subject I won't treat in detail until Chapter 11. But, for now, you can see how this works in Figure 10.5. I've placed a white screen behind the text that we're displaying, with the result that the black type displays well, while the underlying image shows through as if it were being slightly shadowed.

Figure 10.5. Using a Background Screen on Knockout Type Over Non-Neutral Background

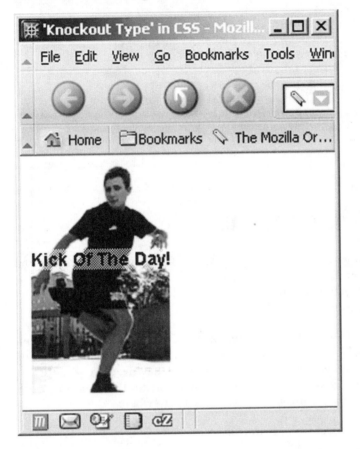

Here's the HTML that produces the effect shown in Figure 10.5. The background graphic, `halfscreen-white.gif`, is available in the images directory of the code archive[1].

```
<!DOCTYPE html PUBLIC "-//W3C//DTD XHTML 1.0 Transitional//EN"
  "http://www.w3.org/TR/xhtml1/DTD/xhtml1-transitional.dtd">
<html xmlns="http://www.w3.org/1999/xhtml">
<head>
  <title>'Knockout Type' in CSS</title>
```

[1] I'm indebted for this trick, as I am for so much of my CSS knowledge, to Eric A. Meyer. He, in turn, credits Todd Fahrner for teaching him this technique.

```
  <meta http-equiv="Content-Type"
    content="text/html; charset=iso-8859-1" />
</head>
<body>
  <div style="position: relative;">
    <img src="/images/kod.jpg" width="112" height="177"
      alt="Jase D performs a perfect Show Pony" />
    <div style="position: absolute; left: 0; top: 65px;
      font: bold 14px Arial, Helvetica, sans-serif;
      background: url(/images/halfscreen-white.gif)
      center repeat;">Kick Of The Day!</div>
  </div>
</body>
</html>
```

The details of how this background is displayed will be explained in Chapter 11.

Clipping HTML Content

There are times when you want to show only part of a large graphic. Perhaps you want to point out a detail that might be missed in the greater image, or you need to emphasize a particular work, which is embedded in a larger piece that isn't relevant to your purpose.

Let's take the "Kick of the Day" graphic we worked on in the previous section. The image is large, and it's used in a couple of different places on the site. Having overlaid it with a text headline, we'd like to avoid having to reproduce the graphic, trim excess content, and redo the styling to create the knockout type, in order to produce a smaller image that we can use elsewhere.

Figure 10.6 shows the effect we're going for.

Figure 10.6. Smaller Image Clipped from Larger One

It looks like we've just taken a slice out of the middle of the larger graphic to use as a pointer or heading of some sort. To do this, we simply:

☐ Define a `div` that's small enough to show only the portion of the larger graphic we wish to display.

☐ Assign the `div` an `overflow` property of `hidden` (I'll cover this point shortly).

☐ Position the larger graphic in the smaller `div` to show the important piece.

Here's the HTML that produces the image in Figure 10.6.

```
<!DOCTYPE html PUBLIC "-//W3C//DTD XHTML 1.0 Transitional//EN"
  "http://www.w3.org/TR/xhtml1/DTD/xhtml1-transitional.dtd">
<html xmlns="http://www.w3.org/1999/xhtml">
<head>
  <title>Clipping a Graphic</title>
  <meta http-equiv="Content-Type"
    content="text/html; charset=iso-8859-1" />
</head>
<body>
  <div style="position: relative; overflow: hidden; height: 30px;
    width: 122px;">
    <img src="/images/kod.jpg" style="position: relative;
      top: -60px;" width="112" height="177"
      alt="Jase D performs a perfect Show Pony"/>
```

```
    <h3 style="position: absolute; left: 0; top: 6px;
       font: bold 14px Arial, Helvetica, sans-serif;
       background: url(/images/halfscreen-white.gif)
       center repeat;">Kick Of The Day!</h3>
  </div>
</body>
</html>
```

The `overflow` property is usable with any content-holding HTML element, but it is most often employed with text and graphic objects. Here, I've defined a "viewport", if you will, which is 30 pixels high and 122 pixels wide (the same width as the entire graphic).

Then, in the `<img>` tag, I've positioned the graphic to moved its top up 65 pixels. This marks the approximate starting point of the knockout type I want to focus on in this snippet of graphic.

The `overflow` property defines how an HTML element displays content whose rendered dimensions exceed the height and/or width of the element itself. The `overflow` property can be assigned any of the values shown in Table 10.1, which produce the results indicated.

Table 10.1. Values for the `overflow` Property and Their Effects

Value	Effect on Content
visible	None. This is the default setting of the `overflow` property. All of the content of the affected element is displayed with no clipping or alteration in the size of the image.
hidden	All content that would normally be displayed outside the boundaries of the constrained size of the element are hidden.
scroll	Horizontal and vertical scrollbars are displayed alongside the visible portion of the content, allowing the user to scroll to see content that is not displayed. Scrollbars appear whether they are actually needed or not.
auto	Horizontal and/or vertical scrollbars display as with the `scroll` value, but only if they are actually needed to permit the viewing of all the content of the affected element.

Summary

This chapter explored the relatively sparse ways CSS and graphical content interact.

As you saw, CSS has little to offer in terms of graphical layout and design. However, CSS properties allow you to achieve more flexible and pleasing alignment of text with graphics, and reuse subsets of larger images, without having to recreate the content.

Chapter 11, begins the fourth and final part of this book, where we'll focus on the non-obvious uses of CSS. Specifically, Chapter 11, explains how to use CSS to create interesting, attractive and interactive menu designs.

IV Non-Obvious Uses of CSS

11

Improving the User Experience

This chapter describes how to use CSS to present a menu that takes the form of an HTML list. This list is used on the *Footbag Freaks* site as the main navigation in the upper left portion of each page, as shown in Figure 11.1. While this navigational menu is a bit simplistic in that it doesn't involve dynamically changing menu items sliding elegantly into and out of visibility, it has the clear advantage of being easy to implement without writing JavaScript.

This chapter first looks at how to use CSS to alter the standard appearance of lists. It starts there because lists of links were a fundamental navigation tool on the Web before the reign of table layout took hold. A basic understanding of how to move away from the default list look will help you see how lists can still be used for primary navigation, even on today's design-centric Web.

The techniques in this chapter were inspired by Jeffrey Zeldman's fantastic A List Apart[1] site. The article on applying CSS to lists[2] to create attractive menus was written by Mark Newhouse. As Mark points out, a navigation system is structurally a list of links and therefore HTML lists are the most appropriate markup with which to code them.

[1] http://www.alistapart.com/
[2] http://www.alistapart.com/stories/taminglists/

Figure 11.1. Navigation Portion of Footbag Freaks Site Based on List

With the basics out of the way, this chapter explains how to manipulate the overall appearance of a list, and of items within a list, using CSS when hyperlinks are involved. This is the heart of the matter when it comes to creating the kind of navigational menu I'm describing here.

Often, when we define list-based navigation menus, we need multiple levels of nesting for navigation within portions of the site. This chapter describes how to accomplish that design goal as well.

While the menu constitutes the majority of the chapter's content, I also offer two other user-interface techniques. In one, you'll see how to modify the cursor on the fly. In the other, you'll learn about using fixed backgrounds to create polished-looking designs.

Menu examples in this chapter are taken from the *Footbag Freaks* site where these tricks are used both in the main navigation menu, and in the list of content on the main page.

Basic List Styling With CSS

The navigational list menu that appears on the front page of the *Footbag Freaks* site is created with the following basic HTML:

```html
<ul id="mainnav">
  <li><a href="categories.htm">Category One</a></li>
  <li><a href="categories.htm">Category Two</a></li>
  <li><a href="categories.htm">Category Three</a></li>
  <li><a href="categories.htm">Category Four</a></li>
  <li><a href="categories.htm">Category Five</a></li>
</ul>
```

Before we apply any CSS rules to this list, it would display as shown in Figure 11.2.

Figure 11.2. Basic Unformatted Link List

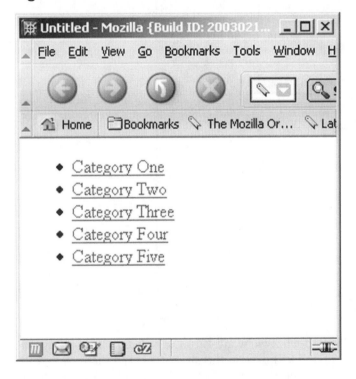

About what you'd expect, right? It's a standard unordered list with an unadorned bullet as its marker.

Now, let's create a style rule that removes the bullet, as, in our final menu, we don't want the bullets hanging around. To do that, simply insert the following style rule into the document:

```
ul#mainnav {
  list-style: none;
}
```

Including a `list-style` property with a value of `none` creates an unordered list with no bullets as shown in Figure 11.3.

Figure 11.3. Unformatted Link List with Bullets Removed

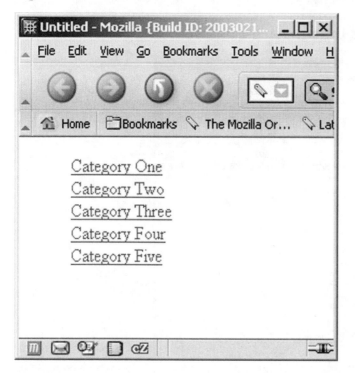

Already, the design is closer to what we want. But, the bulleted list is always indented from the left margin by default, and the ultimate design dictates that we have a colored background behind the menu. Let's take care of those two things in the obvious ways, with the new property assignments shown in bold in the following CSS.

```
ul#mainnav {
  list-style: none;
  margin: 0;
  padding: 0;
  background-color: #D6D6D6;
}
```

The result of applying this rule to the list from which the menu is being created is shown in Figure 11.4.

Figure 11.4. Repositioned Link List With Colored Background

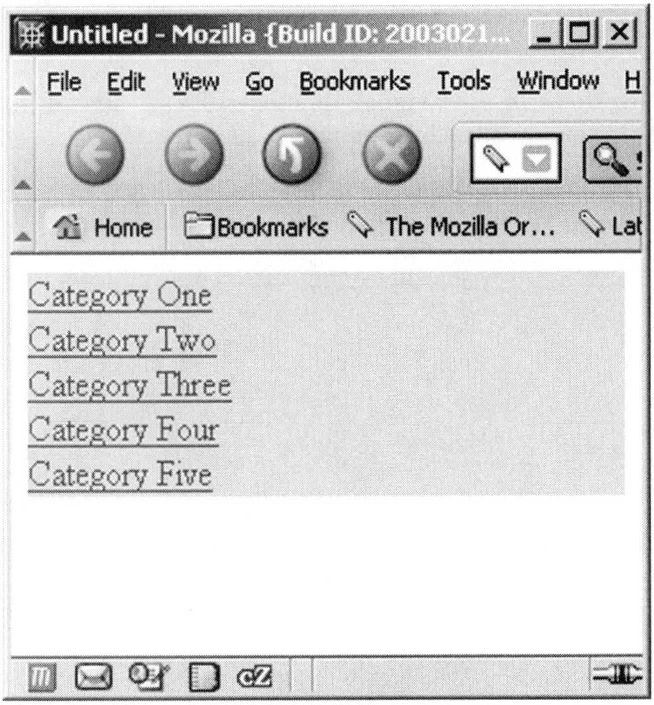

This is getting closer to the final design goal, though we obviously still have some distance to go.

Next, let's deal with the underlining issues in the menu. We want to eliminate the automatic underline placed beneath hyperlinks and add the divider lines between menu items called for by the final design. The hyperlink underlining issue can be addressed by a context rule like this one:

```
ul#mainnav li a:link, ul#mainnav li a:visited {
    text-decoration: none;
}
```

We've seen these before. Note that I've confined the rule's context to hyperlinks (both normal and visited) contained within a list item, in an unordered list identified as mainnav.

Adding a dividing line between each entry in the list is just as simple, thanks to the fact that list items are block elements that can have borders:

```
ul#mainnav li {
    border-top: 1px solid #A5B5C6;
}
```

This rule applies to all list items in the mainnav unordered list. It just adds a colored, one-pixel border to the top of each list item.

Now, the original bullet list looks like Figure 11.5 and you can begin to see it taking shape as an attractive menu like the one on the front page of our site.

Figure 11.5. Border Added, Underline Removed, as Menu Gets Closer to Design Goal

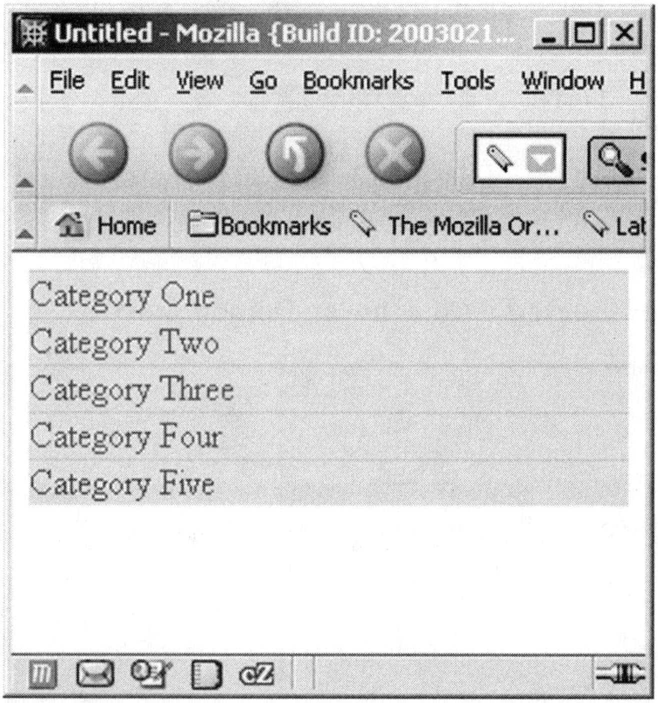

The design specification for the *Foothag Freaks* site calls for the navigation menus to behave like rollover buttons, changing their color as the user positions the cursor over them. Recall that hyperlink objects have a hover pseudo-class that can be used to declare styles. Just create a style rule like this one:

```
ul#mainnav li a:hover {
  background-color: #43616B;
  color: #eee;
}
```

This change dramatically reveals a lingering problem we have ignored until now. Hyperlinks are inline elements by default, so each link in the menu only occupies the area covered by the link text. When you hover your mouse over a link in the menu, you'll see that the colored box only covers the text. In addition to the unattractive visual effect, there is a usability issue to consider as well. To make the menu behave as intended, the user should be able to click anywhere in the rectangle containing one of the links—not necessarily on the link text.

To achieve this, we further modify our links by converting them into block elements with the `display` property:

```
ul#mainnav li a:link, ul#mainnav li a:visited {
  text-decoration: none;
  display: block;
}
```

You can see the result of this change in Figure 11.6.

Figure 11.6. Rollover Created with `a:hover` Pseudo-Class

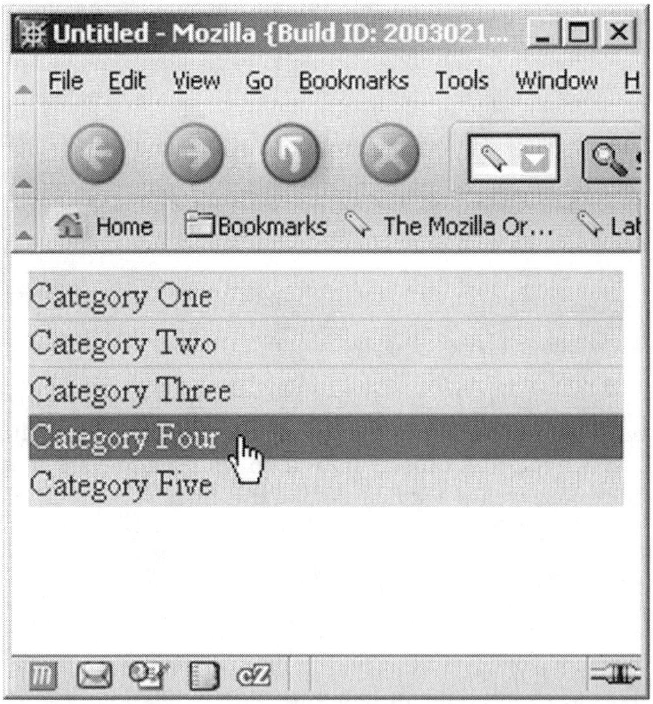

That's the way it looks in *most* browsers, anyway. Unfortunately, Internet Explorer for Windows has a bug that adds a margin to the bottom of each list item when you set the `display` property. To correct this, simply apply a `width` to the list items:

```
ul#mainnav li a:link, ul#mainnav li a:visited {
  text-decoration: none;
  display: block;
  width: 100%;
}
```

This completes the basic modifications that will transform a standard, unordered list into a reasonably professional, interactive, single-level menu. Now, let's take a look at how to spruce it up a bit and give it a more polished appearance.

Enhancing the Look of the Menu

All of the changes we need to make to the menu's appearance relate to the individual list items and how they display, so we'll modify the CSS rule that is applied to the anchors stored in the list items. This is the rule that begins with the line:

```
ul#mainnav li a:link, ul#mainnav li a:visited
```

Right now, that rule deals only with the `display`, `width`, and `text-decoration` properties. To achieve the end result we want, we must change the color scheme of the list as well as its font. We'll also add some padding to the list to give it a less crowded feeling.

Here's what the CSS looks like after we make all the changes we just mentioned:

```
ul#mainnav li a:link, ul#mainnav li a:visited {
  display: block;
  text-decoration: none;
  width: 88%;
  padding: 6px 6%;
  background-color: #5C6F90;
  font: bold 10pt/1.5 arial, sans-serif;
  color: #fff;
}
```

The `padding` value will produce a nicely spaced layout for the menu. Note that we've reduced the `width` to `88%` to make room for the `6%` padding we've added to either side of the link. The `font` property adds further space to the design by placing a 10 point font on a 15 point line (1.5 times the usual line height).

The result of these changes is reflected in Figure 11.7. Other than the font and spacing, it doesn't look so different from Figure 11.6, when it's displayed in black and white.

Figure 11.7. Font, Coloring and Spacing Added to Menu List

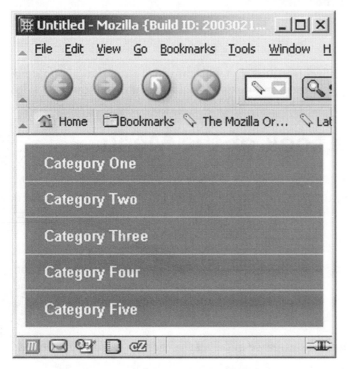

Now, we have a list of links converted into an attractive, interactive menu that works predictably and reliably across platforms and browsers.

Creating a Submenu within the Main Menu

Many sites don't need any more than one level of menu-based navigation. But, sites that have any amount of complexity can probably benefit from at least two-level menus at strategic points, if not throughout the site. In many ways, creating a submenu within the main menu is not so different from creating the main menu.

Figure 11.8 shows a secondary page on the *Foothag Freaks* site, where the main menu has been opened up to reveal a submenu by which we can navigate subcategories.

Figure 11.8. Sub-Menu Navigation on Footbag Freaks Site

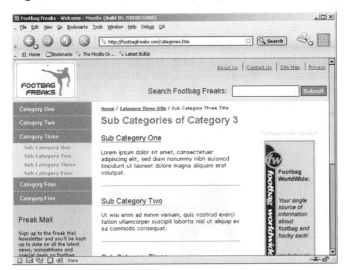

Notice the submenu embedded in the main menu offers the user four choices. The HTML that creates the menu with submenus looks like this:

```
<ul id="mainnav">
  <li><a href="categories.htm">Category One</a></li>
  <li><a href="categories.htm">Category Two</a></li>
  <li><a href="categories.htm">Category Three</a>
    <ul class="subnav">
      <li><a href="subcats.htm">Sub Category One</a></li>
      <li><a href="subcats.htm">Sub Category Two</a></li>
      <li><a href="subcats.htm">Sub Category Three</a></li>
      <li><a href="subcats.htm">Sub Category Four</a></li>
    </ul>
  </li>
  <li><a href="categories.htm">Category Four</a></li>
  <li><a href="categories.htm">Category Five</a></li>
</ul>
```

There's nothing new or mysterious here.

In fact, there's nothing new or mysterious in the CSS that's applied to these newly inserted list elements, either. Note that they belong to class subnav, so the CSS rules you create to control their appearance will also have that identifier.

Here's the basic CSS rule for the sub-navigation list itself.

```
ul#mainnav ul.subnav {
  list-style: none;
  margin: 0;
  padding: 0;
}
```

The rule selector—`ul#mainnav ul.subnav`—is perhaps unnecessarily complex. If we establish by policy the notion that we will use only the class `subnav` for lists that are contained in the `mainnav` or similar menu lists, we could shorten this considerably to `ul.subnav` or even just `.subnav`. But, this selector convention has one advantage over the terser choices: it is readable and its scope and use are readily apparent.

The following CSS rule applies to list items in the `subnav` class of lists:

```
ul#mainnav ul.subnav li {
  border-top: 0 none;
  padding-left: 1.5em;
}
```

The `border-top` property removes the one-pixel border we added to all list item elements within the `mainnav` list, and separates our main menu items. We don't want separator lines between our submenu items, so we set that border to zero in this case. As the selector for this rule is more specific than the selector for all list items within `mainnav` (`ul#mainnav li`), it takes precedence.

By using a `padding-left` setting, we force the submenu to be indented from the left side of the main menu, which makes it easier for the user to spot the menu as something different from the main menu list.

Styling the appearance of the links in the submenu doesn't involve anything particularly new or exciting either:

```
ul#mainnav ul.subnav li a:link, ul#mainnav ul.subnav li a:visited
{
  padding: 1px;
  font: bold 0.7em /1.5 verdana, sans-serif;
  color: #5C6F90;
  background-color: transparent;
}
```

Compared to the equivalent rule for the main navigation list, you can see that we use less padding, a smaller font and a transparent background color. Otherwise, it's quite similar.

Finally, when the user places the cursor over one of these sub-navigation menu links, we want the link to become underlined. So, we define a CSS rule for the a:hover pseudo-class as follows:

```
ul#mainnav ul.subnav li a:hover {
  color: #43616B;
  background-color: transparent;
  text-decoration: underline;
}
```

Modifying the Cursor on the Fly

One aspect of CSS2 that is often overlooked by Web designers but which, when used judiciously, can enhance the user experience at your site, is the ability to define a cursor that appears in conjunction with specific elements of the page. The CSS cursor property sets the mouse cursor to be displayed over each element.

Table 11.1 lists the different cursor values supported by the CSS2 standard and the major browsers that support them. The special value auto is the default, and lets the browser determine what the cursor should look like automatically. The value default sets the cursor to its default appearance, as dictated by the operating system. All of the cursors' exact appearances may vary between browsers and operating systems.

Table 11.1. CSS2 standard cursors

cursor value	Appearance (IE6)	IE (Win)	IE (Mac)	NS/Moz
auto	n/a	4	4	6/1
crosshair	+	4	4	6/1
default		4	4	6/1
e-resize	↔	4	4	6/1
help	??	4	4	6/1
move	✛	4	4	6/1
n-resize	↕	4	4	6/1
ne-resize	↗	4	4	6/1
nw-resize	↖	4	4	6/1
pointer		4	4	6/1
s-resize	↕	4	4	6/1
se-resize	↖	4	4	6/1
sw-resize	↗	4	4	6/1
text	I	4	4	6/1
url(*url*)	n/a	6	–	–
w-resize	↔	4	4	6/1
wait	⏳	4	4	6/1

You must be cautious in using these cursors. Users come to expect that a given cursor has a specific meaning across applications. Arbitrarily modifying the cursor without the context of that specific meaning can be disconcerting to users.

It is possible to define a cursor for any HTML element. If you do so, then the mouse pointer changes shape appropriately whenever the user positions the cursor over that element.

For example, you may have one or more links on a set of pages that lead the user to some help in dealing with the page's content or interaction. You might define a CSS rule that sets up a typical help cursor when the user positions over such links. That rule could look something like this:

```
.helplink {
  cursor: help;
}
```

In the page itself, whenever you define an element (typically a hyperlink but conceptually any element), you could indicate that it should use the help cursor when the user positions the mouse over it, by coding something like this:

```
<a class="helplink" href="helppage.html">Get an explanation</a>
```

The exact appearance of the cursor is system-dependent. The help cursor, for example, appears as an arrow with a question mark tagging along on both Mac and Windows, but the question mark is slightly different and the arrow emphasized differently on each platform.

By combining a cursor change with a script that actually carries out some task, you could accomplish a polished and professional interface for interactive elements of a Web page. However, the details of how to accomplish that are beyond the scope of this discussion.

Using a Background Image as a Fixed Canvas

As you know from your experiences designing and using Websites, if you define a graphic as the background on a page, the graphic will repeat, or tile, itself to fill up the entire client area of the browser. It will also scroll along with any content that is placed on top of it. This is the normal behavior of backgrounds.

However, with CSS, you can change both of those characteristics. You can define the graphic so that rather than tiling, it simply appears once where it is positioned. Also, more interestingly, you can instruct the background graphic to remain in place while other objects, including text, placed on top of it, effectively scroll over it.

Figure 11.9 and Figure 11.10 show this effect as clearly as it can be shown on a "dead" page. Figure 11.9 shows how the page looks before any scrolling takes place. You can see that the picture of our happy fisherman is positioned in the lower right of the page.

Figure 11.9. Fixed Background Image Behind Unscrolled Text

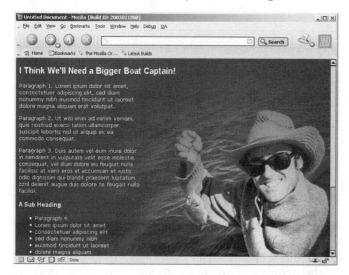

In Figure 11.10, the numbered list has scrolled down several items, but as you can see, the fisherman image that serves as the background for this text remains firmly fixed in place.

Figure 11.10. Scrolled Text Leaves Fixed Background Image in Place

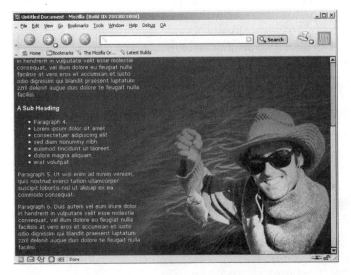

Here is the CSS rule that produces the fixed background effect demonstrated in Figure 11.9 and Figure 11.10.

```
body {
  background: url(fisherman.jpg) fixed no-repeat;
}
```

I used the `background` shorthand and provided the URL of the image to be used as the background (enclosed in a `url()` wrapper), gave it a fixed position and told it not to repeat or tile.

Earlier in the book, backgrounds have all been colors. If you define both a color and an image URL for a background, the image completely covers the colored background, but if the image can't be located or loaded for some reason, the colored background will be visible. If you have artistic talent, you can also define transparent areas of a graphic and then define both an image and a color for the background. In that case, the color will show through the transparent regions of the image.

One of the nicest applications of this fixed-background design I've seen is Eric Meyer's widely applauded Complex Spiral demo[3]. This demo's primary page

[3] http://www.meyerweb.com/eric/css/edge/complexspiral/demo.html

is shown in part in Figure 11.11. Notice that he has achieved the illusion of translucency in the scrolling text block. To do this, he uses a fixed background within the div that contains the content. Unfortunately, that nifty trick works only on a very limited number of browsers with first-rate CSS1 support, so I'm not going to teach you how to do it here. Read Meyer's site if the notion intrigues you; he offers a very clear explanation for how to execute that design. For practical purposes, you'll probably want to stick to using fixed background images only for the body element, which is more widely supported.

Figure 11.11. Illusion of Transparency on Eric Meyer's Complex Spiral Demo Site

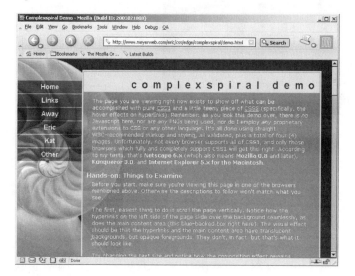

Summary

This chapter has demonstrated how to apply CSS to an ordinary unordered list of links and produce a graphically interesting, interactive menu for site navigation. It also described how to modify cursors dynamically and use fixed backgrounds on HTML pages to create a polished look and feel.

Chapter 12, discusses how to validate your use of CSS to ensure that it conforms to the W3C recommendations, and how to deal with some of the primary issues involved in creating pages that work with nonconforming browsers.

12 Validation and Backward Compatibility

This final chapter discusses two related topics. It begins with a description of the use of W3C and other CSS-validation tools and techniques to ensure that your CSS designs create valid pages. Particularly, as you migrate existing table-centered designs to CSS, validation will be helpful in pointing out areas where you haven't quite lived up to CSS expectations.

The second part of the chapter focuses on some small changes you can make to valid CSS pages so that they will display as correctly as possible in older or in-compatible browsers. It discusses using gateway pages and browser sniffers to route browsers to compatible pages, how to use the @import rule to avoid some potential pitfalls, and how to define a page's DOCTYPE property to gain more direct control over the rendering of that page.

Validating Your CSS

I recommend validating all your external style sheets and all your HTML pages that use internal style sheets as well. It's easy to do and it's free. If you submit a page (or multiple pages) to the W3C's CSS validation service and they pass, you can put a nifty little icon like the one in Figure 12.1 on your page.

Figure 12.1. Valid CSS Badge

To submit a style sheet or HTML page for validation, just go to http://jigsaw.w3.org/css-validator/. The page you'll see looks like Figure 12.2.

Figure 12.2. Main Page of W3C's CSS Validator

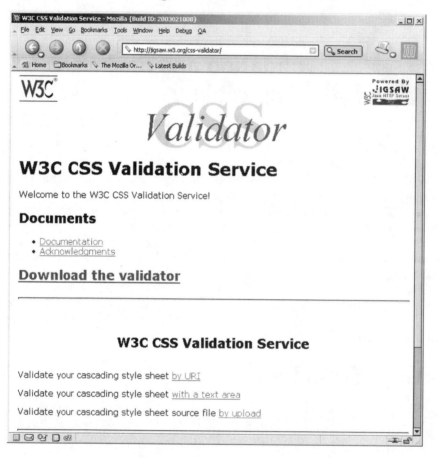

Scroll down this page, if necessary, and decide whether you want to download the validator to your system, submit the URL for the page or style sheet you want validated, or upload a page to the W3C site for validation. Most of the time, I just use the URL validator. Clicking on that link brings you to the page shown in Figure 12.3.

Figure 12.3. URL Validation Page of W3C's CSS Validator

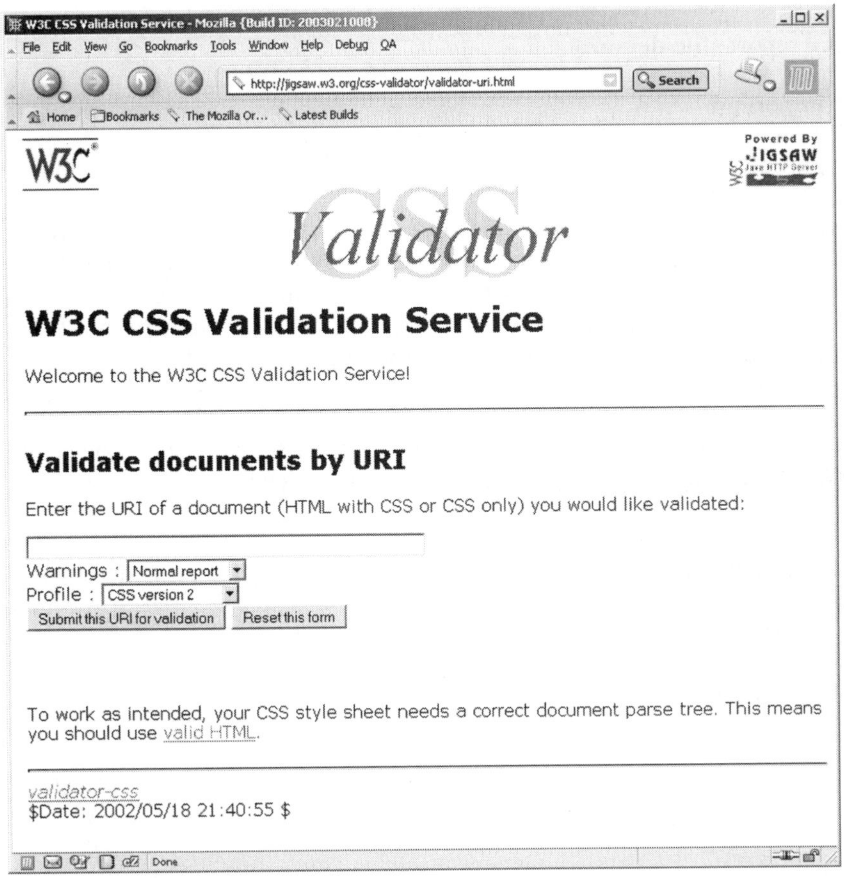

Simply type the URL of the page you want checked into the box, select the appropriate settings in the two popup menus on the form (I discuss these below), and submit the URL for validation. You can submit a page that contains any or all of the types of style information: linked, embedded and/or inline. The validator will load and check any externally-linked style sheets, in addition to looking over the CSS contained within the HTML document itself. You can also submit a CSS style sheet document for validation.

The validation form contains two popup menus. The first, labeled "Warnings", determines how significant a mistake must be before the validator lists it in the litany of warnings it produces as part of its report. It has four options:

❑ all

❑ normal report (the default)

❑ most important

❑ no warnings

Warnings are not the same as errors. If your page has CSS errors in it, it won't validate. But it's possible for a page to validate and still contain markup that is either deprecated or used in inadvisable ways. For example, the CSS validator warns you if you set the color of text and background elements within a block to the same color. This doesn't make the CSS wrong, but it can have an undesirable effect when the page is rendered.

By default, this popup is set to "Normal report" and unless you have some experience or a specific reason to believe that level of warning won't serve your needs, I recommend leaving it at its default value.

The second popup menu on the page is labeled "Profile". This setting determines the CSS recommendation against which your page will be validated. It has four choices:

❑ no special profile

❑ CSS version 1

❑ CSS version 2

❑ mobile

Those options are self-explanatory. By default, the validator sets the profile to CSS2.

When you have set these two popup menus to reflect the options you require, submit the URL for validation. After a brief pause, the validator will let you know that your page contains valid CSS (in which case it provides you with a link to the badge in Figure 12.1, to make it easy to put the graphic on your page). Alternatively, it will tell you what to fix in order to make your page's CSS valid.

It's important to note that to validate the CSS on your page, the validator must be working with a correct HTML page. Specifically, what is called the "document parse tree" must be valid, or the CSS validator will not be able to work as it should.

On the CSS validation page, you'll see a note to this effect and a link to the main W3C validation page, where you can submit the page for HTML validation prior to using the CSS validator. Note that "valid" HTML requires the inclusion of all of the document prologue elements, including DOCTYPE and a character encoding label. If your page lacks either of these, you'll be told that the validator cannot proceed until these points are fixed.

While I find the W3C's HTML and CSS validators to be perfectly adequate, I know Webmasters and Web designers who suggest that the validators maintained by The Web Design Group (WDG) are more stringent and informative.

The WDG's CSSCheck validator[2] does a very decent job of CSS validation. It differs from the W3C validator in two interesting ways.

First, CSSCheck validates only external style sheets. The link you provide must be to a file with a .css extension. Second, CSSCheck will allow you to copy and paste CSS markup into an editing area on its page, and validate that segment. This can be useful during complex CSS markup tasks, when you just want to make sure you have the syntax of something right.

Obviously, there's nothing to prevent you from using both services. That might be a bit like wearing suspenders *and* a belt, but nobody will try to stop you if that's your style!

Adjusting for Backward Compatibility

Throughout this book, I've provided you with CSS that works (as nearly as I can determine, at least) across all modern browsers and platforms. I have also steadfastly ignored browsers that don't support the majority of the CSS1 recommendation.

Browser statistics generally show that you'll reach close to 98% of the total Web browsing audience with those restrictions. But, if you're managing a site to whose stakeholders that missing 2-8% is an issue, and you need to convince your customers or managers that your designs are fine for even the majority of those

---

[2] http://www.htmlhelp.com/tools/csscheck/

outdated browsers, there are a few non-CSS-compliant things you can do to your site to make it work on the older or broken browsers.[1]

I'm going to tackle this subject from the perspective that you're starting with a page that has validated to CSS1 or CSS2 specification, but which has now been declared in need of a retrofit to work with older browsers.

Which Are the Non-Conforming Browsers?

Of the major browsers, the following have no CSS support whatsoever:

❑ Opera (Version 3.5 and earlier)

❑ Netscape Navigator (Version 3.x and earlier)

❑ Internet Explorer (Version 2.x and earlier)

The good news is that these browsers now make up less than 0.5% of all browsers in use on the Web.[2]

The bad news is that Netscape Navigator 4.x, which has a small but inexplicably intransigent following, whose members tend to be quite vocal, is arguably the most maddening of all the browsers. It supports just enough of CSS to do a decent job of rendering most of what I've provided in this book, but it breaks just often enough to be intensely annoying.

---

[1] In reality, the situation (at least in the United States) is that Internet Explorer 5 and 6 combine on the Mac and Windows platforms to own in excess of 90% of the market. If only IE were consistent between Mac and Windows platforms, you could almost safely design pages only for IE and get away with it most of the time (in North America, at least). But, because IE *isn't* consistent across those platforms, and because the Mac still constitutes approximately 8-10% of the browsing public, you can't really adopt an IE-only design strategy and expect anything less than excoriation from certain users. The safe route of coding to W3C recommendations is still the best choice. Philosophically, I'm unalterably opposed to designing Web pages that don't conform to W3C standards and I've been known to stare death rays at sites that demand I use a specific browser and/or operating system "for best viewing."

[2] In truth, it's difficult to say how significant these browsers are. There are virtually no good free sources of reliable browser statistics any longer. Internet.com used to run a service called Browserwatch.com that was quite reliable, but for reasons best known to the owners of that site, they discontinued that service some time ago. Nobody else has rushed in to fill the gap. Statistics like those I'm citing here are an amalgam of quasi-reliable information and personal experience, with a good bit of discussion with other Web designers tossed into the pot. They're certainly accurate within some limits.

In fact, Navigator 4.x deserves and gets its own entire section near the end of this chapter.

Basic Approaches to Non-Conforming Browsers

To make your CSS pages render well in nonconforming browsers, you must choose from the following basic strategies:

- ❏ Combine CSS styles with deprecated HTML elements and attributes.

- ❏ Use redirecting front door pages that allow the user to pick his or her own poison, as it were.

- ❏ Use browser sniffers to automatically send the user to a page designed for his or her browser.

The latter two approaches require that you design and maintain at least two subsites: one for CSS-capable browsers and one for nonconforming browsers. Depending on the size and complexity of the site and the frequency and degree of automation of updates, this can be more or less of a pain.

Combining CSS and Outmoded HTML

Whether mixing deprecated HTML and CSS in your pages is a good idea or not is largely a function of how important it is to you that users of nonconforming browsers have a better-than-ordinary experience when they view your site. This, in turn, depends to some extent on how you've used CSS on your pages.

If, for example, you define CSS styles for various levels of headings and for paragraphs, varying fonts and colors, then any nonconforming browser user can still see your page as if no styles were applied. There's no driving need to recreate the CSS-based user experience beyond aesthetics. In that case, I'd recommend just leaving things as they are. It's probably not worth spending time modifying your HTML for the relatively small number of users who are likely to be affected by the bland standard fonts for headings and text.

At the other extreme, if you're using CSS positioning extensively to create a very specific layout, then you'll probably find that most users' experience of your site will be unacceptable, perhaps even ugly. Unfortunately, that extreme also represents a situation where mixing CSS and deprecated HTML won't help much.

You'll probably end up creating and maintaining two separate sites or sub-sites, one using CSS and one using tables.[3]

Between those extremes, if you find yourself with a layout you particularly like, or that your customer or manager insists be replicated as closely as possible for nonconforming browsers, then you can at least get close to that goal by following the advice in the rest of this section.

The easiest issue to deal with is styles that control the overall appearance of the page. These are usually, but not always, defined in a CSS rule that applies to the body. You can simply add these same characteristics to the <body> tag in the document. As long as the values you include in the <body> tag are identical to those in the body CSS rule, the result is the same in both conforming and non-conforming browsers.

Font colors, styles, families, and related characteristics are similarly easy to deal with. Simply include <font> tags with all of the elements on the page for which you've defined a CSS rule. This is potentially a great deal more time-consuming (and error-prone) than dealing with <body> attributes, because it requires that you replicate the font declarations for every instance of a tag for which you've defined a CSS rule. For example, if you've defined a rule like this:

```
p {
  font-family: Arial, Helvetica, sans-serif;
  color: green;
}
```

you'll need to find every <p> tag and then edit them so they look like this:

```
<font face="Arial, Helvetica, sans-serif" color="green"><p>
  Paragraph text</p></font>
```

You may have noticed in the second code fragment above that I placed the font declaration outside the <p> tags. You've probably become accustomed to the reverse of this order. We place the <font> tags outside the <p> tags to allow the CSS styles to apply to the <p> on browsers that support it; if the <font> tags were placed inside the <p> tags, they would override the style sheet properties even on modern browsers.

---

[3]Fortunately, tools like Macromedia Dreamweaver enable you to do one layout using drag-and-drop direct placement of elements, then save the CSS version and perform a conversion to obtain a separate, table-driven HTML design. That removes much, but not all, of the complexity of maintaining two pages for different categories of browsers. If you find yourself needing to do this, I recommend you look into Dreamweaver as a design tool.

The situation is more complex if you've defined complex selectors so that only certain paragraphs have this special formatting. You'll need to look for all of the appropriate paragraphs and change only those.

Asking the User to Choose an Experience

For a brief period a couple of years ago, there was a trend toward allowing users to determine whether they wanted a "full" experience of the site or something with reduced display capability because of their browser. This was a pretty stupid idea on many fronts, the primary one of which is that most users had no clue what version of a browser they were using or what its capabilities were. Asking them to indicate whether their browser supported CSS, no matter how cleverly worded the inquiry, was likely simply to send them scurrying in fear to the next site they wanted to visit.

Unfortunately, this trend has continued, to some degree, albeit with a little less stupidity associated with it, as Macromedia Flash has become a more widely used technology for creating, well, flashy user experiences. Some site designers have become so enamored of their Flash capabilities and of the admittedly glitzy results they can produce that they've created enormously complex and often irrelevant "intro" pages to their sites. Conventionally, such pages include a (generally tiny and obscure) link or button labeled "skip intro" that allows the user to go directly to the site (presumably the reason they showed up in the first place).[4]

I recommend you avoid using what used to be called "gateway pages" like the plague. They are unhelpful, tasteless, and show a dismaying disregard for the user.

Detecting the User's Browser and Reacting Accordingly

The server from which a Web page is rendered when the user requests it is a full-powered computer. Rather than asking the user whether the browser she's using is capable of rendering CSS or using other fake techniques to determine the browser and version, why not allow the server to handle the task for you? That clearly makes sense.

Since the earliest point at which browsers began to diverge from one another, many people have written scripts to help the server decide which version of a

---

[4]"Skip intro" got to be such a joke that a Dutch company created a Website called skipintro to poke fun at the trend. The site has morphed, the company now claims to be a serious Web design firm (and appear to be), but the historical page is still available for a good chuckle at http://www.skipintro.nl/skipintro.

page to send to the user's machine, depending on the browser type and version they used. As versions proliferated, new browsers were developed, and capabilities diverged, these scripts became incredibly complex.

These "browser sniffers", as they're called, proliferate on the Web. Most of them are pretty similar to one another, even if an examination of the code doesn't necessarily reveal the truth of that observation. They haven't changed much recently, which isn't surprising given that the pace of browser change and diversion has slowed dramatically of late.

Writing or even understanding the workings of a browser sniffer script is not only beyond the scope of this book, it's unnecessary. All you have to do is find a script you like, link to it in your pages, and then be sure you've created appropriately-named pages to send to users once you know their browser's type and version.[5] You may have to make minor modifications to the script, depending on how closely it suits your needs.

Using a browser sniffer script generally involves these steps:

1. Obtain the script and gain access to it either by getting its present URL or copying it to your server.

2. Create a link to the script in a Web page whose sole purpose is to decide which page to send the user based on browser differences. This page is generally not one the user ever sees (or at least sees only fleetingly as the decision gets made).

3. Use any of several techniques to send the user the appropriate page.

4. Design the appropriate pages.

In the case of a simple site consisting of a very small number of pages, and undergoing relatively infrequent updates, you can group pages designed to be served to a particular set of browsers in a directory, and maintain separate directories of pages. This same approach can be used with dynamic sites that consist of a small handful of templates that are used to generate pages on demand; you can just maintain multiple templates.

---

[5]One of the cleanest and most up-to-date scripts for browser sniffing that I've seen lately is on Apple Computer's site [http://developer.apple.com/internet/javascript/internetdev-sniffer.txt]. This script actually needs to be modified to handle redirection (as do many such scripts) but it's accompanied by an excellent tutorial that should make that process fairly easy. Most introductory JavaScript texts would also be quite helpful here. The script, by the way, is completely cross-platform.

With a complex site, the problem is a bit stickier simply because of the sheer volume of content to be managed. In such cases, you should consider using a global variable whose state is preserved either in a server-side session or in a cross-window variable in JavaScript. You can then handle browser detection once, and do a simple variable check when the browser requests a new page.

Whichever method you use to maintain the browser-differentiated pages, the important thing is that the logic of the separation be meaningful, and as intuitive as possible, so that long-term maintenance of what amounts to multiple sites doesn't become a nightmare.

If you use the browser sniffer method with redirection of the user's browser to overcome nonconforming browser problems, I recommend you essentially divide the browsers into "conforming" and "nonconforming", and create only two sets of pages. Don't get bogged down trying to account for minor differences among the ways some CSS properties are addressed by nonconforming minority browsers, or you'll drive yourself more insane than dealing with these browsers will already cause you to become!

That means you should end up with just two sets of pages: one using purely CSS, and one using tables as the primary layout mechanism. There are some ways that you could make the connections across these pages easier to maintain, but that could occupy another entire book, so I'll leave that as an exercise for you, dear reader!

Accommodating Netscape 4.x

Netscape 4 browsers make up less than 2% of the total browser market. This is a good thing, because Navigator 4.x is among the quirkiest and least usable of all the browsers from the designer's perspective. Unfortunately, if you work for clients or managers who insist on backward compatibility, Netscape 4 is as likely as not to be a major emphasis for them. Why? Because Netscape 4 emerged at a time when its publisher was putting on a major push to get its browsers accepted over the rapidly emerging, and soon to be leading, browser from Microsoft.

Tens of thousands of people became convinced that Netscape 4 was the last browser they'd ever need. At the time of its heyday, it was the most nearly standards-compliant browser. To this day, many people who use it believe that if a site doesn't display well in their browser, it's the site's fault.

There are two basic strategies for dealing with Navigator 4: blocking its view of style sheets completely, or modifying a page to accommodate major conflicts between Navigator 4's view of the world and the CSS perspective.

Two Ways to Block Navigator 4 from Style Sheets

There are two ways to prevent Navigator 4 from even seeing the style sheets applied to a particular page. Either of these approaches results in the browser simply ignoring all CSS-related information stored in the external style sheet and, presumably, displaying the page as it would routinely.

The first approach is to use a CSS at-rule called @import.[6] An at-rule is a special kind of CSS directive (or command, if you prefer) that starts with an "at sign" (@). These are used inside styles in a document or, less frequently, in externally linked style sheets. Because Navigator 4 doesn't understand these commands, it ignores them.

To link an external style sheet called corpstyle.css into a page, for example, you could code the head of the document like this:

```
<link rel="stylesheet" type="text/css" href="corpstyle.css" />
```

But, to cause Navigator 4 to ignore this externally-linked style sheet, instead create an embedded style sheet and use an @import rule to reference the external style sheet like this:

```
<style type="text/css">
  @import url(corpstyle.css);
</style>
```

Notice that the name of the style sheet is supplied as an argument to the url() operator. If you use a string instead, as shown below, you will block not only Navigator 4.x but also IE4 on Mac and Windows.

```
<style type="text/css">
  @import "corpstyle.css";
</style>
```

The other simple way to block Navigator 4 from seeing a style sheet is to take advantage of an error in the way that browser implements the media attribute of a CSS <link> tag. The media attribute is optional and generally not included

---

[6]The other at-rules are described in Appendix A.

but if it is and if it contains a value other than `screen`, then Netscape Navigator
4.x ignores it. Here's an example of how to accomplish this:

```
<link rel="stylesheet" type="text/css" href="corpstyle.css"
  media="all" />
```

Generally, you should use `all` as the value for the `media` attribute if you want
Navigator 4 to ignore the style sheet. You may, however, be more comfortable
using `screen` along with some other value, such as `screen, print`, which will
also have the desired effect on Navigator 4.

Identifying and Dealing With Navigator 4 Problems

Just about the only way to identify CSS markup that will break in Navigator 4.x
is to use a compatibility chart, and go through your documents looking for possibly
offending properties. You can find a comprehensive CSS property reference, including browser compatibility information, in Appendix C. Since books tend to
slip out of date quicker than online information, however, I'll also provide some
online reference sources for you.

The most exhaustive online reference to Web browser compatibility I've seen is
at Web Review Magazine's site[5]. Although it tends to slip out of date because
it's maintained by volunteers, the information it has is accurate. It doesn't keep
pace with new browser releases, but that's generally not a problem because of
the lag time from a browser's release and its broad market penetration.

The other good Web browser compatibility chart is at Western Civilisation's
Website[6]. This company publishes a CSS editor and other Web design tools,
and maintains this chart as a service to its customers and prospects. I've generally
found the data here to be current and accurate, as well.

If you look down the Navigator 4.x columns in either of these online tables, or
peruse Appendix C, you'll see the aspects of CSS design that tend to be problematic for Navigator 4. Among the most pronounced areas of nonconformance are:

☐ the cascade itself

☐ `font-variant`

☐ backgrounds (particularly positioning and attachment)

---

[5] http://www.webreview.com/style/css1/charts/mastergrid.shtml
[6] http://www.westciv.com/style_master/academy/browser_support/index.html

❑ word and letter spacing

❑ `vertical-align`

❑ most of the box-related CSS properties (these are buggy at best)

❑ much border-related control

❑ `list-style` properties

Other, less obvious errors abound as well. For example, Navigator 4 incorrectly causes an element to inherit the font size set in the parent element rather than the relative value, when you use relative units (see Chapter 9).

In general, I advise you to spend as little time as possible worrying about Navigator 4.x support and very little energy trying to get your pages to display well (let alone perfectly) in this flawed browser.

Keep the Quirks: DOCTYPE Switching

Web pages that are coded to display in earlier browsers (versions that don't offer full CSS support) may look ugly, or fail to display at all in later browsers that do support CSS. Badly formed HTML, which earlier browsers forgave, breaks in newer browsers that must render HTML more meticulously because of the strict rules that come with standards like CSS.

The opposite is also true, as we've seen. Pages designed to display well in recent and new browsers may not display well, or may fail to display at all, in older browsers. IE5 for Macintosh, IE6 for Windows, Netscape 6, and Mozilla browsers support a technology called **DOCTYPE Switching**. Simply stated, this technology allows these browsers to adapt their display characteristics based on the document type (`DOCTYPE`) declared at the beginning of a Web page.

I should point out that this `DOCTYPE` statement has always been recommended for inclusion on Web pages. Most Web designers have ignored the advice, and Web design tool manufacturers have failed to enforce it. As a result, updating all your current Web pages with this type of statement may be a bit of a task. If you're using a good editor or design tool, the burden won't be onerous.

A browser that supports DOCTYPE Switching gives the appearance of supporting two different compatibility modes: a standards mode, and a quirks mode. The former is more strict about its interpretation of tags and CSS instructions than is the latter.

Assuming your pages don't already make use of this feature, you can add a DOCTYPE statement as the first statement on every Web page you've designed. If the page uses style sheet rules, whether embedded, external, or both, you should provide a "strict" DOCTYPE statement like this one for the HTML 4.0 standard:

```
<!DOCTYPE HTML PUBLIC "-//W3C/DTD HTML 4.0//EN"
  "http://www.w3.org/TR/html4/strict.dtd">
```

The equivalent DOCTYPE for the newer, XHTML 1.0 standard is:

```
<!DOCTYPE html PUBLIC "-//W3C//DTD XHTML 1.0 Strict//EN"
  "http://www.w3.org/TR/xhtml1/DTD/xhtml1-strict.dtd">
```

If one or more pages on your site does *not* support CSS, but requires older-style rendering using embedded HTML tags, the following DOCTYPE will ensure that *most* browsers that support DOCTYPE Switching will render the page cleanly and correctly:

```
<!DOCTYPE HTML PUBLIC "-//W3C//DTD HTML 4.0 Transitional//EN"
  "http://www.w3.org/TR/html4/loose.dtd">
```

And, if you prefer to adhere to the new XHTML 1.0 standard:

```
<!DOCTYPE html PUBLIC "-//W3C//DTD XHTML 1.0 Transitional//EN"
  "http://www.w3.org/TR/xhtml1/DTD/xhtml1-transitional.dtd">
```

Notice that the second pair of DOCTYPE statements refers to the "loose" or "transitional" versions of the two standards, both through the public identifiers and URLs provided. The result is that browsers that support DOCTYPE Switching technology act in "quirks" mode and, again, display the documents correctly even if there are standards compliance issues with the HTML on the page.

Unfortunately, Internet Explorer 6 requires a little more mangling of the DOCTYPE statement before it will switch into "quirks" mode. In addition to specifying the "transitional" version of HTML 4.0, you must also leave out the URL portion of the DOCTYPE to enable "quirks" mode:

```
<!DOCTYPE HTML PUBLIC "-//W3C//DTD HTML 4.0 Transitional//EN">
```

Any HTML DOCTYPE that specifies a URL, and any XHTML DOCTYPE *whatsoever* will put IE6 in "strict" mode, so if you do want it to operate in compatibility mode you must use this last DOCTYPE. For full details, consult MSDN[7].

Most browsers (including IE6) will also go into "quirks" mode if the DOCTYPE statement is missing; however, as both the HTML and XHTML standards specify that this statement is required, I don't recommend this practice.

XML DOCTYPE Switching Bug in Internet Explorer

In this book, I have endeavoured to present 100% XHTML 1.0 compliant HTML code, except where it was necessary to show code for older browsers. Every sample document in this book begins the same way:

```
<!DOCTYPE html PUBLIC "-//W3C//DTD XHTML 1.0 Transitional//EN"
  "http://www.w3.org/TR/xhtml1/DTD/xhtml1-transitional.dtd">
<html xmlns="http://www.w3.org/1999/xhtml">
<head>
  <title>Page Title Here</title>
  <meta http-equiv="Content-Type"
    content="text/html; charset=iso-8859-1" />
```

As you can see, the DOCTYPE declaration on the first line will ensure that modern browsers operate in standards-compliant mode.

XML purists may wonder why our XHTML documents don't start with an XML version declaration like this:

```
<?xml version="1.0" encoding="iso-8859-1"?>
```

Indeed, the XML standard prescribes that a document should begin with an <?xml ...?> declaration, which is then followed by the DOCTYPE declaration.

Unfortunately, when a document begins with an <?xml ...?> declaration, Internet Explorer 6 for Windows does not see the DOCTYPE, and lapses into "quirks" mode. For this reason, you must leave out the XML version declaration to get the best CSS support out of all current browsers.

Thankfully, the XML standard allows you to omit the declaration if you're happy with the default settings, which in the case of most XHTML documents, we are.

---

[7] http://msdn.microsoft.com/library/en-us/dnie60/html/cssenhancements.asp

Summary

In this final chapter, you've seen how to validate the CSS and HTML on your Web pages in order to ensure that they comply with W3C recommendations. You've seen how to deal with the question of backward compatibility in those rare cases where it should be necessary to do so. In particular, you've learned how to isolate the misbehaving Navigator 4.x browser from your otherwise excellent pages.

This brings the book to a close. I hope you've enjoyed our journey together and that you are now confident going forward as a Web designer who does it with style!

Appendix A. CSS Miscellany

This appendix pulls together information about CSS that I thought was particularly interesting and potentially useful but which didn't fit the main flow of the text. The operative word in the title of the appendix is "miscellaneous." There's no particular order to what's here. The following list represents the topics covered in this appendix, shown in the order in which they are presented:

☐ at-rules

☐ aural style sheets

☐ CSS and JavaScript

At-Rules

The CSS2 recommendation from the W3C defines a new type of CSS rule. It's called an "at-rule" because all the rules of this type start with an "at" sign (@). This type of rule is meant to be extensible. In other words, future editions of the W3C recommendation, browser developers, and others may define new sets of rules that begin with @.

For now, there are four groups of @ rules:

☐ `@import`

☐ `@media`

☐ `@page`

☐ `@font-face`

The `@import` rule is discussed in Chapter 12.

The `@media` rule allows you to define different output options for various media in a single style sheet. Browser support is somewhat inconsistent, though it seems to be getting better with each release. Right now, support for this rule is at least usable in most modern browsers (the most notable exception being IE 5.2 on Macintosh).

Initially, W3C defines that the following media types are valid for use with the @media rule. However, you should note that the list is not guaranteed to be complete. As new technologies and display platforms emerge, more keywords will undoubtedly be added.

- ❑ all

- ❑ aural

- ❑ braille

- ❑ embossed

- ❑ handheld

- ❑ print

- ❑ projection

- ❑ screen

- ❑ TTY

- ❑ TV

The purpose of all of these is largely self-explanatory with the exception of "embossed", which is intended to define output for a Braille printer. The following HTML produces two decidedly different appearances, depending on whether you're viewing the page on your computer screen or printing it out. It demonstrates the syntax and use of the @media rule.

```
<!DOCTYPE html PUBLIC "-//W3C//DTD XHTML 1.0 Transitional//EN"
  "http://www.w3.org/TR/xhtml1/DTD/xhtml1-transitional.dtd">
<html xmlns="http://www.w3.org/1999/xhtml">
<head>
  <title>Demonstrating @media Rules</title>
  <style type="text/css">
  <!--
  @media print {
    body {
      font-size: 12pt;
      font-family: courier;
    }
  }
```

```
@media screen {
  body {
    font-size: 36px;
    font-family: arial;
  }
}

@media screen, print {
  body {
    line-height: 1.2;
  }
}
-->
</style>
</head>
<body>
Let's see if this actually works and, if so, in which browsers.
I've defined an @media rule for print that makes it print
12-point Courier, but another @media rule that displays in
36-pixel Arial on the screen. Both devices produce output with a
line-height 120% of the default value.
</body>
</html>
```

Notice that it's OK to define a single @media rule to apply to multiple media. In that case, the names of the media must be separated by commas. There are two other ways to specify the medium to be used with a given style sheet or rule. You can use the @import rule and supply the media type as a parameter, as in this example:

```
@import url(bossvoice.css) aural;
```

This rule tells the browser to import the CSS stylesheet called bossvoice.css, and that it is to be applied to aural output devices.

The second way to define a style's medium is to use the media attribute of the style tag, as shown here:

```
<style type="text/css" media="projection">
body {
  color: blue;
  background-color: white;
}
</style>
```

If you define a style sheet for a medium that understands the notion of a "page," you can use the @page at-rule to declare sizes, borders, page breaks, and the presence or absence of crop marks on the output page.[1]

For example, to define an 8.5-inch by 11-inch page with a 0.5-inch border all the way around, you would write a @page rule like this:

```
@page {
    size: 8.5in 11in;
    margin: 0.5in;
}
```

The size property can be given one of three constant values, in addition to the specific size values shown earlier:

❏ auto, which tells the browser to use the default page size for the browser application

❏ landscape, where the larger dimension is the width

❏ portrait, where the larger dimension is the height

The margin property is a shorthand for the following, more specific properties, which may be specified individually:

❏ margin-top

❏ margin-right

❏ margin-bottom

❏ margin-left

You can also define special, overriding dimensions and margins for the first page of a document, and separate dimensions for left- and right-hand pages using the :first, :left, and :right pseudo-classes. Here's a set of @page rules that defines the layout for a document to be printed on both sides, with a special setting for the front page:

---

[1] The @page rule has some complexity associated with it that I'm not going to attempt to cover here. If you're curious, I suggest you go to the W3C page where the @page rule is defined [http://www.w3.org/TR/REC-CSS2/page.html#page-box].

```
@page {
  margin: 2cm; /* All margins set to 2cm */
}
@page:first {
  margin-top: 10cm; /* Top margin on first page 10cm */
}

/* 1cm larger margins near binding */
@page:left {
  margin-left: 3cm;
  margin-right: 4cm;
}
@page:right {
  margin-left: 4cm;
  margin-right: 3cm;
}
```

Under the CSS2 Recommendation, you can control page breaks in paged output as well. Page control is a very complex topic and one that is probably beyond not only the scope of this discussion, but also the interest level of the vast majority of Web designers. So, I'm not going to go into it here, except to say that if you ever get into a position where you want or need to prepare a Web page for printed (or other paged) output, you can confidently state that you can control the page break situation... The relevant properties are described in detail in Appendix C.

Aural Style Sheets

Sound is, in the view of some Web designers at least, a vastly under-utilized aspect of communication on the Internet. Most applications for aural presentation of Web content today revolve around people with hearing loss, but in the future, I anticipate that we will see far more use of spoken language, background music, and mixtures of voice and music to enliven some user experiences.

The CSS2 Recommendation from the W3C defines a whole range of sound (aural) presentation qualities that can be defined in CSS. Collectively, these make up the components of an aural style sheet.

Here's a snippet of an aural style sheet, borrowed directly from the W3C's Web page on aural style sheets[2]:

```
h1, h2, h3, h4, h5, h6 {
  voice-family: paul;
```

[2] http://www.w3.org/TR/REC-CSS2/aural.html

```
    stress: 20;
    richness: 90;
    cue-before: url(ping.au);
}
p.heidi {
    azimuth: center-left;
}
p.peter {
    azimuth: right;
}
p.goat {
    volume: x-soft;
}
```

Let's go over this style sheet fragment, line by line.

All headings will be spoken using a voice-family called "paul." A voice family is much like a font family; it contains a collection of minor variations on a voice. The headings will apply a stress value (determining the "contour" of a voice, i.e. the degree of difference in inflection in various parts of the sentences), of 20, which is pretty low.

The code defines a richness of 90, which is very high. Richness determines how far a voice carries, and affects what we might think of as "loudness." Before any heading is pronounced, an "auditory icon" called ping.au will be played. You can define cues to be played before and after any sound segment.

Any paragraph marked as an instance of the class "heidi" will appear to originate from the listener's left, in a vertical center of space. Paragraphs that are instances of the class "peter" will come from the listener's right side. All paragraphs spoken by the "goat" voice will be extremely soft.

You get the idea. Again, a full treatment of this topic is beyond the scope of this book, but I wanted you to gain something of an appreciation for the scope of what *can* be done.

With aural style rules, you can control the following characteristics of a voice or the spoken presentation of the information on your Web page:

❏ volume

❏ whether to speak words or spell them out

❏ pausing

❑ cue sounds before and after

❑ mixing (playing two sounds simultaneously)

❑ spatial location of the sound in 3-D space

❑ speech rate

❑ pitch and range of pitch

❑ stress

❑ richness

❑ how to speak punctuation (pronounce it or use it as pause cues)

❑ how to speak numerals (separate digits or numerical values)

The properties that control all of these factors are listed in Appendix C.

CSS and JavaScript

When you combine XHTML, JavaScript and CSS, you get something called Dynamic HTML, or DHTML. Many people mistakenly believe that DHTML is a technology. It's not. It's a term used to refer to the potential for high levels of interactivity (dynamism) in pages generated using (X)HTML.

Many books have been written about DHTML. Without any doubt, in my opinion, the best of breed is my friend Danny Goodman's massive *Dynamic HTML: The Definitive Guide, 2nd Edition*, published by O'Reilly. This 1,400-page volume not only provides wonderful tutorials and insights into the workings of all the technologies that comprise DHTML, but also includes an exhaustive, 99% accurate reference to all the arcana as well.

I've omitted teaching you JavaScript or DHTML here because the subject is so vast. This book is intended principally for beginning-to-intermediate Web designers, not advanced folks using scripting and programming techniques.

Still, it's important, as you begin to move beyond what's in this book and develop your skills as a Web designer, that you have a basic appreciation of the potential for DHTML. So, here I'll provide a brief overview of the topic, just to whet your appetite and perhaps forestall some of your budding questions about what could be done with CSS.

At the core of DHTML is something called the Document Object Model, or DOM. While the comparison is a bit simplistic, you can think of the DOM as a specification or definition of the way you can refer to individual pieces of your Web pages. This, in turn, enables you to tell them to change something about their display or behavior. JavaScript is the language that's most often used to write these instructions.

Essentially, each CSS property can be accessed and modified from a JavaScript. Within the JavaScript code, you simply refer to the object by its ID or name, identify the property whose value you wish to retrieve or change, and, if appropriate, supply a new value. When the script is executed, the CSS modification occurs.

For example, you could create a button on a Web page that would hide some particular piece of content (whose ID we'll assume to be hereandgone). You would define a JavaScript function called, for example, hideshow. It would look something like this:

```
function hideShow() {
  document.getElementById("hereandgone").style.visibility="hidden";
}
```

Where you define the script, when and how it gets executed, and other similar details are beyond the scope of our discussion here. The point is simply that you can access and modify element styles in an HTML page, even after the page has been rendered in the user's browser using JavaScript. The syntax varies very little from the example above, which is one of the reasons why the DOM has been defined as it has. It seems cumbersome to have to type getelementById every time you want to get an element's style or other property, but the fact is that since this operator is the same in every instance, you can quickly learn to handle lots of different scripting situations with very little additional knowledge.

Appendix B. CSS Color Reference

As covered in detail in Chapter 7, there are five methods to specify color values in CSS:

❏ Descriptive color names

```
color: red;
```

❏ System color names

```
color: AppWorkspace;
```

❏ RGB hexadecimal values (including a three-character shorthand)

```
color: #ff0000;
color: #f00;
```

❏ RGB decimal values

```
color: rgb(255, 0, 0);
```

❏ RGB percentage values

```
color: rgb(100%, 0%, 0%);
```

This appendix provides a complete reference to the first two methods—color names. The CSS2 Recommendation[1] prescribes a set of 16 descriptive color names, which are presented in Table B.1. Netscape proposed an additional 124 color names, which are supported by practically every graphical browser available today, and are presented in Table B.2. Finally, CSS2 also provides a set of 28 system color names, which correspond to the colors used for different parts of the GUI presented by the user's operating system, and are presented in Table B.3. System color names are supported in most current browsers, but older browsers typically do not support them.

---

[1] http://www.w3.org/TR/REC-CSS2/syndata.html#color-units

Table B.1. Standard CSS Color Names

Color Name	Hex Equivalent	Red	Green	Blue
aqua	#00FFFF	0	255	255
black	#000000	0	0	0
blue	#0000FF	0	0	255
fuchsia	#FF00FF	255	0	255
gray	#808080	128	128	128
green	#008000	0	128	0
lime	#00FF00	0	255	0
maroon	#800000	128	0	0
navy	#000080	0	0	128
olive	#808000	128	128	0
purple	#800080	128	0	128
red	#FF0000	255	0	0
silver	#C0C0C0	192	192	192
teal	#008080	0	128	128
white	#FFFFFF	255	255	255
yellow	#FFFF00	255	255	0

Table B.2. Netscape Extended Color Names

Color Name	Hex Equivalent	Red	Green	Blue
aliceblue	#F0F8FF	240	248	255
antiquewhite	#FAEBD7	250	235	215
aquamarine	#7FFFD4	127	255	212
azure	#F0FFFF	240	255	255
beige	#F5F5DC	245	245	220
bisque	#FFE4C4	255	228	196
blanchedalmond	#FFEBCD	255	235	205
blueviolet	#8A2BE2	138	43	226
brown	#A52A2A	165	42	42
burlywood	#DEB887	222	184	135
cadetblue	#5F9EA0	95	158	160
chartreuse	#7FFF00	127	255	0
chocolate	#D2691E	210	105	30
coral	#FF7F50	255	127	80
cornflowerblue	#6495ED	100	149	237
cornsilk	#FFF8DC	255	248	220
crimson	#DC143D	220	20	61
cyan	#00FFFF	0	255	255
darkblue	#00008B	0	0	139
darkcyan	#008B8B	0	139	139
darkgoldenrod	#B8860B	139	134	11
darkgray	#A9A9A9	169	169	169
darkgreen	#006400	0	100	0
darkkhaki	#BDB76B	189	183	107
darkmagenta	#8B008B	139	0	139
darkolivegreen	#556B2F	85	107	47
darkorange	#FF8C00	255	140	0
darkorchid	#9932CC	153	50	204

Color Name	Hex Equivalent	Red	Green	Blue
darkred	#8B0000	139	0	0
darksalmon	#E9967A	233	150	122
darkseagreen	#8FBC8F	143	188	143
darkslateblue	#483D8B	72	61	139
darkslategray	#2F4F4F	47	79	79
darkturquoise	#00CED1	0	206	209
darkviolet	#9400D3	148	0	211
deeppink	#FF1493	255	20	147
deepskyblue	#00BFFF	0	191	255
dimgray	#696969	105	105	105
dodgerblue	#1E90FF	30	144	255
firebrick	#B22222	178	34	34
floralwhite	#FFFAF0	255	250	240
forestgreen	#228B22	34	139	34
gainsboro	#DCDCDC	220	220	220
ghostwhite	#F8F8FF	248	248	255
gold	#FFD700	255	215	0
goldenrod	#DAA520	218	165	32
greenyellow	#ADFF2F	173	255	47
honeydew	#F0FFF0	240	255	240
hotpink	#FF69B4	255	105	180
indianred	#CD5C5C	205	92	92
indigo	#4B0082	75	0	130
ivory	#FFFFF0	255	255	240
khaki	#F0E68C	240	230	140
lavender	#E6E6FA	230	230	250
lavenderblush	#FFF0F5	255	240	245
lawngreen	#7CFC00	124	252	0
lemonchiffon	#FFFACD	255	250	205

Color Name	Hex Equivalent	Red	Green	Blue
lightblue	#ADD8E6	173	216	230
lightcoral	#F08080	240	128	128
lightcyan	#E0FFFF	224	255	255
lightgoldenrodyellow	#FAFAD2	250	250	210
lightgreen	#90EE90	144	238	144
lightgrey	#D3D3D3	211	211	211
lightpink	#FFB6C1	255	182	193
lightsalmon	#FFA07A	255	160	122
lightseagreen	#20B2AA	32	178	170
lightskyblue	#87CEFA	135	206	250
lightslategray	#778899	119	136	153
lightsteelblue	#B0C4DE	176	196	222
lightyellow	#FFFFE0	255	255	224
limegreen	#32CD32	50	205	50
linen	#FAF0E6	250	240	230
magenta	#FF00FF	255	0	255
mediumaquamarine	#66CDAA	102	205	170
mediumblue	#0000CD	0	0	205
mediumorchid	#BA55D3	186	85	211
mediumpurple	#9370DB	147	112	219
mediumseagreen	#3CB371	60	179	113
mediumslateblue	#7B68EE	123	104	238
mediumspringgreen	#00FA9A	0	250	154
mediumturquoise	#48D1CC	72	209	204
mediumvioletred	#C71585	199	21	133
midnightblue	#191970	25	25	112
mintcream	#F5FFFA	245	255	250
mistyrose	#FFE4E1	255	228	225
moccasin	#FFE4B5	255	228	181

Color Name	Hex Equivalent	Red	Green	Blue
navajowhite	#FFDEAD	255	222	173
oldlace	#FDF5E6	253	245	230
olivedrab	#6B8E23	107	142	35
orange	#FFA500	255	165	0
orangered	#FF4500	255	69	0
orchid	#DA70D6	218	112	214
palegoldenrod	#EEE8AA	238	232	170
palegreen	#98FB98	152	251	152
paleturquoise	#AFEEEE	175	238	238
palevioletred	#DB7093	219	112	147
papayawhip	#FFEFD5	255	239	213
peachpuff	#FFDAB9	255	218	185
peru	#CD853F	205	133	63
pink	#FFC0CB	255	192	203
plum	#DDA0DD	221	160	221
powderblue	#B0E0E6	176	224	230
rosybrown	#BC8F8F	188	143	143
royalblue	#4169E1	65	105	225
saddlebrown	#8B4513	139	69	19
salmon	#FA8072	250	128	114
sandybrown	#F4A460	244	164	96
seagreen	#2E8B57	46	139	87
seashell	#FFF5EE	255	245	238
sienna	#A0522D	160	82	45
skyblue	#87CEEB	135	206	235
slateblue	#6A5ACD	106	90	205
slategray	#708090	112	128	144
snow	#FFFAFA	255	250	250
spinggreen	#00FF7F	0	255	127

Color Name	Hex Equivalent	Red	Green	Blue
steelblue	#4682B4	70	130	180
tan	#D2B48C	210	180	140
thistle	#D8BFD8	216	191	216
tomato	#FF6347	255	99	71
turquoise	#40E0D0	64	224	208
violet	#EE82EE	238	130	238
wheat	#F5DEB3	245	222	179
whitesmoke	#F5F5F5	245	245	245
yellowgreen	#9ACD32	154	205	50

Table B.3. Standard CSS System Color Names

Color Name	Description
ActiveBorder	active window border color
ActiveCaption	active window caption color
AppWorkspace	background color of a multiple document interface
Background	desktop background color
ButtonFace	face color for three-dimensional display elements
ButtonHighlight	highlight color for three-dimensional display elements (edges facing light source)
ButtonShadow	shadow color for three-dimensional display elements (edges opposite light source)
ButtonText	text color on push buttons
CaptionText	text color in caption, size box, and scrollbar arrow box
GrayText	grayed-out (disabled) text color
Highlight	background color for selected items in a control
HighlightText	text color for selected items in a control
InactiveBorder	inactive window border color
InactiveCaption	inactive window caption color
InactiveCaptionText	inactive caption text color
InfoBackground	tooltip background color
InfoText	tooltip text color
Menu	menu background color
MenuText	menu text color
Scrollbar	scrollbar background color
ThreeDDarkShadow	dark shadow color for three-dimensional display elements
ThreeDFace	face color for three-dimensional display elements
ThreeDHighlight	highlight color for three-dimensional display elements

Color Name	Description
ThreeDLightShadow	light color for three-dimensional display elements
ThreeDShadow	shadow color for three-dimensional display elements
Window	window background color
WindowFrame	window frame color
WindowText	text color in windows

Appendix C. CSS Property Reference

This appendix contains a complete reference to all CSS properties at the time of this writing. This includes properties defined in the CSS1[1] and CSS2[2] specifications, as well as browser-specific extensions to the CSS recommendations.

Where a browser-specific extension exposes the same functionality as a planned feature in CSS3, which is currently a working draft, this is indicated with a reference to the relevant draft.

azimuth

`azimuth` sets the direction in horizontal space from which the sound comes when the content is presented aurally (e.g. in a speaking browser for the blind).

For full details on this property, see the CSS2 specification[3].

Inherited: Yes

See also: `elevation`

Value

An angle (`-360deg` to `360deg`, where `0deg` is in front of the listener), or a descriptive constant (e.g. `far-right behind`).

Initial value: `center`

Compatibility

CSS Version: 2

Not yet supported by any browser.

---

[1] http://www.w3.org/TR/REC-CSS1
[2] http://www.w3.org/TR/REC-CSS2/
[3] http://www.w3.org/TR/REC-CSS2/aural.html#spatial-props

Examples

This style rule will cause all headings to be heard from the front-left of the sound field:

```
h1, h2, h3, h4, h5, h6 {
  azimuth: -45deg;
}
```

background

A shorthand property that allows you to set all the background properties of an element with a single property declaration.

Inherited: No

See also: `background-attachment`, `background-color`, `background-image`, `background-position`, and `background-repeat`

Value

You can specify any of the values permitted by the five `background-` properties, in any order, separated by spaces. The properties you do not specify take on their initial value.

Initial value: none

Compatibility

CSS Version: 1

Is supported by Internet Explorer 4 or later, Netscape 6 or later, Opera 5 or later, and all Mozilla browsers. Is partially supported by Netscape 4.x; however, this support is undocumented and unreliable.

Examples

This rule gives the page a fixed (non-scrolling) background image, which will display over a solid white background:

```
body {
  background: #fff url(/images/texture.gif) fixed;
}
```

background-attachment

This property determines whether the background image assigned to an element scrolls in sync with the element's content or remains fixed in relation to the browser window. For example, if you wanted the top-left corner of your page background image to remain in the top-left corner of the browser window, even as the page was scrolled, you would set background-attachment to fixed.

Inherited: No

See also: background-image

Value

fixed or scroll

Initial value: scroll

Compatibility

CSS Version: 1

Supported by Internet Explorer 4 or later, Netscape 6 or later, Opera 5 or later, and all Mozilla browsers.

Internet Explorer for Windows (at least up to version 6) and Opera browsers (up to version 6), do not correctly support background-attachment: fixed on elements besides body. Opera 7, Internet Explorer 5 for Macintosh, Netscape 6.2.1 or later, and Mozilla browsers all get this right.

Examples

This style rule applies a background image to the page and specifies that the image should not scroll with the page content:

```
body {
  background-image: url(/images/texture.gif);
```

```
    background-attachment: fixed;
}
```

background-color

Sets the background color for an element.

Note that the default background color is transparent, so even though this property is not inherited, nested elements will allow the background to show through by default. The reason for this arrangement is to allow background images to be displayed behind nested elements.

It is considered good practice always to specify a foreground color (with the color property) whenever you specify a background color, and vice versa.

Inherited: No

See also: color

Value

Any CSS color value (see Appendix B) or transparent.

Initial value: transparent

Compatibility

CSS Version: 1

Works in all CSS-compatible browsers, including Internet Explorer 4 or later and Netscape 4 or later.

Netscape 4 does not correctly fill a block element with its assigned background color, unless it has a border assigned (even a zero-width border will do), and setting any visible border leaves a transparent gap between the padding area of the block and its border in that browser. The Netscape 4 specific layer-back-ground-color property lets you fill that transparent gap.

Example

This style rule fills `blockquote` tags of class `warning` with a tomato red background color. Note the zero-width border, which coerces Netscape 4 into filling the entire block with the color.

```
blockquote.warning {
  background-color: #ff6347;
  border: 0 solid #ff6347;
}
```

background-image

This property sets the background image for an element. By default, element backgrounds are transparent, so the background image will show through nested elements, unless they have been assigned background colors or images of their own.

The positioning and tiling of a background image may be customized with the `background-position` and `background-repeat` properties, respectively.

Inherited: No

See also: `background-attachment`, `background-color`, `background-position`, `background-repeat`

Value

A URL or none. In CSS, URLs must be surrounded by the `url()` wrapper, not quotes. See the examples below.

Initial value: `none`

Compatibility

CSS Version: 1

Works in all CSS-compatible browsers, including Internet Explorer 4 or later and Netscape 4 or later.

Netscape 4 does not correctly fill a block element with its assigned background image, unless it has a border assigned (even a zero-width border will do), and setting any visible border leaves a transparent gap between the padding area of the block and its border in that browser. The Netscape 4 specific `layer-background-image` property lets you fill that transparent gap.

Example

These style rules demonstrate assigning background images with relative, absolute, and fully-qualified URLs, respectively:

```
body {
    background-image: url(../images/texture.gif);
}

body {
    background-image: url(/images/texture.gif);
}

body {
    background-image: url(http://www.mysite.com/images/texture.gif);
}
```

background-position

By default, an element's background image (assigned with the `background-image` property) is aligned so that its top and left edges are flush with the top and left edges of the element (including any padding), respectively. With the `background-position` property, you can assign a different position for the image.

Inherited: No

See also: `background-image`

Value

One position specifier, or two position specifiers separated by a space.

Each of the position specifiers may be a CSS length measurement (pixels, points, ems, etc.), a percentage, or one of the constants from Table C.1.

Table C.1. background-position constants

Vertical	Horizontal
top, center, bottom	left, center, right

If you specify only one measurement or percentage, it applies to the horizontal position; the vertical position of the image will default to 50%. If you specify two measurements or percentages, the first specifies the horizontal position, the second specifies the vertical. Negative measurements/percentages are allowed, but are rarely useful.

If you specify only one constant, the other dimension defaults to center. The order of constants is not significant.

You can mix length measurement types and percentages (i.e. specify vertical position in one format, horizontal in another). You cannot mix lengths/percentages with constants, however.

Percentages and constants differ from length measurements in the way they position the image. In an element 500 pixels wide, a horizontal position of center or 50% will center the image within the horizontal area of the element. A horizontal position of 250px, however (or any equivalent length measurement), positions the *left edge* of the image exactly 250 pixels from the left edge of the element.

Initial value: 0 0

Compatibility

CSS Version: 2

Works in Internet Explorer 4 or later, Netscape 6 or later, Opera, and Mozilla browsers.

Setting a non-default value for this property in Internet Explorer 4 for Windows reveals a bug in that browser's support of background-repeat. See the compatibility section of background-repeat for details.

Examples

In this style rule, the background image is centered in the element area:

```
body {
  background-position: center;
}
```

In both of these style rules, the background image is placed flush against the bottom-right corner of the element:

```
body {
  background-position: 100% 100%;
}
```

```
body {
    background-position: bottom right;
}
```

In this style rule, the background image's left edge will be positioned 20 pixels from the left of the element, and the image will be centered vertically:

```
body {
  background-position: 20px;
}
```

In this style rule, the background image's top edge is 20 pixels from the top of the element, and the image will be centered horizontally across the element's width:

```
body {
  background-position: 50% 20px;
}
```

The following style rule is illegal, as it mixes a length measurement with a constant:

```
body {
  background-position: 20px center; /* This is illegal! */
}
```

background-position-x, background-position-y

These nonstandard properties are supported only by Internet Explorer browsers, and let you individually specify the two components of the background-position property. These properties are most useful in Dynamic HTML scripting in an Internet Explorer only environment.

Inherited: No

See also: background-position

Value

Both of these properties support values specified in CSS lengths and percentages. Additionally, background-position-x and background-position-y support the horizontal and vertical position constants listed in Table C.1. Important differences between positions specified with CSS length measurements, and positions specified with percentages or constants, are described under background-position.

Initial value: 0

Compatibility

CSS Version: n/a

Supported by Internet Explorer 4 or later only.

Example

This style rule places the background image 20 pixels from the top and centered horizontally on the page:

```
body {
  background-position-x: center;
  background-position-y: 20px;
}
```

background-repeat

By default, a background image, specified with the background-image property, will repeat horizontally and vertically to fill the element (this is often referred to as *tiling*). The background-repeat property lets you override that behavior with your own preferences.

Inherited: No

See also: background-image, background-position

Value

`repeat`, `no-repeat`, `repeat-x`, or `repeat-y`

The first two options are self-explanatory. `repeat-x` causes the image to repeat only horizontally, effectively forming a horizontal band with the background image. `repeat-y` causes the image to repeat only vertically, forming a vertical band.

Initial value: `repeat`

Compatibility

CSS Version: 1

Works in all CSS-compatible browsers, including Internet Explorer 4 or later and Netscape 4 or later.

Internet Explorer 4 for Windows, however, only tiles images down and to the right (not up or to the left), so if you specify a `background-position` other than the default, you may get incomplete tiling in that browser.

Example

This style rule uses `background-repeat` and `background-position` to create a horizontal band 50 pixels down from the top of the page. We keep the left edge of the background image flush against the left margin to avoid the bug in Internet Explorer 4 for Windows.

```
body {
  background-repeat: repeat-x;
  background-position: 0 50px;
}
```

behavior

An Internet Explorer only property, `behavior` lets you assign packaged Dynamic HTML code to HTML elements in bulk. For a full description of the Behaviors feature in Internet Explorer, refer to the MSDN Web site[4].

---

[4] http://msdn.microsoft.com/workshop/author/behaviors/overview.asp

Inherited: No

Value

A URL (specified with the CSS url() wrapper) or an object ID.

Initial value: none

Compatibility

CSS Version: n/a

Attached behaviors are supported by Internet Explorer 5 for Windows or later. Other behavior types are supported by Internet Explorer 5.5 for Windows or later.

Example

The following style rule applies the behavior defined in the draganddrop.htc file to any element of class draganddrop:

```
.draganddrop {
  behavior: url(draganddrop.htc);
}
```

border

A shorthand property that lets you set the same width, color, and style for all four borders of an element with a single property declaration. This property sets up identical borders on all four sides, but can be followed by side-specific border properties that modify them.

Inherited: No

See also: border-width, border-style, and border-color

Value

You can specify a border-width value, a border-style value, and a border-color value, or any combination of the three, in any order, separated by spaces.

Initial value: none

Compatibility

CSS Version: 1

Works on all CSS-compatible browsers, with the same browser-specific limitations as the individual `border-` properties.

Example

This style rule puts a dashed, yellow border 1 pixel wide around `div` tags of class `advertisement`:

```
div.advertisement {
  border: dashed yellow 1px;
}
```

border-bottom, border-left, border-right, border-top

These four properties are shorthand properties that let you set the style, width, and color of the border on a particular side of an element with single property declaration.

Inherited: No

See also: `border-width`, `border-style`, and `border-color`

Value

You can specify a `border-width` value, a `border-style` value, and a `border-color` value, or any combination of the three, in any order, separated by spaces.

Initial value: none

Compatibility

CSS Version: 1

Works in all CSS-compatible browsers, with exception of Netscape 4.

Example

Applies a 1 pixel thick, dashed, blue border to the bottom of elements with a `title` attribute:

```
[title] {
  border-bottom: dashed blue 1px;
}
```

Note that attribute selectors are not yet supported by many browsers.

border-bottom-color, border-left-color, border-right-color, border-top-color

Each of these properties sets the color of the border along one side of an element.

Inherited: No

See also: `border-color`

Value

Any CSS color value (see Appendix B).

Initial value: none

Compatibility

CSS Version: 2

Works in all CSS-compatible browsers, with exception of Netscape 4.

Example

```
p.funky {
  border-style: solid;
  border-top-color: blue;
  border-right-color: yellow;
  border-bottom-color: #ff0000;
  border-left-color: #0f0;
}
```

border-bottom-style, border-left-style, border-right-style, border-top-style

Each of these properties sets the style of the border along one side of an element.

Inherited: No

See also: `border-style`

Value

Any of the constants allowed for `border-style`.

Initial value: none

Compatibility

CSS Version: 2

Works in all CSS-compatible browsers, with exception of Netscape 4.

Example

This style rule puts double lines along the left and right and single lines along the top and bottom of `blockquote` elements:

```
blockquote {
  border-top-style: solid;
  border-bottom-style: solid;
  border-left-style: double;
  border-right-style: double;
}
```

border-bottom-width, border-left-width, border-right-width, border-top-width

Each of these properties sets the width of the border along one side of an element.

Inherited: No

See also: `border-width`

Value

thin, `medium`, `thick`, or any CSS length measurement.

Initial value: `medium` (0 in Netscape 4)

Compatibility

CSS Version: 1

Works in all CSS-compatible browsers, including Internet Explorer 4 or later and Netscape 4 or later.

Note that Netscape 4's default value is 0, so you need to set the border width as well as the style for borders to appear in that browser.

Example

This style rule puts 2-pixel borders along the left and right and 1-pixel borders along the top and bottom of `blockquote` elements:

```
blockquote {
  border-style: solid;
  border-top-width: 1px;
  border-bottom-width: 1px;
  border-left-width: 2px;
  border-right-width: 2px;
}
```

border-collapse

This property lets you choose which of two systems for defining table borders you want the browser to use.

The default system, which you can select with the value `separate`, is the familiar "separate borders" system, where each table cell has its own borders separated by the cell spacing of the table. The new system, which you can select with the `collapse` value, gets rid of any cell spacing, combines the borders of adjacent cells, and lets you assign borders to row and column groups. For full details, refer to the CSS2 specification[5].

Inherited: Yes

See also: `empty-cells`

Value

`collapse` or `separate`

Initial value: `separate`[1]

Compatibility

CSS Version: 2

Works in Internet Explorer 5 for Windows, Netscape 6, and Mozilla browsers.

Example

This style rule sets tables of class `data` to use the collapsed border model:

```
table.data {
  border-collapse: collapse;
}
```

border-color

The `border-color` property sets the color of the border surrounding the selected element(s).

The colors for each side may be set individually using the `border-bottom-color`, `border-left-color`, `border-right-color`, and `border-top-color` properties.

Inherited: No

---

[5] http://www.w3.org/TR/REC-CSS2/tables.html#borders

[1]The initial value prescribed by the CSS2 specification is actually `collapse`; however, all current browsers' default table rendering corresponds to `separate`. The CSS Working Group has therefore proposed changing the default value of this property to `separate` in a future version of the CSS specification. This proposal may be found in the Errata for the CSS2 specification.

Value

You can specify from one to four different color values (see Appendix B) to specify different colors for each side of the element, as shown in Table C.2. Note that Netscape 4 supports only a single border color value.

Table C.2. Effects of multiple values on border properties

Number of values	Effect on borders
1	All four borders receive the value specified.
2	Top and bottom (horizontal) borders receive the first value, left and right (vertical) borders receive the second.
3	Top border receives the first value, vertical borders receive the second, bottom border receives the third.
4	Values are applied to top, right, bottom, and left borders, respectively.

Initial value: The color property of the element, which may be inherited if not explicitly specified.

Compatibility

CSS Version: 1

Works in all CSS-compatible browsers, including Internet Explorer 4 or later and Netscape 4 or later. Netscape 4 supports only a single border color value.

Example

This style rule puts blue borders on the top and bottom and red borders on the left and right sides of blockquote elements:

```
blockquote {
  border-style: solid;
  border-color: blue red;
}
```

border-spacing

This property is the CSS equivalent to the `cellspacing` attribute of the HTML `<table>` tag. It lets you specify the spacing that will appear between cells in a table. This property is ignored if `border-collapse` is set to `collapse` for the table.

Inherited: Yes

See also: `border-collapse`

Value

A single CSS length measurement, or two lengths separated by a space. A single value will be applied as both the horizontal and vertical spacing between cells. Two values will be applied as horizontal and vertical spacing, respectively.

Initial value: 0

Compatibility

CSS Version: 2

Supported by Netscape 6 and Mozilla browsers only at this time.

Example

This style rule allows 5 pixels of spacing between all table cells in tables of class `spacious`.

```
table.spacious {
  border-spacing: 5px;
}
```

border-style

The `border-style` property sets the style of the border surrounding the selected element(s).

The style for each side may be set individually, using the `border-bottom-style`, `border-left-style`, `border-right-style`, and `border-top-style` properties.

Inherited: No

Value

The CSS specifications provide a set of constants for a range of border styles. Table C.3 shows the available constants and the browsers that support them.

You can specify from one to four different style values to specify different styles for each side of the element, as shown in Table C.2. Note that Netscape 4 supports only a single border style value.

The difference between none and hidden, though not visible in Table C.3, arises in HTML tables where the border-collapse property is set to collapse. When two cells share a border and one of them specifies a style of none for the border, the other cell's border style takes precedence and the border is drawn.

The hidden border style, however, takes precedence over all other border styles; therefore, if the first cell in the previous example specified a style of hidden, the other cell's border style would be ignored and no border would be drawn. See the CSS2 Specification[6] for a full discussion of table border conflict resolution.

Initial value: none

---

[6] http://www.w3.org/TR/REC-CSS2/tables.html#border-conflict-resolution

Table C.3. CSS border style constants

Constant	CSS Spec	Supporting Browsers	Sample
double	CSS1	All CSS Browsers	double
groove	CSS1	All CSS Browsers	groove
inset	CSS1	All CSS Browsers	inset
none	CSS1	All CSS Browsers	none
outset	CSS1	All CSS Browsers	outset
ridge	CSS1	All CSS Browsers	ridge
solid	CSS1	All CSS Browsers	solid
dashed	CSS1	Netscape 6, Mozilla, IE 5.5/Win, IE 4/Mac	dashed
dotted	CSS1	Netscape 6, Mozilla, IE 5.5/Win, IE 4/Mac	dotted
hidden	CSS2	Netscape 6, Mozilla, IE 5.5/Win, IE 4/Mac	hidden

Compatibility

CSS Version: 1

Works in all CSS-compatible browsers, including Internet Explorer 4 and Netscape 4. For specific compatibility information, see above.

Note that Netscape 4 defines a default border width of 0, so in addition to a border-style, you must also specify a border-width for the border to appear in that browser.

Example

This style rule makes any element of class fauxbutton look like a button by giving it an outset border style, a light grey background, and black text:

```
.fauxbutton {
  border-style: outset;
  border-color: grey;
  border-width: medium;
  background: lightgrey;
  color: black;
}
```

border-width

The border-width property sets the width of the border surrounding the selected element(s).

The widths for each side may be set individually using the border-bottom-width, border-left-width, border-right-width, and border-top-width properties.

Inherited: No

Value

thin, medium, thick, or any CSS length measurement.

You can specify from one to four different values to specify different border widths for each side of the element, as shown in Table C.2.

Initial value: medium (0 in Netscape 4)

Compatibility

CSS Version: 1

Works in all CSS-compatible browsers, including Internet Explorer 4 and Netscape 4.

Note that Netscape 4 defines a default border width of 0, so in addition to a border-style, you must also specify a border-width for the border to appear in that browser.

Example

This style rule puts thick borders on the top and bottom and thin borders on the left and right sides of blockquote elements:

```
blockquote {
  border-style: solid;
  border-width: thick thin;
}
```

bottom

This property lets you set the distance between the bottom edge of an `absolute` positioned element (including its padding, border, and margin)[2] and the bottom edge of the positioning context in which it resides. The positioning context is the content area of the element's nearest ancestor that has a `position` property value other than `static`, or the `body` element.

In Internet Explorer for Windows, Netscape 6, and Mozilla browsers, when the positioning context is the document body, the element is positioned relative to the bottom edge of the *browser window* (when no scrolling has yet occurred) instead of the document area, as the CSS Specification requires. Internet Explorer 5 for Macintosh follows the specification and positions the block relative to the bottom of the document area.

For `relative` positioned elements, this property sets a relative offset from the normal position of its bottom edge. So, a setting of `10px` will shift the bottom edge of the box up by 10 pixels, and a setting of `-10px` will shift it down by the same amount.

Inherited: No

See also: `position`, `left`, `top`, and `right`

Value

A CSS length measurement, a percentage value, or the `auto` constant. Percentages are based on the height of the parent element. The `auto` constant tells the browser to determine the position of the bottom edge itself, based on whatever other constraints may exist on the size/position of the element.

Initial value: `auto`

---

[2]The CSS2 specification contains an error that suggests that the padding, border, and margin of the positioned element should not be considered. This has been acknowledged as a mistake by the CSS Working Group in the Errata document for CSS2.

Compatibility

CSS Version: 2

Works in Internet Explorer 5 or later, Netscape 6 or later, and Mozilla browsers.

Often, the same effect can be achieved by setting the **top** property of a box. Since **top** is supported by more browsers than **bottom**, this should be done whenever possible.

Example

This style rule positions the element with ID menu at the bottom of the window (or the bottom of the document in Internet Explorer for Macintosh):

```
#menu {
  position: absolute;
  bottom: 0;
  width: 100px;
  height: 200px;
}
```

caption-side

This property lets you specify the side of a table on which its caption (specified with the <caption> tag) should appear.

Inherited: Yes

Value

Any of the following constants: **top**, **bottom**, **left**, or **right**.

Initial value: top

Compatibility

CSS Version: 2

Works in Internet Explorer 5 for Macintosh, Netscape 6 or later, and Mozilla browsers. The values **left** and **right** do not yet work in most browsers.

Example

This style rule places captions at the bottom of all tables that occur within other tables.

```
table table {
  caption-side: bottom;
}
```

clear

Setting a `clear` property on an element lets you specify that it should appear below any floating elements that would normally cut into it. You can specify that the element should be clear of left-floated elements, right-floated elements, or both.

Inherited: No

See also: `float`

Value

`left`, `right`, `none`, or `both`.

Initial value: `none`

Compatibility

CSS Version: 1

Works in all CSS-compatible browsers, including Internet Explorer 4 or later, Netscape 4 or later, and Mozilla browsers.

Example

This style rule ensures that the element with ID `footer` will be clear of any floating elements above it in the page:

```
#footer {
  clear: both;
}
```

clip

This property clips the visible region of the absolute- or fixed-positioned element(s) to which it is applied. The element occupies the same amount of space on the page as usual, but only the area specified by this property is displayed.

In contrast to the `overflow` property, this property only affects the *visible* area of an element (including its padding, borders, etc.). The size and position of an element for layout purposes is not affected by this property.

Inherited: No

See also: `overflow`

Value

The current CSS specification allows only for rectangular clipping regions. You specify such a region by wrapping four measurement values in the CSS `rect()` wrapper as follows:

```
clip: rect(top right bottom left);
```

For an element x pixels wide and y pixels high, the default clipping region (assuming it has no borders or padding to increase its rendered area) would be `rect(0px xpx ypx 0)`. To trim off 10 pixels from each side of the image, you'd change this to `rect(10px x-10px y-10px 10px)`, where you would calculate and substitute the actual values of $x-10$ and $y-10$.

The default value, `auto`, lets the browser determine the area of the element to draw, as usual.

Initial value: `auto`

Compatibility

CSS Version: 2

Works in all CSS-compatible browsers, including Internet Explorer 4 or later, Netscape 4 or later, and Mozilla browsers. This property is buggy in Internet Explorer 4 for Macintosh and can cause affected elements to be left out of scrollbar size calculations in Netscape 4.

Note that Opera browsers will clip only the rendered content of the element—not its background. This is actually correct according to the CSS2 specification, although it does not match the established behavior of other browsers.

Example

This style rule will clip 10 pixels off the left and right sides of the element with ID logo, which is a 100 x 100 pixel image:

```
#logo {
  position: absolute;
  clip: rect(0px 90px 100px 10px);
}
```

color

This property sets the foreground (text) color of the element. This property also defines the default border color of the element.

In general, you should always specify a background color when you specify a foreground color, and vice versa.

Inherited: Yes

See also: background-color

Value

Any CSS color value (see Appendix B).

Initial value: black

Compatibility

CSS Version: 1

Works in all CSS-compatible browsers including Internet Explorer 4 or later, Netscape 4 or later, and Mozilla browsers.

Example

This style rule sets paragraphs of class `warning` to have white text on a tomato red background.

```
p.warning {
  color: white;
  background-color: #ff6347;
}
```

content

Sometimes it makes sense to generate some text at the beginning or end of an element as part of that element's style. Termed **generated content**, this text is not part of the HTML document, but is generated purely by the style sheet. The CSS `content` property is intended for this purpose. You must apply it to the `:before` or `:after` pseudo-elements, as shown in the examples below.

Inherited: No

See also: `counter-increment`, `counter-reset`, `quotes`

Value

The CSS2 specification mandates a number of different generated content formats, but several are not yet supported by current browsers (see the Compatibility section for details). You can use any combination of the following content formats by listing them one after the other, separated by spaces.

`"arbitrary string"`
  This format lets you place a string of text before or after the actual content of the element. You cannot format this text by placing HTML code in the string—the browser will display the tags as text. Instead, use CSS to style the string, as in the examples below. The special code \A in the string produces a line break (same effect as an HTML <br> tag).

`url(http://url.goes.here)`
  This format lets you place some external resource before or after the actual content of the element. For example, if you supply a URL to an image, the browser should place that image before/after the content of the element. If you supply a URL to an HTML document, the browser should display the contents of the document before/after the content of the element.

There are obvious complexities that come into play here, but since no browsers yet support this format, any further discussion would be purely academic.

```
counter(name)
counter(name, style)
counters(name, string)
counters(name, string, style)
```

These formats let you generate numbered elements (for example, numbered section headings) without having to resort to an ordered list (`<ol>`) in the HTML document. You must define, increment, and reset your counters when appropriate using the `counter-increment` and `counter-reset` CSS properties, and then use one of the above formats to display the value of a counter where desired.

`counter(name)` will display the value of the named counter in decimal format, while `counter(name, style)` lets you specify the style in which to display the counter value (you can use any style allowed by the `list-style-type` CSS property). You can also define hierarchical counters to produce multiple-level numbering (e.g. "Section 5.2.3"), the values of which you can output with `counters(name, string)` or `counters(name, string, style)`. The `string` argument specifies the string that is used to separate the numbers, and is typically a period (`"."`).

```
attr(attribute)
```

This format lets you output the value of an attribute of the element (e.g. the `title` attribute of an `<a>` tag) before or after the actual content of the element.

```
open-quote
close-quote
```

These formats let you display opening or closing quotation marks, the exact appearance of which are dictated by the CSS `quotes` property.

```
no-open-quote
no-close-quote
```

These formats let you put "fake" opening or closing quotes that don't actually display anything, but which still jump in and out of nesting levels defined in the `quotes` property.

Initial value: `" "` (the empty string)

Compatibility

CSS Version: 2

Netscape 6, Mozilla, and Opera browsers support a subset of the formats discussed above. Specifically, they support the *"arbitrary string"* and quote-related formats. Internet Explorer browsers do not support this property up to and including IE6 for Windows.

Examples

This style rule puts the text "Note: " in bold at the start of a paragraph of class `note`:

```
p.note:before {
  content: "Note: ";
  font-weight: bold;
}
```

These style rules puts angle brackets (< >) around `span` elements of class `tagname` by using generated content and the `quotes` property:

```
span.tagname {
  quotes: "<" ">";
}
span.tagname:before {
  content: open-quote;
}
span.tagname:after {
  content: close-quote;
}
```

These style rules put quotation marks around `<blockquote>` elements. The third style rule (which is not supported by current browsers because of the use of `attr(attribute)`) applies to `blockquote` elements that have a `cite` attribute, and modifies the `content` property to close the quotation marks and then display the source of the citation on a new line.

```
blockquote:before {
  content: open-quote;
}
blockquote:after {
  content: close-quote;
}
```

```
blockquote[cite]:after {
  content: close-quote "\Afrom " attr(cite);
}
```

Also unsupported by current browsers, these style rules should place a standard HTML header and footer on the current page:

```
body:before {
  content: url(standardheader.html);
}
body:after {
  content: url(standardfooter.html);
}
```

counter-increment

This property increments or decrements a named counter (for display with the `content` property) for each occurrence of the selected element(s).

On nested elements, a hierarchical counter is automatically created, so that you effectively have a separate counter at each level of the structure.

Inherited: No

See also: `content`, `counter-reset`

Value

A counter name, optionally followed by a positive or negative integer to indicate how much to increment (positive) or decrement (negative) the counter. If you want to increment/decrement multiple counters for a single element, you can separate their names (and optional integers) by spaces.

The default value, `none` is also supported, but is of little practical use.

Initial value: none

Compatibility

CSS Version: 2

Not supported by any currently-available browser.

Examples

This simple example will keep track of the number of h1 tags in the document and will output a chapter number at the start of each:

```
h1 {
  counter-increment: chapter;
}
h1:before {
  content: "Chapter " counter(chapter) " - ";
}
```

This example uses a counter to number div elements in the document, and then displays the counter value in h1 tags appearing within them. Because the counters() format is used to output the counter value, nested div elements will be numbered hierarchically (e.g. "Division 2.1.3").

```
div {
  counter-increment: division;
}
div > h1:before {
  content: "Division " counters(division,".") ": ";
}
```

counter-reset

This property sets a named counter (for display with the content property), to a particular value, each time the enclosing style rule is matched.

By default, the counter is reset to zero, but you can specify any value you like.

Inherited: No

See also: counter-increment

Value

A counter name, optionally followed by a positive or negative integer that specifies the new value for the counter (the default it 0). If you want to set multiple counters for a single element, you can separate their names (and optional integers) by spaces.

The default value, none is also supported, but is of little practical use.

Initial value: none

Compatibility

CSS Version: 2

Not supported by any currently-available browser.

Example

This example lets you use h1 elements to mark chapters, h2 elements to mark subsections, and have hierarchical numbering on section headings:

```
h1 {
  counter-increment: chapter;
  counter-reset: section;
}
h1:before {
  content: "Chapter " counter(chapter) " - ";
}
h2 {
  counter-increment: section;
}
h2:before {
  content: "Section " counter(chapter) "." counter(section) " - ";
}
```

cue

Sound cues are used by aural (speaking) browsers for the visually impaired as "audio icons". This is a shorthand property that lets you specify the cue-before and cue-after properties with a single property declaration.

Inherited: No

See also: cue-before, cue-after

Value

One or two URLs (specified with CSS url() syntax) that point to sound files. If one URL is provided, it is assigned to cue-before and cue-after—the sound is played before and after the element. If two URLs are provided, the first is assigned to `cue-before` and the second to `cue-after`.

Initial value: none

Compatibility

CSS Version: 2

Not supported by any currently-available browser.

Example

This example plays `ding.wav` before and after each `div` element:

```
div {
  cue: url(/sounds/ding.wav);
}
```

cue-after, cue-before

Sound cues are used by aural (speaking) browsers for the visually impaired as "audio icons". `cue-before` and `cue-after` let you set cues to be played before and after an element, respectively.

Inherited: No

See also: cue

Value

A URL, specified with CSS `url()` syntax, that points to a sound file.

The default value, `none` is also supported, but is of little practical use.

Initial value: none

Compatibility

CSS Version: 2

Not supported by any currently-available browser.

Example

This example plays `ding.wav` before each `h1` element, with the exception of `h1` elements of class `silent`:

```
h1 {
  cue-before: url(/sounds/ding.wav);
}
h1.silent {
  cue-before: none;
}
```

cursor

This property lets you modify the appearance of the mouse cursor when the mouse is over a selected element.

Inherited: Yes

Value

Table C.4 lists the different cursor values supported by the CSS2 standard and the major browsers that support them. The special value `auto` is the default, and lets the browser determine what the cursor should look like automatically. The value `default` sets the cursor to its default appearance, as dictated by the operating system.

The value `url(url)`, which is currently supported only in Internet Explorer 6 for Windows, lets you define your own cursor by pointing to a `.cur` (Windows static cursor) or `.ani` (Windows animated cursor) file on your site. Presumably, this property will support more standard image formats when it is implemented in other browsers.

Table C.5 lists additional, nonstandard cursors supported by various versions of Internet Explorer.

All of the cursors' exact appearances may vary between browsers and operating systems.

Table C.4. CSS2 standard cursors

cursor value	Appearance (as in IE6)	IE (Win)	IE (Mac)	NS/Moz
auto	n/a	4	4	6/1
crosshair	+	4	4	6/1
default	↖	4	4	6/1
e-resize	↔	4	4	6/1
help	↖?	4	4	6/1
move	✛	4	4	6/1
n-resize	↕	4	4	6/1
ne-resize	↗	4	4	6/1
nw-resize	↖	4	4	6/1
pointer	👆	4	4	6/1
s-resize	↕	4	4	6/1
se-resize	↘	4	4	6/1
sw-resize	↙	4	4	6/1
text	I	4	4	6/1
url(url)	n/a	6	–	–
w-resize	↔	4	4	6/1
wait	⧗	4	4	6/1

Table C.5. Internet Explorer-only cursors

cursor value	Appearance (as in IE6)	IE (Win)	IE (Mac)
all-scroll		6	–
col-resize		6	–
hand		4	4
no-drop		6	–
not-allowed		6	–
progress		6	–
row-resize		6	–
vertical-text		6	–

Initial value: auto

Compatibility

CSS Version: 1

Supported by all CSS-compatible browsers, with the notable exception of Netscape 4.

Some values of this property are not be supported by all browsers—refer to Table C.4 and Table C.5.

Example

This style rule (which doesn't work in browsers that don't support attribute selectors) displays the pointer cursor when the mouse is over any element with a onclick attribute.

```
[onclick] {
  cursor: pointer;
}
```

direction

Most western languages are written left-to-right (LTR). As you probably know, many other languages (e.g. Hebrew) are written right-to-left (RTL). Documents written with the Unicode character set[7] can contain text from both LTR and RTL languages. The Unicode standard includes a complicated algorithm that should be used for displaying such mixed text. It also defines special characters that let you "group" text.

For example, consider the following imaginary string of text, where the lowercase text represents LTR characters and the uppercase text represents RTL:

```
english1 HEBREW1 english2 HEBREW2 english3
```

Now, the obvious way to render this would be "english1 1WERBEH english2 2WERBEH english3", but what if we add some HTML tags to the mix?

```
<p>english1 <q>HEBREW1 english2 HEBREW2</q> english3</p>
```

As you can see, the text beginning with HEBREW1 and ending with HEBREW2 is intended as an inline quotation in Hebrew, which just happens to contain an English word. Since HEBREW1 and HEBREW2 belong to the same block of Hebrew text, "2WERBEH" should be rendered to the left or "1WERBEH". With this in mind, the complete paragraph should be rendered as "english1 2WERBEH english2 1WERBEH english3".

The HTML 4.0 standard (along with XHTML 1.0) defines the dir attribute and the bdo element to handle these complexities. To obtain the desired rendering in an HTML4-compatible browser, the code should be:

```
<p>english1 <q lang="he" dir="rtl">HEBREW1 english2 HEBREW2</q>
  english3</p>
```

The dir attribute of the q tag is what specifies the rendering order; the lang attribute won't have any actual visible effect. For full details on language and bidirectional text rendering in HTML, refer to Section 8 of the HTML 4.0 standard[8].

So, where does CSS come into play, you ask? Well, the direction property, in combination with a unicode-bidi property setting of embed, performs the same

[7] http://www.unicode.org/
[8] http://www.w3.org/TR/REC-html40/struct/dirlang.html

role as the HTML `dir` attribute. In combination with a `unicode-bidi` property setting of `bidi-override`, `direction` has the same effect as the HTML `bdo` tag. It is still considered best practice, however, to include bidirectional text attributes as part of the HTML code. The `direction` and `unicode-bidi` properties are intended for use in styling XML documents that do not have the benefit of HTML 4's bidirectional text features. Since the focus of this book is on Web development, I'll therefore refer you to the CSS2 standard[9] for full details on these properties.

Inherited: Yes

See also: `unicode-bidi`

Value

`ltr` or `rtl`.

Initial value: `ltr`

Compatibility

CSS Version: 2

Not supported by any currently-available browser.

Example

This style rule sets the text direction of an imaginary XML element named `hebrew` to `rtl`. The `unicode-bidi` property is there to ensure that this setting will "group" any elements within it according to this direction, even if `hebrew` is rendered as an inline element.

```
hebrew {
  direction: rtl;
  unicode-bidi: embed;
}
```

display

In HTML, there are different *types* of elements. `div` and `blockquote`, for example, are both block elements, while `strong` and `em` are both inline elements. For each

---

[9] http://www.w3.org/TR/REC-CSS2/visuren.html#direction

type of element, a browser supports a "display mode". All block elements are essentially displayed the same way, just with varying margins, padding, borders, etc. by default.

The `display` property lets you set the "display mode" for an element. For example, you can set a hyperlink (a) to be displayed as a block instead of inline text.

The most common use for the display property is to show and hide portions of an HTML document. Setting `display` to `none` causes the element not only to be hidden (as with the `visibility` property), but not to occupy any space on the page either. Using Dynamic HTML to set this property in JavaScript event handlers lets you create, for instance, hierarchical menus that expand and collapse to display submenus on the fly.

Inherited: No

See also: `visibility`

Value

block
> CSS version: 1
>
> **Browser support:** All CSS-compatible, including Netscape 4.
>
> The default display mode for p, div, ul, blockquote, and many others, block causes the element to occupy a rectangular area of the page, stacked vertically with its sibling elements, so that previous siblings are above it, and subsequent siblings are below it.

inline
> CSS version: 1
>
> **Browser support:** All CSS-compatible, including Netscape 4.
>
> The default display mode for strong, u, a, code, and many others, this causes the element to flow "inline" as a string of text within the parent block, possibly broken by word wrapping.

list-item
> CSS version: 1

Browser support: Netscape 4 or later, Internet Explorer 6 for Windows, Internet Explorer 5 for Mac.

The default display mode for `li` elements, `list-item` causes the element to be rendered as a list item. The `list-style` family of properties control the position and appearance of the list item marker (i.e. the bullet or number).

marker

CSS version: 2

Browser support: No currently-available browsers.

This display mode can be applied only to `:before` and `:after` pseudo-elements, and tells the browser to treat generated content (created with the `content` property) as a "marker" to be displayed in its own box in the margin of the main content. The formatting is similar to, although somewhat more flexible than, the formatting applied to the bullets or numbers preceding list items. The `marker-offset` property is specifically provided to format generated content with this display mode.

none

CSS version: 1

Browser support: All CSS-compatible, including Netscape 4.

This display mode causes the element not to be rendered at all. The element will not occupy any space on the page (unlike `visibility: hidden`, which hides the element but reserves space for it on the page).

compact

CSS version: 2

Browser support: No currently-available browsers.

This display mode causes the element to appear in the left margin (or right margin in right-to-left languages) of the block immediately following it if it can fit all on one line. If the element is too big to fit in the next block's margin on one line, it is displayed as a normal block instead. The effect is illustrated in Figure C.1.

Figure C.1. Effect of compact display mode

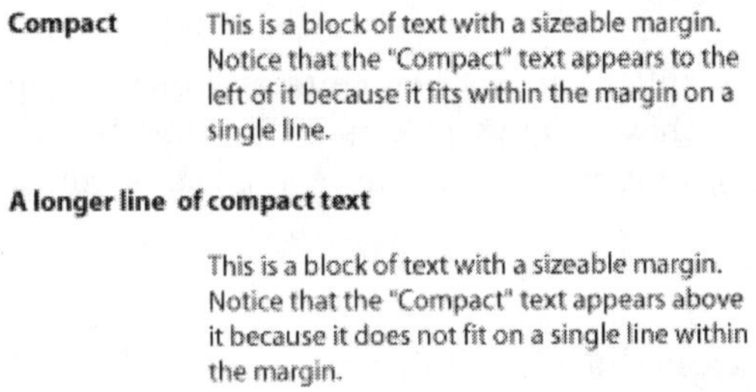

Compact   This is a block of text with a sizeable margin. Notice that the "Compact" text appears to the left of it because it fits within the margin on a single line.

A longer line of compact text

This is a block of text with a sizeable margin. Notice that the "Compact" text appears above it because it does not fit on a single line within the margin.

`run-in`
CSS version: 2

Browser support: No currently-available browsers.

This display mode causes the element to appear as an inline element at the start of the block immediately following it. If there is no block following a run-in element, it is displayed as a normal block instead. The effect is illustrated in Figure C.2.

Figure C.2. Effect of run-in display mode

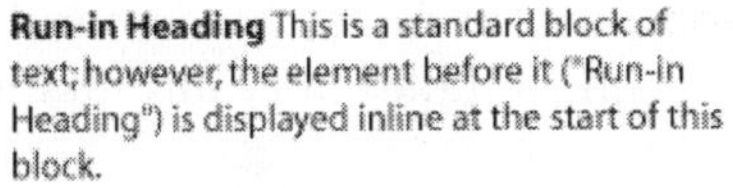

Run-in Heading This is a standard block of text; however, the element before it ("Run-in Heading") is displayed inline at the start of this block.

```
table
inline-table
table-row
table-column
table-row-group
table-column-group
table-header-group
table-footer-group
table-cell
table-caption
```
CSS version: 2

Browser support: Fully supported by IE5 (Macintosh). IE5 (Win) supports only `table-header-group`, while IE5.5 (Win) adds support for `table-footer-group`. There is no additional support in IE6 (Win). NS6/Mozilla supports all of these except `inline-table`, `table-caption`, `table-column`, and `table-column-group`.

These display modes let you display various elements as tables (or parts thereof). The practical utility of these display modes is questionable, which is why most browsers have yet to fully implement them. For full details, refer to the CSS2 Specification[10].

inline-block
CSS version: 3 (according to early draft specification)

Browser support: Internet Explorer 5.5 or later for Windows only.

This display lets you place a block inline with the content of its parent element.

Initial value: `inline`[3]

Compatibility

CSS Version: 1 (many display modes added in CSS2, with more coming in CSS3)

All CSS-compatible browsers support this property, but none yet supports the full range of CSS2 display modes. See above for full compatibility information.

Example

This style rule hides unordered list (`ul`) elements nested within an unordered list of class `menu`. In a practical application, JavaScript code could be used to display these submenus, by changing the `display` property to `block`, when the user clicks one of the main menu items.

```
ul.menu ul {
  display: none;
}
```

---

[10] http://www.w3.org/TR/REC-CSS2/tables.html

[3]Elements like **p**, **div**, **blockquote**, etc. have a default **display** value of **block**, and other elements have their own default **display** values. These defaults come from the browser's built-in default style sheet, rather than from the CSS specification. If you were to create your own tag (which you can do with XHTML), its **display** property would be **inline** by default.

elevation

elevation sets the angle to the horizontal, from which the sound comes when the content is presented aurally (e.g. in a speaking browser for the blind).

Inherited: Yes

See also: azimuth

Value

An angle (-90deg to 90deg, where 90deg is directly above the listener, -90deg is directly below, and 0deg is at the listener's ear level), or a descriptive constant (e.g. above)

Initial value: level

Compatibility

CSS Version: 2

Not yet supported by any browser.

Example

This style rule will cause all elements of class commandment to be heard from 80 degrees above the horizontal:

```
.commandment {
  elevation: 80deg;
}
```

empty-cells

This property lets you set whether empty table cells are displayed in a table operating in "separate borders" mode (see border-collapse) or not.

Inherited: Yes

See also: border-collapse

Value

show or hide. When set to hide, empty table cells, their borders, and their backgrounds are not drawn—the table background is visible in their place.

Initial value: show[4]

Compatibility

CSS Version: 2

Supported by Netscape 6 and Mozilla browsers. Not yet supported by any version of Internet Explorer.

Example

This style rule sets tables of class seethru to hide empty table cells:

```
table.seethru {
  border-collapse: separate;
  empty-cells: hide;
}
```

filter

Internet Explorer for Windows offers this property, which lets you apply static special effects, and animated transitions, to any HTML element.

Inherited: No

Value

Internet Explorer 4 or later for Windows supports a set of 14 static filters and two animated transition filters. Internet Explorer 5.5 or later supports a new filter technology that offers all the filters supported by IE4 and a bunch more besides, with a total of 2 procedural surface filters, 16 static effect filters, and 17 animated transition filters.

Static filters offer effects such as translucent elements, drop shadows, glows, blurs, flips, rotations, lighting, and distortions. Animated transition filters let you wrap

---

[4]Netscape 6 and Mozilla browsers default to **hide** when running in "quirks mode".

an element's change from one appearance to another in an animated effect. Available transitions include simple PowerPoint™-style wipes and slides, smooth fades and gradient wipes, and a fanciful pixelation effect.

You need to apply animated transition filters with CSS and then trigger them with JavaScript code to see the animated effect.

Internet Explorer 4 filters have the following syntax:

```
filter: filter(param=value, ...)
```

Internet Explorer 5.5 filters look like this:

```
filter: progid:DXImageTransform.Microsoft.filter(param=value, ...)
```

You can apply filters in any sensible combination by specifying them one at a time, separated by spaces, in the value of the `filter` property.

For complete documentation that covers all the available filters as well as how to use them in various ways, Microsoft's Introduction to Filters and Transitions[11] and it's Visual Filters and Transitions Reference[12].

Initial value: none

Compatibility

CSS Version: n/a

Internet Explorer 4 or later supports a basic set of filters and transitions. These basic filters are superseded in Internet Explorer 5.5 by an entirely new set of filters, but support for the original set is maintained for backwards compatibility.

Examples

This style rule uses the IE4 static filter `dropShadow` to show a shadow beneath any element of class `floating`:

```
.floating {
  filter: dropShadow(color=#000000, offx=5, offy=5);
}
```

---

[11] http://msdn.microsoft.com/workshop/author/filter/filters.asp
[12] http://msdn.microsoft.com/workshop/author/filter/reference/reference.asp

The style rule in this example assigns the IE5.5 animated transition filter `Pixelate` to the element with the ID `toolbar`. The JavaScript code then assigns an event handler that gets triggered when the page finishes loading. The event handler enables the filter (it's disabled in the CSS code), sets the starting state for the transition with `Apply()`, makes the element visible (it's hidden in the CSS code), then plays the transition with `Play()`.

```
<style type="text/css">
#toolbar {
  visibility: hidden;
  filter: progid:DXImageTransform.Microsoft.Pixelate(MaxSquare=50,
Duration=1, Enabled=false);
}
</style>
<script type="text/javascript" language="JavaScript">
window.onload = function() {
  var toolbar = document.getElementById('toolbar');
  toolbar.filters[0].enabled = true;
  toolbar.filters[0].Apply();
  toolbar.style.visibility='visible';
  toolbar.filters[0].Play();
}
</script>
```

float

When set to a value besides the default (`none`), this property causes the element to float against the left or right margin of its parent element. A floated element will not affect the placement of any of the blocks on the page, but the content within those blocks (including other floated elements) will flow around it. The `clear` property lets you create elements that will be displaced downwards to prevent their content from flowing around floated elements.

Inherited: No

See also: `clear`

Value

`left`, `right`, or `none`.

Initial value: `none`

Compatibility

CSS Version: 1

Supported by all CSS-compatible browsers, including Netscape 4, Internet Explorer 4, and Mozilla browsers.

Example

This style rule sets images of class `headshot` to float against the left side of their parent elements:

```
img.headshot {
  float: left;
}
```

font

A shorthand property that allows you to set many font properties of an element with a single property declaration. With this one property, you can set the values of `font-style`, `font-variant`, `font-weight`, `font-size`, `line-height`, and `font-family`.

Unless you use one of the CSS2 constants (described below), you must specify a `font-size` and `font-family`. All the other properties are optional, and will be reset to their initial values if they are not specified (overriding any previous declarations of equal or lesser precedence for their values). The properties `font-stretch` and `font-size-adjust` are also reset to their default values by this property, even though you don't have the option of specifying your own values.

Inherited: Yes

See also: The individual font properties, listed above.

Value

The syntax of this property is as follows:

```
font: [style] [variant] [weight] size [/ line-height] family
```

The values in square brackets are optional. The first three values—*style*, *variant*, and *weight*—may be specified in any order, and can take values allowed for font-style, font-variant, and font-weight, respectively. *size* is required, and can take any font-size value. *line-height* must come right after *size* if it is specified, can take any line-height value, and it is preceded by a slash (/). Finally, the *family* value can take any font-family value.

As of CSS2, an alternative syntax is available for this property:

```
font: constant
```

constant is one of the following constants, each of which corresponds to a full font specification (family, size, weight, etc.):

❑ caption

❑ icon

❑ menu

❑ message-box

❑ small-caption

❑ status-bar

The fonts associated with these constants vary between browsers, operating systems, and individual system configurations. The idea is that they should match the fonts in use elsewhere on the system so that user interface elements of the Web page can be made to match up with equivalent elements in local applications.

Initial value: none

Compatibility

CSS Version: 1 (constants added in CSS2)

All CSS-compatible browsers support this to some extent—generally one that's compatible with the limits of each browser's support for individual font properties.

Examples

This style rule uses all possible values to define a font for paragraph elements:

```
p {
  normal normal normal 11pt/12pt Myriad, Helvetica, sans-serif;
}
```

This style rule applies the system caption font to caption elements:

```
caption {
  font: caption;
}
```

font-family

This property lets you set the typeface used to display text in an element. Like the HTML font tag, this property lets you specify a list of fonts, each of which will be tried in order.

If the first font is not available on the user's system, or if a particular character is not present in the font, the browser will check the second font in the list, and so on. This per-character fallback method (which is specified only as of CSS2, and is therefore not yet supported in all browsers) lets you create multilingual content and then list a font for each language; the browser should pick and choose characters from the fonts in the list, always giving preference to those listed first.

Any time you set this property, the font list should end with a **generic font name** (see below), so that the browser will always have some idea of the type of font you're after.

Be aware that browsers will not fall back on fonts specified in lower-priority style rules. For example, if you set paragraph elements to Verdana, sans-serif and paragraphs of class note to Myriad, a user that does not have Myriad installed will see paragraphs of class note displayed in the browser's default font, not Verdana. In this example, you should set paragraphs of class note to Myriad, Verdana, sans-serif to achieve the desired effect.

Inherited: Yes

See also: font

Value

A comma-separated list of font names. Font names that contain spaces should be quoted (e.g. "Times New Roman").

In addition to actual font names, the list can contain any of the following generic font names:

☐ serif

The browser selects a font with serifs.[5].

☐ sans-serif

The browser selects a font without serifs.

☐ cursive

The browser selects a handwritten font.

☐ fantasy

The browser selects an elaborate, stylized font.

☐ monospace

The browser selects a font where all characters have the same dimensions—suitable for showing code.

Since browsers will always be able to find a font for each of these generic font names, it only makes sense for the last font in the font-family list to be one of these.

Initial value: browser specific

Compatibility

CSS Version: 1

All CSS-compatible browsers, including Netscape 4, Internet Explorer 4, and Mozilla browsers.

Example

This style rule assigns a very common set of fonts to the body of the document:

---

[5]Serifs are those little horizontal flares that you see at the tops and bottoms of vertical lines in fonts like Times New Roman.

```
body {
  font-family: Verdana, Arial, Helvetica, sans-serif;
}
```

font-size

This property lets you set the size of the font displayed in an element.

You have several different methods to choose from. You can select an absolute font size, or specify the size relative to the font size of the parent element. If you choose an absolute size, you can specify an exact CSS length (e.g. in pixels or points), or a font size constant (e.g. small), which yields a fixed, browser-specific size. If you choose a relative size, again you have the choice between a CSS relative length (e.g. in ems or a percentage), or a relative size constant (larger or smaller).

Inherited: Yes, but in the case of relative measurements, the *computed* value is inherited.

See also: font

Value

As outlined above, this property supports a range of different value formats:

Absolute CSS measurements
A CSS length measurement in pixels (px), points (pt), picas pi, centimeters cm, millimeters (mm), or inches (in).

Absolute size constants
Any of the following absolute size constants:

❑ xx-small

❑ x-small

❑ small

❑ medium

❑ large

☐ x-large

☐ xx-large

The actual sizes of these constants are up to the browser to determine, and are generally smaller in Mac OS than in Windows browsers. The differences between font sizes are also browser-specific, but the standard suggests a factor of 20% between adjacent values (i.e. large is 20% bigger than medium).

Relative CSS measurements

A relative CSS measurement, in ems (em), exes (ex), or percentages (%). This will set the font size of an element relative to that of its parent element.

Relative size constants

Either of the following size constants:

☐ smaller

☐ larger

The amount by which to adjust the parent's font size for the element is left up to the browser, but the spec suggests a factor of 20%. According to this suggestion, smaller is roughly equivalent to 80% or 0.8em, and larger is roughly equivalent to 120% or 1.2em.

Initial value: medium (see compatibility note for Internet Explorer for Windows).

Compatibility

CSS Version: 1

All CSS-compatible browsers support this property.

In Internet Explorer for Windows (up to and including version 6.0), the initial (default) font size is small instead of medium. In other words, Internet Explorer takes a font-size setting of small to mean the user's selected default font size. medium, therefore, becomes one step larger than the default font size. IE 6.0 corrects this in standards-compliant mode[13], but for all previous versions you'll need to use a separate, browser-specific style sheet if you intend to design for them with absolute font size constants.

---

[13] http://msdn.microsoft.com/library/en-us/dnie60/html/cssenhancements.asp

Examples

This style rule sets the default font size for all elements in the document to 11 points. Because `font-size` is inherited, all elements that don't define their own `font-size` should inherit this value:

```
body {
    font-size: 11pt;
}
```

In practice, many older browsers do not allow font properties to be inherited by certain elements (tables, for example), so a more aggressive rule is needed:

```
body, p, blockquote, li, td, th, pre {
    font-size: 11pt;
}
```

This style rule illustrates a common *faux pas* among inexperienced developers:

```
ul, ol {
    font-size: 80%;
}
```

Because the *computed* value of the `font-size` property is inherited, not only will lists have a font 20% smaller than the body text, but lists nested within other lists will have a font size 20% smaller than *that*! Similarly, lists nested two levels deep will be 20% smaller again (just over half the size of the body text). To avoid this unwanted domino effect, you must add a second style rule so that they inherit their parent's font-size:

```
ul ul, ul ol, ol ul, ol ol {
    font-size: inherit;
}
```

font-size-adjust

If you've ever compared two different fonts at the same point size and thought that one looked considerably smaller than the other, you have encountered the reason for this property. Correctly setting this property lets the browser adjust for font differences to preserve the *apparent* size if it needs to use a different font than the one you specified (e.g. if the font you specified was not available on the user's system).

The apparent size of a font has more to do with the height of lowercase letters (the **x-height**) than with the actual font size. At 100 points, Myriad Web has an x-height of 48 points—lowercase letters are 48% as tall as the font size. This ratio is called the **aspect value** of the font. In other words, Myriad Web has an aspect value of 0.48. Verdana, however, has an aspect value of 0.58. If you specified Myriad Web as your desired font, but the user's browser substituted Verdana for it because Myriad Web was not available, the text would look larger because of the substitute font's higher aspect value.

If you set the `font-size-adjust` property to the aspect value of your preferred font, the browser should be able to adjust the sizes of substitute fonts to give them the x-height you were after. This assumes the browser knows (or can detect) the aspect value of the substitute font.

Inherited: Yes

See also: `font`

Value

The aspect value of your preferred font. This is used in combination with the `font-size` property, to adjust the size of a substitute font, so that it is displayed with the same x-height. The special value `none` disables font size adjustment for the element.

Initial value: `none`

Compatibility

CSS Version: 2

Not supported in any currently-available browser.

Example

This style rule assigns a set of fonts to the body element and uses `font-size-adjust` to ensure that whatever font is used, it will have the same x-height as Myriad Web (the preferred font) at 11 points.

```
body {
  font-family: "Myriad Web", Verdana, Helvetica, sans-serif;
  font-size-adjust: 0.48; /* The aspect value of Myriad Web */
}
```

font-stretch

Many font families (Futura comes to mind) have not only different weights (e.g. normal, light, bold) and styles (e.g. normal, italic, oblique), but also different densities (e.g. normal, condensed, extended). This property lets you select the density of the font to be displayed in an element.

The CSS2 specification makes no mention of whether a browser should artificially condense or expand a font that does not have different density versions available; however, since most browsers do this for other font properties (e.g. font-style, font-weight, font-variant), this would not be unreasonable to expect. The property name certainly suggests that function.

Inherited: Yes

See also: font

Value

One of 11 constants: 9 absolute and 2 relative.

The absolute constants are:

❏ ultra-condensed

❏ extra-condensed

❏ condensed

❏ semi-condensed

❏ normal

❏ semi-expanded

❏ expanded

❏ extra-expanded

❏ ultra-expanded

The relative constants are:

☐ narrower

☐ wider

The relative constants take the font-stretch value of the parent element and sets the current element's value to the next narrower or wider value, respectively.

Initial value: normal

Compatibility

CSS Version: 2

Not supported by any currently-available browsers.

Example

This style rule sets any element of class languid to be displayed in an extra-expanded font:

```
.languid {
  font-stretch: extra-expanded;
}
```

font-style

This property lets you choose between the normal, italic, and oblique styles of a font.

Inherited: Yes

See also: font

Value

normal, oblique, or italic.

Initial value: normal

Compatibility

CSS Version: 1

Supported by all CSS-compatible browsers.

Most browsers will artificially skew a normal font to create an italic style if none is available. Additionally, most browsers will treat the `oblique` setting as a synonym for `italic`, rather than select or generate an actual oblique font style.

Example

The default style sheets employed by most browsers specify that emphasis (`em`) elements should be displayed in an italic font. If you wanted to display emphasis with an underline instead, you would have to make a point of setting the `font-style` to `normal`:

```
em {
  font-style: normal;
  text-decoration: underline;
}
```

font-variant

This property lets you specify that the current element be rendered with a small-caps version of the font assigned to it. In a small-caps font, the lowercase letters look just like uppercase letters, but smaller.

The Latin alphabet (used by most Western languages) is actually the exception in that it has uppercase and lowercase versions of each letter. Most other writing systems in the world have a single case, and therefore are unaffected by this property.

Inherited: Yes

See also: `font`

Value

`normal` or `small-caps`.

Initial value: `normal`

Compatibility

CSS Version: 1

Supported by most CSS-compatible browsers, with the notable exception of Netscape 4.

Internet Explorer 6 (when not running in standards-compliant mode[14]) and all previous versions for Windows, as well as Internet Explorer 4 for Macintosh, display the `small-caps` value as all-caps (i.e. all characters in the element are capitalized). Internet Explorer 6 (Windows), in standards-compliant mode, and Internet Explorer 5 for Macintosh, artificially shrink the capitals corresponding to lowercase characters in the text to simulate a `small-caps` font.

No currently-available browsers will actually use the small-caps variant of a font if one is available.

Example

This style rule displays all headings on the page in small-caps:

```
h1, h2, h3, h4, h5, h6 {
   font-variant: small-caps;
}
```

font-weight

This property sets the boldness of the font to be displayed in the element.

Inherited: Yes, but in the case of relative settings, the *computed* value is inherited.

See also: `font`

Value

The CSS specification defines the following absolute values:

❏ `normal` (equivalent to 400)

❏ `bold` (equivalent to 700)

❏ 100

❏ 200

---

[14] http://msdn.microsoft.com/library/en-us/dnie60/html/cssenhancements.asp

☐ 300

☐ 400

☐ 500

☐ 600

☐ 700

☐ 800

☐ 900

Also available are the following relative values:

☐ `bolder`

☐ `lighter`

According to the CSS2 specification, `bolder` and `lighter` should select the next version that is bolder or lighter than the font inherited from the parent element, respectively.

Initial value: `normal`

Compatibility

CSS Version: 1

Supported by all CSS-compatible browsers.

Most browsers only really support `normal` and `bold`, mapping the numerical and relative values to those two absolute settings.

Example

This style rule overrides the default style sheets of most browsers that specify that `strong` elements should be rendered bold. On browsers that support more than one level of boldness, such elements will be displayed bolder than text in the parent element. Thus, a `strong` element inside a heading that is rendered bold will be rendered with even greater boldness.

```
strong {
  font-weight: bolder;
}
```

height

This property sets the height of the contents of a block or replaced[6] element. This height does not include padding, borders, or margins.

If the contents of a block require more vertical space than the height you assign, the behavior is defined by the overflow property.

Inherited: No

See also: max-height, min-height, overflow, width

Value

Any CSS length value, a percentage of the parent element's height, or auto.

Initial value: auto

Compatibility

CSS Version: 1

This property is supported in some form by all CSS-compatible browsers. Current, standards-compliant browsers (Netscape 6, Opera 7, Mozilla, Internet Explorer 5 for Mac) support it fully.

Internet Explorer for Windows (up to and including version 6.0) incorrectly includes padding, borders, and margins in the height value. This is known as the **box model bug**. IE 6.0 corrects this in standards-compliant mode[15], but for all previous versions you'll need to use a separate, browser-specific style sheet or live with smaller boxes whenever borders, margins, or padding come into play (which is almost always). A third alternative is commonly known as the **box**

---

[6]A replaced element is any element whose appearance and dimensions are defined by an external resource. Examples include images (img tags), plug-ins (object tags), and form fields (input and select tags). Another way to think of replaced elements is any element that can be displayed inline with text and that acts as a single, big character for the purposes of wrapping and layout.
[15] http://msdn.microsoft.com/library/en-us/dnie60/html/cssenhancements.asp

model hack[16], and exploits a more obscure bug in IE6's CSS support to work around the box model bug.

In Internet Explorer 4, this property is supported only for a limited subset of block elements (`div` is a safe bet).

In Netscape 4, this property is only really supported for images and absolute-positioned elements.

Example

This style rule assigns a fixed height of 100 pixels to paragraphs within the element with ID `blurbs`.

```
#blurbs p {
  height: 100px;
}
```

ime-mode

Chinese, Japanese and Korean writing systems have more characters than can fit on a typical keyboard. Windows deals with this with an Input Method Editor (IME). When the IME is active, the user can type a few keyboard characters to describe the actual character he or she wishes to insert, then choose it from a popup list. When the IME is inactive, the actual keyboard characters are inserted as typed.

This nonstandard property lets you set the default IME mode for a form field (`input` or `textarea`)—active or inactive—or even disable the IME entirely for that field.

Inherited: No

Value

`active`, `auto`, `disabled`, or `inactive`.

Initial value: auto

---

[16] http://css-discuss.incutio.com/?page=BoxModelHack

Compatibility

CSS Version: n/a

Internet Explorer 5 for Windows or later only.

Example

This style rule sets the IME to inactive by default in `input` and `textarea` elements of class `latin`:

```
input.latin, textarea.latin {
  ime-mode: inactive;
}
```

layout-flow

This nonstandard property lets you choose between two common layout methods for text: left-to-right horizontal lines stacked top to bottom on the page (the usual layout for western languages like English), and top-to-bottom vertical lines stacked right to left on the page (the usual layout for East Asian languages like Chinese).

This property has been deprecated in favour of the more flexible `writing-mode` property.

Inherited: Yes

See also: `writing-mode`

Value

`horizontal` or `vertical-ideographic`

Initial value: `horizontal`

Compatibility

CSS Version: n/a

Internet Explorer for Windows version 5 or later only.

Example

This style rule sets the `layout-flow` of the `body` and all its children (unless otherwise specified) to the East Asian style:

```
body {
  layout-flow: vertical-ideographic;
}
```

layout-grid

East Asian writing systems generally call for character layout to be performed in a grid. This nonstandard shorthand property lets you set all the properties associated with that grid in a single property declaration.

Inherited: Yes

See also: `layout-grid-char`, `layout-grid-line`, `layout-grid-mode`, and `layout-grid-type`

Value

The format of this property is as follows:

```
layout-grid: [mode] [type] [line [char]]
```

The values in square brackets are optional, and have the following meanings:

❏ *mode* is a valid value for `layout-grid-mode`

❏ *type* is a valid value for `layout-grid-type`

❏ *line* is a valid value for `layout-grid-line`

❏ *char* is a valid value for `layout-grid-char`

Initial value: `both loose none none`

Compatibility

CSS Version: n/a

Internet Explorer 5 or later for Windows only.

Equivalent functionality is planned for inclusion in CSS3, but final property names and values are likely to differ. To follow the work on this front, see the CSS Working Group Web site[17].

Example

This is a basic example of the `layout-grid` property in use:

```
div.fullgrid {
  layout-grid: both fixed 12px 12px;
}
```

layout-grid-char

East Asian writing systems generally call for character layout to be performed in a grid. This property sets the character size enforced by that grid.

`layout-grid-mode` must be set to `char` or `both` for this property to have any effect.

Inherited: Yes

See also: `layout-grid`

Value

This property can take a CSS length value, a percentage of the parent element's width, `auto` (use the largest character in the font as the grid size), or `none` (character grid disabled).

Initial value: `none`

Compatibility

CSS Version: n/a

Internet Explorer 5 or later for Windows only.

---

[17] http://www.w3.org/TR/2003/WD-css3-text-20030226/#document-grid

Equivalent functionality is planned for inclusion in CSS3, but final property names and values are likely to differ. To follow the work on this front, see the CSS Working Group Web site[18].

Example

This style rule specifies that characters should be positioned according to a 12pt grid:

```
div.monospaced {
   layout-grid-char: 12pt;
}
```

layout-grid-line

East Asian writing systems generally call for character layout to be performed in a grid. This property sets the line size enforced by that grid.

layout-grid-mode must be set to line or both for this property to have any effect.

Inherited: Yes

See also: layout-grid and layout-grid-mode

Value

This property can take a CSS length value, a percentage of the parent element's height, auto (use the largest character in the font as the grid size), or none (line grid disabled).

Initial value: none

Compatibility

CSS Version: n/a

Internet Explorer 5 or later for Windows only.

---

[18] http://www.w3.org/TR/2003/WD-css3-text-20030226/#document-grid

Equivalent functionality is planned for inclusion in CSS3, but final property names and values are likely to differ. To follow the work on this front, see the CSS Working Group Web site[19].

Example

This style rule specifies that lines should be positioned according to a 12pt grid:

```
div.monospaced {
  layout-grid-line: 12pt;
}
```

layout-grid-mode

East Asian writing systems generally call for character layout to be performed in a grid. This property lets you set which character dimensions (character width or line height) are regulated by the grid.

Inherited: Yes

See also: layout-grid, layout-grid-char, and layout-grid-line

Value

Any one of the following constants:

❑ both

❑ char

❑ line

❑ none

Initial value: both

Compatibility

CSS Version: n/a

---

[19] http://www.w3.org/TR/2003/WD-css3-text-20030226/#document-grid

Internet Explorer 5 or later for Windows only.

Equivalent functionality is planned for inclusion in CSS3, but final property names and values are likely to differ. To follow the work on this front, see the CSS Working Group Web site[20].

Example

This style rule sets span elements with the attribute lang="jp", to display characters according to a 12 point grid, but to leave the line height alone:

```
span[lang=jp] {
  layout-grid-mode: char;
  layout-grid-char: 12pt;
}
```

Note that since Internet Explorer for Windows doesn't currently support attribute selectors, this style rule has no practical use.

layout-grid-type

East Asian writing systems generally call for character layout to be performed in a grid. Different East Asian languages have different conventions as to which characters should be aligned to the grid. This property lets you set the convention to use.

For full details on this property, see the reference page at MSDN[21].

Inherited: Yes

See also: layout-grid and layout-grid-mode

Value

Any one of the following constants:

❑ fixed

❑ loose

---

[20] http://www.w3.org/TR/2003/WD-css3-text-20030226/#document-grid
[21] http://msdn.microsoft.com/workshop/author/dhtml/reference/properties/layoutgridtype.asp

❏ strict

Initial value: loose

Compatibility

CSS Version: n/a

Internet Explorer 5 or later for Windows only.

Equivalent functionality is planned for inclusion in CSS3, but final property names and values are likely to differ. To follow the work on this front, see the CSS Working Group Web site[22].

Example

This style rule sets span elements with the attribute lang="jp" to use a strict layout grid:

```
span[lang=jp] {
  layout-grid-type: strict;
}
```

Note that since Internet Explorer for Windows doesn't currently support attribute selectors, this style rule has no practical use.

layer-background-color

Longtime users of CSS Positioning will be familiar with Netscape 4's unwelcome penchant for leaving a space between the content of an absolute-positioned block and its border. This three-pixel space is in addition to the padding, and is left transparent, even if the block was assigned a background.

This little-known nonstandard property, which works only in Netscape 4, sets the background color of both the main background area as well as that three-pixel space! Although there is still no way to get rid of that three-pixel space, a browser-specific style sheet can reduce the padding by three pixels to achieve the desired rendering, as long as the intended padding of the box is at least 3 pixels!

---

[22] http://www.w3.org/TR/2003/WD-css3-text-20030226/#document-grid

If `background-color` is set as well as `layer-background-color`, the `background-color` will fill the content area and actual padding, while the `layer-background-color` will fill the three-pixel space.

Inherited: No

See also: `background-color`

Value

Any CSS color value.

Initial value: `transparent`

Compatibility

CSS Version: n/a

Netscape 4 only.

Example

This demonstrates how to achieve identical rendering of a box in standards-compliant browsers and in Netscape 4:

```
/* This style rule appears in the common style sheet */
#thebox {
  position: absolute;
  padding: 10px;
  border: 1px solid black;
  background-color: red;
}

/* This style rule appears in the NS4-only style sheet */
#thebox {
  padding: 7px;
  layer-background-color: red;
}
```

layer-background-image

Longtime users of CSS Positioning will be familiar with Netscape 4's unwelcome penchant for leaving a space between the content of an absolute-positioned block and its border. This three-pixel space is in addition to the padding, and is left transparent even if the block was assigned a background.

This little-known nonstandard property, which works only in Netscape 4, sets the background image of both the main background area as well as that three-pixel space! Although there is still no way to get rid of that three-pixel space, a browser-specific style sheet can reduce the padding by three pixels to achieve the desired rendering, as long as the intended padding of the box is at least 3 pixels!

If background-image is set as well as layer-background-image, the background-image will fill the content area and actual padding, while the layer-background-image will fill the three-pixel space.

Inherited: No

See also: background-image

Value

A URL or none. In CSS, URLs must be surrounded by the url() wrapper, not quotes. See the example below.

Initial value: none

Compatibility

CSS Version: n/a

Netscape 4 only.

Example

This demonstrates how to achieve identical rendering of a box in standards-compliant browsers and in Netscape 4:

```
/* This style rule appears in the common style sheet */
#thebox {
  position: absolute;
  padding: 10px;
  border: 1px solid black;
  background-image: url(/images/checker.gif);
}
```

```
/* This style rule appears in the NS4-only style sheet */
#thebox {
  padding: 7px;
  layer-background-image: url(/images/checker.gif);
}
```

left

This property lets you set the distance between the left edge of an absolute positioned element (including its padding, border, and margin)[7] and the left edge of the positioning context in which it resides. The positioning context is the content area of the element's nearest ancestor that has a position property value other than static, or the body element.

For relative positioned elements, this property sets a relative offset from the normal position of its left edge. So, a setting of 10px will shift the left edge of the box 10 pixels to the right, and a setting of -10px will shift it 10 pixels to the left.

Inherited: No

See also: position, bottom, top, and right

Value

A CSS length measurement, a percentage value, or the auto constant. Percentages are based on the width of the parent element. The auto constant tells the browser to determine the position of the left edge itself, based on whatever other constraints may exist on the size/position of the element.

Initial value: auto

Compatibility

CSS Version: 2

Supported by all CSS-compatible browsers, including Internet Explorer 4 or later, Netscape 4 or later, and Mozilla browsers.

---

[7]The CSS2 specification contains an error that suggests that the padding, border, and margin of the positioned element should not be considered. This has been acknowledged as a mistake by the CSS Working Group in the Errata document for CSS2.

Example

This style rule positions the element with ID menu 80% of the way from the left edge of the window and gives it a width of 19.9%. We don't use a full 20% for the width to prevent rounding errors in some browsers from generating a horizontal scrollbar.

```
#menu {
    position: absolute;
    left: 80%;
    width: 19.9%;
    height: 200px;
}
```

letter-spacing

This property lets you either increase or decrease the amount of spacing between characters in an element.

Inherited: Yes

See also: word-spacing

Value

Any CSS length or normal. Percentages are *not* allowed.

Positive lengths increase letter spacing by the specified amount, while negative lengths decrease it. In most cases, it is preferable to specify the spacing in ems (e.g. 0.5em), as this will preserve the relative spacing of letters, even if you change the font size (one em is equal to the height of the current font).

Initial value: normal

Compatibility

CSS Version: 1

Supported by all CSS-compatible browsers, with the notable exception of Netscape 4.

Examples

This style rule sets all elements of class **spacy** to have extra spacing one half the height of the font between each character:

```
.spacy {
  letter-spacing: 0.5em;
}
```

This style rule sets all elements of class **crowded** to display characters one half the font size closer together than usual:

```
.crowded {
  letter-spacing: -0.5em;
}
```

line-break

This nonstandard property controls line-breaking policy (*Kinsoku*) for Japanese text.

By default, a relaxed line-breaking routine is used. This is the preferred method for modern typography, especially where narrow columns may exist. With this property, you can specify that a stricter, more traditional method is applied.

Inherited: Yes

Value

normal or strict

Initial value: normal

Compatibility

CSS Version: n/a

Internet Explorer 5 or later for Windows only.

Equivalent functionality is planned for inclusion in CSS3, and early drafts indicate that the property name and values will be the same as shown here. To follow the work on this front, see the CSS Working Group Web site[23].

[23] http://www.w3.org/TR/2003/WD-css3-text-20030226/#line-breaking

Example

This style rule will instruct the browser to use strict (traditional) line-breaking rules for any element of class `tradbreak`:

```
.tradbreak {
  line-break: strict;
}
```

line-height

By default, the browser will determine the amount of vertical space allocated to a line by simply taking the tallest element (or font). The `line-height` property is what is used in this process, and setting it lets you artificially increase, decrease, or arbitrarily set the line height for an element. If more than one element appears on a line, the one with the highest `line-height` property still determines the rendered height of the line.

Inherited: Yes, but see below for differences in inheritance rules based on the value format.

See also: `font` and `font-size`

Value

This property supports any of the following formats for its value:

normal

This constant is the initial value of this property, and is equivalent to a number setting somewhere between `1.0` and `1.2`, according to the CSS2 specification.

number

A number (e.g. `1.5`), which is multiplied by the font size to get the rendered height of the line. A setting of `1.0` will crowd the lines together as closely as possible without overlapping characters, while a setting of `1.2` will leave a more natural amount of space between the lines. The value inherited by child elements will be this number, not the resultant line height, so a child element with a larger font will leave a proportionally larger space between lines.

length
> A CSS absolute length (e.g. 50px). A setting in ems will look the same as a number setting with the same face value, but child elements will inherit the actual line height, rather than the proportion of the font size.

percentage
> A percentage, which is multiplied by the font size, to obtain the displayed line height. As with a setting in ems, the rendered line height may be proportional to the font size, but child elements inherit the absolute height, rather than the relative percentage.

Initial value: normal

Compatibility

CSS Version: 1

Supported by all CSS-compatible browsers, including Netscape 4 or later, Internet Explorer 4 or later, and Mozilla browsers.

Example

This style rule sets all elements of class spacy to have line height one and a half times the font size:

```
.spacy {
  line-height: 1.5;
}
```

Because a number value is used, child elements will also have line heights 1.5 times *their* font sizes. If a value of 150% or 1.5em was used here, child elements would instead have the same line height as this element.

list-style

This shorthand property lets you set the three list-style properties with a single property declaration.

All three elements are optional, but any property you do not specify will be implicitly set to its initial value (overriding any value specified in a rule of lesser or equal priority).

For this property to have any effect, the target element (or one of its descendants, which will inherit this property) must have it display property set to list-item. The recommended method to set the list-style properties for a list, is to apply the properties to the list element so that the individual list items inherit them.

Inherited: Yes

See also: list-style-image, list-style-position, and list-style-type.

Value

The syntax for this property is as follows:

```
list-style: [type] [position] [image]
```

Each of the three values is optional (as indicated by the square brackets); however, at least one must appear. *type* is any valid value for list-style-type, *position* is any valid value for list-style-position, and *image* is any valid value for list-style-image. These three values may appear in any order.

If you specify both *type* and *image*, the type will be used when the image fails to load.

Setting this property to none will set both list-style-image and list-style-type to none.

Initial value: none

Compatibility

CSS Version: 1

This property is supported by all CSS-compatible browsers.

Netscape 4 does not support list-style-image and list-style-position; consequently, those elements of this property are nonfunctional in that browser.

Examples

These style rules set an image for unordered lists and a Roman numeral format for ordered lists:

```
ul {
  list-style: url(/images/bullet.gif);
}
ol {
  list-style: upper-roman;
}
```

Compare these rules to the following:

```
ul {
  list-style-image: url(/images/bullet.gif);
}
ol {
  list-style-type: upper-roman;
}
```

If we had an ordered list (ol) nested inside an unordered list (ul), the first set of rules above would have the intended effect of displaying Roman numerals for the ordered list. The second set of rules, however, would display images for *all* the list elements—in both the ordered and unordered lists—because the nested, ordered list would inherit the list-style-image property from the unordered list. This doesn't happen with the first set of style rules because list-style: upper-roman implicitly sets the list-style-image property to none.

list-style-image

This property lets you assign an image to be displayed, instead of a standard marker for list items. You can set this property for individual list items (li) if needed; however, the recommended method for specifying an image for all elements in a list is to apply the property to the list element (ol, ul, etc.) and let the list items inherit it.

You should usually specify a list-style-type value with your list-style-image; the browser will use the list-style-type as a fallback if the image fails to load.

Be aware of the fact that this property is inherited by descendant elements, including nested lists. See the discussion in the example for the list-style property to learn how to avoid this pitfall.

Inherited: Yes

See also: list-style, list-style-type

Value

A CSS URL (using the url() wrapper), or none.

Initial value: none

Compatibility

CSS Version: 1

Works in all CSS-compatible browsers, with the notable exception of Netscape 4.

Example

These style rules will set all unordered list (ul) elements to display an image as a marker (with square as the fallback list-style-type). The second rule specifically sets the list-style-image and list-style-type of ordered list elements (ol) to prevent them from inheriting the unordered list properties if they are nested inside one.

```
ul {
  list-style-image: url(/images/bullet.gif);
  list-style-type: square;
}
ol {
  list-style-image: none;
  list-style-type: decimal;
}
```

list-style-position

As shown in Figure C.3, list-style-position controls whether or not the markers for list elements hang in the margin of list items or appear within the block.

Figure C.3. Effects of list-style-position

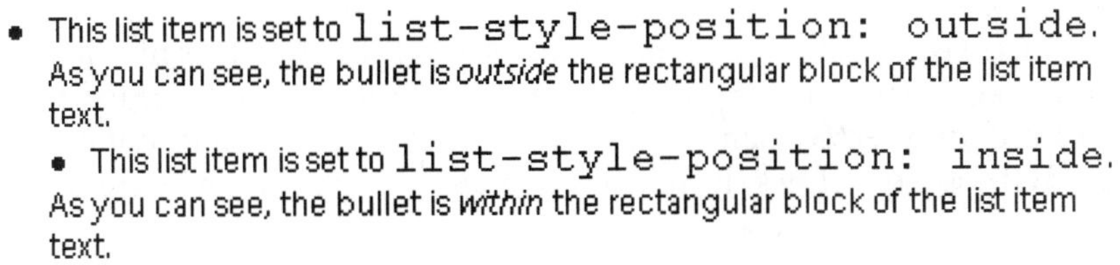

- This list item is set to `list-style-position: outside`. As you can see, the bullet is *outside* the rectangular block of the list item text.
    - This list item is set to `list-style-position: inside`. As you can see, the bullet is *within* the rectangular block of the list item text.

Inherited: Yes

See also: `list-style`

Value

`inside` or `outside`

Initial value: `outside`

Compatibility

CSS Version: 1

This property works in all CSS-compatible browsers, with the notable exception of Netscape 4.

Internet Explorer 4 for Macintosh exhibits rendering glitches when this property is set to `inside`.

Example

This style rule sets lists of class compact to display markers within the rectangular block of the list item text and removes the associated left margin:

```
ul.compact, ol.compact {
  list-style-position: inside;
  margin-left: 0;
}
```

list-style-type

This property lets you set the type of marker displayed list items. This may include actual list item (li) elements, or other elements with their display property set to list-item. If an affected element also has a list-style-image value other than none, this property defines the fallback marker to display if the image cannot be loaded.

Inherited: Yes

See also: list-style, list-style-image

Value

There are a wide range of constants available for this property.

The following "glyph" markers display a single symbol for all list items, and are commonly used for unordered lists:

- ❏ circle
- ❏ disc
- ❏ square

The following "numbering" markers display a number in the chosen format for each list item:

- ❏ decimal
- ❏ decimal-leading-zero
- ❏ lower-roman
- ❏ upper-roman
- ❏ hebrew
- ❏ georgian
- ❏ armenian

☐ `cjk-ideographic`

☐ `hiragana`

☐ `katakana`

☐ `hiragana-iroha`

☐ `katakana-iroha`

The following "alphabetic" markers display a letter in the chosen format for each list item:

☐ `lower-alpha` or `lower-latin`

☐ `upper-alpha` or `upper-latin`

☐ `lower-greek`

The special constant `none` displays no marker at all.

Initial value: none[8]

Compatibility

CSS Version: 1 (with multilingual constants added in CSS2)

This property is supported by all CSS-compatible browsers; however, most support only the CSS1 constants: `circle`, `disc`, `square`, `lower-alpha`, `upper-alpha`, `lower-roman`, `upper-roman`, and `none`.

Netscape 4 for Macintosh does not correctly support the `none` value—it displays question marks as list markers.

Example

This set of style rules sets top-level unordered lists to use square bullets, nested unordered lists to use circle bullets, and doubly-nested unordered lists to use disc bullets:

---

[8]This initial value applies to generic elements. Web browsers generally use a default internal style sheet that specifies a `list-style-type` of `disc` for unordered lists and `decimal` for ordered lists. Most browsers also assign unique default types to nested lists.

```
ul {
  list-style-type: square;
  list-style-image: none;
}
ul ul {
  list-style-type: circle;
}
ul ul ul {
  list-style-type: disc;
}
```

margin

This property sets the size of the margins surrounding the selected element(s).

The size for each side may be set individually using the margin-bottom, margin-left, margin-right, and margin-top properties.

Inherited: No

See also: margin-bottom, margin-left, margin-right, margin-top

Value

You can specify from one to four different values to specify different margin sizes for each side of the element, as shown in Table C.6.

Each value can be a CSS length (px, pt, em, etc.), a percentage of the parent element's *width* (even for the top and bottom margins[9]), or the auto constant, which tells the browser automatically to calculate and use a margin that will allow the element to assume its default (or assigned) width.

---

[9]This is true with one exception. When the parent element is the **body**, percentage values for top and bottom margins are based on the document's *height* instead. This exception does *not* apply to borders or padding.

Table C.6. Effects of multiple values on `margin` property

Number of values	Effect on margins
1	All four margins receive the value specified.
2	Top and bottom (horizontal) margins receive the first value, left and right (vertical) margins receive the second.
3	Top margin receives the first value, vertical margins receive the second, bottom margin receives the third.
4	Values are applied to top, right, bottom, and left margins, respectively.

Initial value: 0

Compatibility

CSS Version: 1

Works in all CSS-compatible browsers, including Internet Explorer 4 and Netscape 4.

Example

This style rule sets `blockquote` elements to be 80% of the width of their parent block. The margin property leaves a 10 pixel margin above and below these elements, and sets the left and right margins to `auto` so that the block will be centered horizontally.

```
blockquote {
  width: 80%;
  margin: 10px auto;
}
```

margin-bottom, margin-left, margin-right, margin-top

These properties let you set sizes of the individual margins around an element.

Inherited: No

See also: `margin`

Value

Each value can be a CSS length (`px`, `pt`, `em`, etc.), a percentage of the parent element's *width* (even for the top and bottom margins[9]), or the `auto` constant, which tells the browser automatically to calculate and use a margin that will allow the element to assume its default (or assigned) width.

Initial value: 0[10]

Compatibility

CSS Version: 1

Works in all CSS-compatible browsers, including Internet Explorer 4 and Netscape 4.

Example

These style rules modify the default margins, assigned by the browser to headings and paragraphs, to make headings "stick to" the first paragraph that follows:

```
h1, h2, h3, h4, h5, h6 {
  margin-bottom: 0;
  margin-top: 12pt;
}
p {
  margin-top: 0;
  margin-bottom: 6px;
}
```

marker-offset

When a `:before` or `:after` pseudo-element has its `display` property set to `marker`, it is rendered outside the main content box of the element, to the left of the first line (`:before`), or to the right of the last line (`:after`) in left-to-right writing systems. This property sets the distance between the two closest border edges of the main content and the marker, as shown in Figure C.4.

---

[10]This initial value is for generic elements. Browsers use an internal style sheet that defines default margins for elements such as headings, paragraphs, block quotes, and list items.

Figure C.4. The effect of `marker-offset`

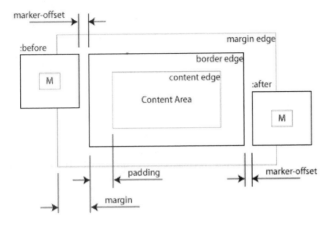

Note that the marker box has padding and borders, but no margins.

Inherited: No

See also: `display`

Value

Any CSS length value (px, pt, em, etc.), or the `auto` constant, which lets the browser choose the distance.

Initial value: `auto`

Compatibility

CSS Version: 2

Not supported by any currently-available browser.

Example

This style rules place stylistic quotation marks around `blockquote` elements. The `marker-offset` property ensures that there will be 5 pixels' space between the quotation marks and the content of the element (plus any padding that may be added to the `blockquote`).

```
blockquote:before, blockquote:after {
  display: marker;
  marker-offset: 5px;
  content: '"';
  font-size: 150%;
  color: blue;
}
```

marks

This property, which can appear only within a @page at-rule (see the section called "At-Rules") specifies whether crop marks, page alignment crosses, or both should appear on the printed page.

Value

Either the none constant, or crop, cross, or both (separated by a space).

Initial value: none

Compatibility

CSS Version: 2

Not supported by any currently-available browser.

Example

This at-rule specifies that pages should be printed with crop marks (to indicated where the page should be cut) and crosses (to help in the alignment of pages):

```
@page {
  marks: crop cross;
}
```

max-height, min-height

Instead of setting a fixed height, it is sometimes useful to set *limits* on the height of an element. These two properties let you set a maximum and/or minimum height. The height of the element is calculated normally, and then these limits are applied.

Remember to set the `overflow` property to `hidden` (or another appropriate value) if you set a `max-height`; otherwise, the content will overflow the specified height, even if the element does not.

Inherited: No

See also: `height`, `max-width`, `min-width`

Value

A CSS length (px, pt, em, etc.), a percentage of the parent element's content area height, or (in the case of `max-height` only) `none`.

Initial value:

❏ `max-height: none`

❏ `min-height: 0`

Compatibility

CSS Version: 2

This property is fully supported on Netscape 6 and Mozilla browsers and Opera 7 or later only.

Internet Explorer 6 for Windows supports `min-height` only, and then only on `td`, `th`, and `tr` elements in fixed-layout tables (see `table-layout`). The CSS2 specification specifically states that this property should *not* apply to table elements.

Example

This style rule specifies that the element with ID `sidemenu` should have a height between 200 and 1000 pixels, and should display a scrollbar if the content's height is greater than the maximum.

```
#sidemenu {
  min-height: 200px;
  max-height: 1000px;
  overflow: auto;
}
```

max-width, min-width

Instead of setting a fixed width, it is sometimes useful to set *limits* on the width of an element. These two properties let you set a maximum and/or minimum width. The width of the element is calculated normally, and then these limits are applied.

Remember to set the overflow property to hidden (or another appropriate value) if you set a max-width; otherwise, the content will overflow the specified width, even if the element does not.

Inherited: No

See also: width, max-height, min-height

Value

A CSS length (px, pt, em, etc.), a percentage of the parent element's content area height, or (in the case of max-height only) none.

Initial value:

☐ max-height: none

☐ min-height: 0

Compatibility

CSS Version: 2

This property is fully supported on Netscape 6 and Mozilla browsers and Opera 7 or later only.

Example

This style rule specifies that the element with ID topmenu should have a width between 200 and 1000 pixels, and should display a scrollbar if the content's width is greater than the maximum.

```
#topmenu {
  min-width: 200px;
  max-width: 1000px;
```

```
    overflow: auto;
}
```

-moz-border-radius

Mozilla-based browsers (including Netscape 6 or later) support a number of nonstandard CSS properties that were implemented for the skinning engines of those browsers. These properties all begin with the prefix `-moz-` to indicate their nonstandard nature. Several of these properties are useful for general Web site design as well, and have equivalents in current drafts of future CSS standards.

`-moz-border-radius` is a shorthand property that lets you add rounded corners to the border of an element by setting the radius to use for each of the corners of the box. The content of the box is not clipped by these rounded corners, so you'll usually want to define an appropriate amount of padding to prevent overlaps. The background *is* clipped, however.

Inherited: No

See also: `-moz-border-radius-corner`

Value

You can specify from one to four values for this property, separated by spaces. Each value can be a CSS length value or a percentage of the width of the element from 0% to 50%. The maximum corner radius will always be 50% of the maximum dimension (width or height) of the element. The effects of specifying multiple values are shown in Table C.7.

Table C.7. Effects of multiple values on `margin` property

Number of values	Effect on margins
1	All four corners receive the value specified.
2	Top left and bottom right corners receive the first value, top right and bottom left corners receive the second.
3	Top left corner receives the first value, top right and bottom left corners receive the second, bottom right corner receives the third.
4	Values are applied to top left, top right, bottom right, and bottom left corners, respectively.

Initial value: 0

Compatibility

CSS Version: n/a

This property works in Mozilla-based browsers, including Netscape 6 or later, only.

Equivalent functionality is planned for inclusion in CSS3, but final property names and values are likely to differ. To follow the work on this front, see the CSS Working Group Web site[24].

Example

This style rule creates a circular element 100 pixels in diameter:

```
.circle {
  border: 1px solid red;
  width: 100px;
  height: 100px;
  -moz-border-radius: 50%;
}
```

-moz-border-radius-bottomleft, -moz-border-radius-bottomright, -moz-border-radius-topleft, -moz-border-radius-topright

Mozilla-based browsers (including Netscape 6 or later) support a number of nonstandard CSS properties that were implemented for the skinning engines of those browsers. These properties all begin with the prefix -moz- to indicate their nonstandard nature. Several of these properties are useful for general Web site design as well, and have equivalents in current drafts of future CSS standards.

The -moz-border-radius-*corner* properties let you add rounded corners to the border of an element by setting the radius to use for each of the corners of the

---

[24] http://www.w3.org/TR/2002/WD-css3-border-20021107/#the-border-radius

box. The content of the box is not clipped by these rounded corners, so you'll usually want to define an appropriate amount of padding to prevent overlaps. The background *is* clipped, however.

Inherited: No

See also: `-moz-border-radius`

Value

The value can be a CSS length value or a percentage of the width of the element from 0% to 50%. The maximum corner radius will always be 50% of the maximum dimension (width or height) of the element.

Initial value: 0

Compatibility

CSS Version: n/a

This property works in Mozilla-based browsers, including Netscape 6 or later, only.

Equivalent functionality is planned for inclusion in CSS3, but final property names and values are likely to differ. To follow the work on this front, see the CSS Working Group Web site[25].

Example

This style rule creates an interesting rounded shape:

```
.roundthing {
  border: 1px solid red;
  width: 100px;
  height: 100px;
  -moz-border-radius-bottomleft: 25%;
  -moz-border-radius-bottomright: 50%;
  -moz-border-radius-topleft: 50%;
  -moz-border-radius-topright: 25%;
}
```

---

[25] http://www.w3.org/TR/2002/WD-css3-border-20021107/#the-border-radius

-moz-opacity

Mozilla-based browsers (including Netscape 6 or later) support a number of nonstandard CSS properties that were implemented for the skinning engines of those browsers. These properties all begin with the prefix -moz- to indicate their nonstandard nature. Several of these properties are useful for general Web site design as well, and have equivalents in current drafts of future CSS standards.

The -moz-opacity property lets you create translucent elements that allow elements behind them partially to show through.

Inherited: No

See also: filter

Value

You can set the opacity as a decimal number between 0.0 (totally transparent) and 1.0 (totally opaque), or as a percentage between 0% (transparent) and 100% (opaque). You should generally use decimal numbers, as the draft CSS3 standard does not currently allow for percentages.

Initial value: 1.0

Compatibility

CSS Version: n/a

This property works in Mozilla-based browsers, including Netscape 6 or later, only.

Equivalent functionality is planned for inclusion in CSS3, but final property names and values are likely to differ. To follow the work on this front, see the CSS Working Group Web site[26].

Example

This style rule makes the element with ID sidebar 50% transparent:

---

[26] http://www.w3.org/TR/2003/WD-css3-color-20030214/#transparency

```
#sidebar {
  -moz-opacity: 0.5;
}
```

orphans

This property affects the position of page breaks, when the user prints the page from his or her browser. With this property, you can specify the minimum number of lines in a block before a page break can occur.

For example, if a paragraph element had six lines and the page size called for a page break to occur after the second line, then an orphans setting of 3 would force the page break to occur *before* the paragraph so that the first 3 lines could appear on the same page.

Inherited: Yes

See also: widows

Value

A positive integer.

Initial value: 2

Compatibility

CSS Version: 2

This property is supported by Mozilla browsers (including Netscape 6 or later), Opera 7, and Internet Explorer 5 for Macintosh.

Example

This style rule indicates that page breaks must allow at least four lines of a broken paragraph to appear at the bottom of the page before the break occurs:

```
p {
  orphans: 4;
}
```

outline

Outlines are very similar to borders; however, they do not occupy any space in the CSS box model (i.e. turning off and on an element's outline or changing its outline width should not affect the position of that element, or any other elements on the page). Additionally, an outline should follow the actual shape of the element's content (e.g. hugging the jagged right edge of a left-aligned paragraph) rather than forming a rectangular box around it. The outline of an inline element that flows over several lines is closed at the starts and ends of lines, whereas the border is not.

`outline` is a shorthand property that lets you set all three of the outline-related properties for an element with a single property declaration.

Inherited: No

See also: `border`, `outline-color`, `outline-style`, `outline-width`

Value

The syntax for this property is as follows:

```
outline: [color] [style] [width]
```

`color` is any valid value for `outline-color`. `style` is any valid value for `outline-style`. `width` is any valid value for `outline-width`.

All three of the values are optional (as indicated by the square brackets), but you must specify at least one. They can be specified in any order. Any unspecified value causes the corresponding property to be set to its initial value.

Initial value: none

Compatibility

CSS Version: 2

Only Internet Explorer 5 for Macintosh and Opera 7 browsers support this property, and they only render rectangular outlines as opposed to the content-hugging style prescribed by the CSS2 specification.

Example

This style rule makes use of the `:focus` pseudo-class to draw a medium, dashed, red outline around any form element that has focus:

```
input:focus, select:focus, textarea:focus {
  outline: medium dashed red;
}
```

outline-color

Outlines are very similar to borders; however, they do not occupy any space in the CSS box model (i.e. turning off and on an element's outline or changing its outline width should not affect the position of that element, or any other elements on the page). Additionally, an outline should follow the actual shape of the element's content (e.g. hugging the jagged right edge of a left-aligned paragraph) rather than forming a rectangular box around it. The outline of an inline element that flows over several lines is closed at the starts and ends of lines, whereas the border is not.

The `outline-color` property sets the color of the outline drawn around the selected element(s).

Inherited: No

See also: `border-color`

Value

Any CSS color value, or `invert`, which will reverse the color(s) of the background over which it is drawn.

Initial value: `invert` (`black` in current browsers)

Compatibility

CSS Version: 2

Only Internet Explorer 5 for Macintosh and Opera 7 browsers support this property, and they render only rectangular outlines, as opposed to the content-hugging style prescribed by the CSS2 specification. Both of these browsers use an initial value of `black`, as they do not support `invert`.

Example

This style rule puts red outlines around hyperlinks when the user hovers the mouse over them:

```
a:hover {
  outline-style: solid;
  outline-color: red;
}
```

outline-style

Outlines are very similar to borders; however, they do not occupy any space in the CSS box model (i.e. turning off and on an element's outline or changing its outline width should not affect the position of that element, or any other elements on the page). Additionally, an outline should follow the actual shape of the element's content (e.g. hugging the jagged right edge of a left-aligned paragraph) rather than forming a rectangular box around it. The outline of an inline element that flows over several lines is closed at the starts and ends of lines, whereas the border is not.

The outline-style property sets the style of the outline drawn around the selected element(s).

Inherited: No

See also: border-style

Value

This property accepts the same set of constants as border-style (see Table C.3), with the exception of hidden.

Initial value: none

Compatibility

CSS Version: 2

Only Internet Explorer 5 for Macintosh and Opera 7 browsers support this property, and they render only rectangular outlines as opposed to the content-hugging style prescribed by the CSS2 specification.

Example

This style rule adds an outline of style `inset` around active hyperlinks:

```
a:active {
  outline-style: inset;
  outline-color: grey;
  outline-width: medium;
}
```

outline-width

Outlines are very similar to borders; however, they do not occupy any space in the CSS box model (i.e. turning off and on an element's outline or changing its outline width should not affect the position of that element, or any other elements on the page). Additionally, an outline should follow the actual shape of the element's content (e.g. hugging the jagged right edge of a left-aligned paragraph) rather than forming a rectangular box around it. The outline of an inline element that flows over several lines is closed at the starts and ends of lines, whereas the border is not.

The `outline-width` property sets the width of the outline drawn around the selected element(s).

Inherited: No

See also: `border-width`

Value

`thin`, `medium`, `thick`, or any CSS length measurement.

Initial value: `medium`

Compatibility

CSS Version: 2

Only Internet Explorer 5 for Macintosh and Opera 7 browsers support this property, and they render only rectangular outlines as opposed to the content-hugging style prescribed by the CSS2 specification.

Example

This style rule adds a three pixel outline of style `outset` around hyperlinks when the user hovers the mouse over them:

```
a:hover {
    outline-style: outset;
    outline-color: grey;
    outline-width: 3px;
}
```

overflow

This property lets you control how the browser treats an element when it is not big enough to hold all its content. In practice, this occurs only when you have assigned a fixed or maximum width and/or height for the element. Most often, content will overflow the height of the element, because inline content will reflow to accommodate limited width; however, if an element contains children with their own fixed widths, they can overflow the width as well.

When you apply the `overflow` property to an element whose dimensions cause part of its contents to be cropped, the size of the element is cropped for layout purposes as well. Decorations such as borders are applied to the element after cropping has taken place. This is quite different to the `clip` property, which affects only the *visible* area of the element, and which crops borders and other decorations along with the element content.

Inherited: No

See also: `clip`, `height`, `text-overflow`, `max-width`, `max-height`, `width`

Value

This property can be set to any of these four constant values:

auto

This setting causes scrollbars to appear when needed, to allow the content of the element to be scrolled within the defined width/height limits. Be aware that the scrollbars themselves will occupy a browser-specific amount of space within the element area.

hidden

> This setting hides any overflowing content. Affected content will be invisible and inaccessible to the user.

scroll

> This setting behaves just like auto, except that horizontal and vertical scrollbars are displayed, whether they are needed or not. This lends predictability to the appearance of the block, when you're not sure whether the scrollbars will be needed or not.

visible

> This setting specifies that content that overflows the assigned boundaries of the element should be rendered anyway. The overflowing content should be drawn outside the visible box (its background and borders).

Initial value: visible

Compatibility

CSS Version: 2

This property works on all CSS-compatible browsers, with the notable exception of Netscape 4, which will always expand the height of an element to accommodate its content.

Internet Explorer for Windows (up to and including version 6 in standards-compliant mode) incorrectly expands the size of the box to accommodate overflowing content when this property is set to visible, rather than drawing the content outside the bounds of the box.

Internet Explorer 4 for Macintosh does not support adding scrollbars to elements with the auto and scroll settings.

Example

This style rule assigns a width and height to the element with ID mainmenu, but allows scrollbars to be added, if necessary, to make overflowing content accessible:

```
#mainmenu {
  width: 150px;
  height: 400px;
  overflow: auto;
}
```

overflow-x, overflow-y

These nonstandard properties, supported by Internet Explorer for Windows version 5 or later, work the same as the `overflow` property, except that they apply only to one dimension. `overflow-x` controls how/if content that overflows the horizontal limits of the element is rendered and `overflow-y` controls the content protruding from the vertical limits.

Inherited: No

See also: `overflow`

Value

These properties can each take any one of the constant values supported by the `overflow` property.

Initial value: `visible`

Compatibility

CSS Version: n/a

These properties work with Internet Explorer for Windows version 5 or later only.

Equivalent functionality is planned for inclusion in CSS3, but final property values may differ. To follow the work on this front, see the CSS Working Group Web site[27].

Example

This style rule assigns a width and height to the element with ID `mainmenu`, and allows a vertical scrollbar to be added if the content is too high to fit within the allocated 400 pixels. Content that does not fit horizontally will be visibly clipped:

```
#mainmenu {
  width: 150px;
  height: 400px;
  overflow-x: hidden;
```

---

[27] http://www.w3.org/TR/2002/WD-css3-box-20021024/#the-overflow-x

```
  overflow-y: auto;
}
```

padding

This shorthand property sets the size of the padding surrounding the selected element(s) on all four sides with a single property declaration. Padding is extra space added around the content of an element, but within its borders. Any background color or image assigned to an element will also fill the padding area of the element.

The amount of padding for each side may be set individually using the padding-bottom, padding-left, padding-right, and padding-top properties.

Inherited: No

See also: padding-bottom, padding-left, padding-right, padding-top

Value

You can specify from one to four different values to specify different padding sizes for each side of the element, as shown in Table C.8.

Each value can be a CSS length (px, pt, em, etc.), or a percentage of the parent element's *width*, even for the top and bottom paddings.

Table C.8. Effects of multiple values on padding property

Number of values	Effect on padding
1	All four sides receive the value specified.
2	Top and bottom (horizontal) paddings receive the first value, left and right (vertical) paddings receive the second.
3	Top padding receives the first value, vertical paddings receive the second, bottom padding receives the third.
4	Values are applied to top, right, bottom, and left paddings, respectively.

Initial value: 0

Compatibility

CSS Version: 1

Works in all CSS-compatible browsers, including Internet Explorer 4 and Netscape 4.

On any element with a border, Netscape 4 adds an extra 3 pixels of padding on all four sides of the element outside the normal padding area. This three-pixel space cannot be removed, and unlike the padding area, is transparent even when a background is assigned to the element. The `layer-background-color` and `layer-background-image` properties will allow you to fill the area in most cases; however, you'll still need to deal with the extra padding.

Examples

This style rule adds a thin border and red background around elements of class warning. It also adds 5 pixels of padding on the top and bottom and 10 pixels of padding on the left and right, between the content and the borders, to allow the content to breathe a little:

```
.warning {
  border: 1px solid;
  background-color: red;
  padding: 5px 10px;
}
```

This style rule sets a padding of 3 pixels around all cells in tables of class spacy. This is the CSS equivalent of `cellpadding="3"` in the `<table>` tag.

```
table.spacy td, table.spacy th {
  padding: 3px;
}
```

padding-bottom, padding-left, padding-right, padding-top

These properties let you set sizes of the individual padding sizes around an element. Padding is extra space added around the content of an element, but within its borders. Any background color or image assigned to an element will also fill the padding area of the element.

Inherited: No

See also: `padding`

Value

Each value can be a CSS length (`px`, `pt`, `em`, etc.), a percentage of the parent element's *width* (even for the top and bottom paddings).

Initial value: 0

Compatibility

CSS Version: 1

Works in all CSS-compatible browsers, including Internet Explorer 4 and Netscape 4.

On any element with a border, Netscape 4 adds an extra 3 pixels of padding on all four sides of the element outside the normal padding area. This three-pixel space cannot be removed, and unlike the padding area, is transparent even when a background is assigned to the element. The `layer-background-color` and `layer-background-image` properties will allow you to fill the area in most cases; however, you'll still need to deal with the extra padding.

Example

This style rule adds a thin border and red background around elements of class `warning`. It also adds 5 pixels of padding on the top and bottom and 10 pixels of padding on the left and right, between the content and the borders, to allow the content to breathe a little:

```
.warning {
  border: 1px solid;
  background-color: red;
  padding-top: 5px;
  padding-bottom: 5px;
  padding-left: 10px;
  padding-right: 10px;
}
```

See the example for the `padding` property to see how this same effect can be achieved with less typing.

page

The @page at-rule can be given an identifier so that you can declare different page types for use by a site when printing. For example, this style rule sets up a page type named mylandscape:

```
@page mylandscape {
  size: 11in 8.5in;
  margin: 1in;
  marks: crop;
}
```

The page property lets you assign a named page type to selected elements. Those elements will then be printed on the specified page type.

Inherited: Yes

Value

An identifier assigned to a @page rule declared elsewhere, or auto.

Initial value: auto

Compatibility

CSS Version: 2

Internet Explorer 5 for Macintosh, Netscape 6, Mozilla, and Opera browsers support this property, but do not actually apply it.

Example

This style rule ensures that all div elements of class overhead are rendered on a page of type mylandscape (as declared above) and are followed by a page break:

```
div.overhead {
  page: mylandscape;
  page-break-after: always;
}
```

page-break-after

When printing a Web page, the browser simply places page breaks where they need to occur in the content so that all printed pages are as full as possible by default. This property affords you greater control over the placement of page breaks during printing, by letting you manually add or suppress a page break after a given element.

Inherited: No

See also: orphans, page-break-before, page-break-inside, widows

Value

This property can take any of the following values:

always
> The browser will always put a page break after the selected element(s).

avoid
> The browser will try to avoid placing a page break after the selected element(s).
>
> The practical effect of this setting is to keep an element on the same page as the next sibling element.

auto
> The browser will put a page break after the selected element(s) if it ended at the bottom of a page.

left
> The browser will always put one or two page breaks after the selected element(s) so that the next element begins at the top of a left-hand (i.e. even-numbered) page in double-sided printing.

right
> The browser will always put one or two page breaks after the selected element(s) so that the next element begins at the top of a right-hand (i.e. odd-numbered) page in double-sided printing.

Initial value: auto

Compatibility

CSS Version: 2

This property works in Internet Explorer 4 or later, Netscape 7 or later, Mozilla, and Opera browsers. All of these browsers treat `left` and `right` the same as `always`.

The `avoid` value is not directly supported by Internet Explorer for Windows; however, if you use a JavaScript to set the property to an empty string (`""`) it will have the same effect.

Example

This style rule keeps every heading on the same page as the first element that follows it, whenever possible:

```
h1, h2, h3, h4, h5, h6 {
  page-break-after: avoid;
}
```

page-break-before

When printing a Web page, the browser simply places page breaks where they need to occur in the content so that all printed pages are as full as possible by default. This property affords you greater control over the placement of page breaks during printing, by letting you manually add or suppress a page break before a given element.

Inherited: No

See also: `orphans`, `page-break-after`, `page-break-inside`, `widows`

Value

This property can take any of the following values:

`always`
    The browser will always put a page break before the selected element(s).

avoid

The browser will try to avoid placing a page break before the selected element(s).

The practical effect of this setting is to keep an element on the same page as the previous sibling element.

auto

The browser will put a page break before the selected element(s) if the previous element ended at the bottom of a page.

left

The browser will always put one or two page breaks before the selected element(s) so that they begin at the top of a left-hand (i.e. even-numbered) page in double-sided printing.

right

The browser will always put one or two page breaks before the selected element(s) so that they begin at the top of a right-hand (i.e. odd-numbered) page in double-sided printing.

Initial value: auto

Compatibility

CSS Version: 2

This property works in Internet Explorer 4 or later, Netscape 7 or later, Mozilla, and Opera browsers. All of these browsers treat left and right the same as always.

The avoid value is not directly supported by Internet Explorer for Windows; however, if you use a JavaScript to set the property to an empty string ("") it will have the same effect.

Example

This style rule adds the necessary page breaks to place all div elements of class section at the top of a right-hand page:

```
div.section {
  page-break-before: right;
}
```

page-break-inside

When printing a Web page, the browser simply places page breaks where they need to occur in the content so that all printed pages are as full as possible by default. This property affords you greater control over the placement of page breaks during printing, by letting you manually prevent page breaks from occurring in the middle of selected elements.

Inherited: Yes

See also: orphans, page-break-after, page-break-before, widows

Value

This property can take any of the following values:

avoid

> The browser will try to avoid placing a page break within the selected element(s).
>
> The practical effect of this setting is to keep all of an element on one page.

auto

> The browser will put a page break within the selected element(s) if the bottom of a page is reached while rendering it.

Initial value: auto

Compatibility

CSS Version: 2

Not supported by any currently-available browser.

Example

This style rule keeps pre elements of class programlisting on one page whenever possible:

```
pre.programlisting {
  page-break-inside: avoid;
}
```

pause

Pauses are used by aural (speaking) browsers for the visually impaired to provide clues to document structure. This is a shorthand property that lets you specify the pause-before and pause-after properties with a single property declaration.

Inherited: No

See also: pause-before, pause-after, speech-rate

Value

One or two time values, each of which is a floating-point number followed by either s (seconds) or ms (milliseconds), or a percentage of the average word time (which is 1/*rate*, where *rate* is the value of the element's spech-rate property).

If one value is specified, it is applied to both the pause-before and pause-after properties. If two values are specified, the first is applied to pause-before, the second to pause-after.

Initial value: Browser-specific

Compatibility

CSS Version: 2

Not supported by any currently-available browser.

Example

This example pauses for half the length of the average word before and after each div element:

```
div {
  pause: 50%;
}
```

pause-after, pause-before

Pauses are used by aural (speaking) browsers for the visually impaired to provide clues to document structure. `pause-before` and `pause-after` let you set the amount of time to pause before and after an element, respectively.

Inherited: No

See also: `pause`, `speech-rate`

Value

Each of these properties takes a time value, each of which is a floating-point number followed by either `s` (seconds) or `ms` (milliseconds), or a percentage of the average word time (which is 1/*rate*, where *rate* is the value of the element's `spech-rate` property).

Initial value: Browser-specific

Compatibility

CSS Version: 2

Not supported by any currently-available browser.

Example

This example pauses for half the length of the average word before each h1 element, with the exception of h1 elements of class `minor`:

```
h1 {
   pause-before: 50%;
}
h1.minor {
   pause-before: none;
}
```

pitch

For use by aural (speaking) browsers for the visually impaired, this property sets the average pitch (frequency) of the voice that reads a selected element's content aloud. Typical male voices are around 120Hz, while female voices average about 210Hz.

Inherited: Yes

See also: `pitch-range`, `richness`, `stress`, `voice-family`, `volume`

Value

A frequency in Hertz (`Hz`) or kiloHertz (`kHz`), or any of the following constants:

- [ ] `x-low`

- [ ] `low`

- [ ] `medium`

- [ ] `high`

- [ ] `x-high`

The actual frequencies that correspond to these constants depend on the `voice-family` property in use.

Initial value: `medium`

Compatibility

CSS Version: 2

Not supported by any currently-available browser.

Example

This example causes aural browsers to speak elements of class `ominous` in a low pitch:

```
.ominous {
  pitch: low;
}
```

pitch-range

For use by aural (speaking) browsers for the visually impaired, this property controls the amount of pitch variation (which affects the perceived level of animation and excitement) in the voice that reads a selected element's content aloud.

Inherited: Yes

See also: `pitch`, `richness`, `stress`, `voice-family`, `volume`

Value

Any integer between 0 and 100, where 0 is a complete monotone, 50 is an average speaking voice, and 100 is extremely animated.

Initial value: 50

Compatibility

CSS Version: 2

Not supported by any currently-available browser.

Example

This example causes aural browsers to speak elements of class `ominous` with an added level of animation:

```
.ominous {
  pitch-range: 75;
}
```

play-during

Intended for use by aural browsers for the visually impaired, this property could have at least one practical use in mainstream browsers: providing a standard way to add background audio to a page. In aural browsers, this property sets the sound played in the background while the contents of a selected element are read aloud.

Inherited: No

See also: cue

Value

Values for this property can take the following format:

```
play-during: url(uri) [mix] [repeat]
```

uri is the relative or absolute URL of the sound file you wish to have played during the reading of this element. The optional keyword mix, when present, causes the element's background sound to be mixed with the background sound of its parent element, instead of replacing it. The optional keyword repeat, when present, causes the sound to be played repeatedly, if it is shorter than the reading of the element content.

Alternatively, this property may be set to either of the following constants:

- ❏ auto

- ❏ none

auto allows the parent element's play-during sound to continue playing while the element is read (as opposed to setting this value to inherit, which would cause it to start again from the beginning). none suppresses the parent element's play-during sound during the reading of the element, allowing it to resume afterward.

Initial value: auto

Compatibility

CSS Version: 2

Not supported by any currently-available browser.

Example

This example plays dirge.wav in the background of a div element of class epitaph:

```
div.epitaph {
  play-during: url(/sounds/dirge.wav) repeat;
}
```

position

This property sets the method used to position an element on the page.

Inherited: No

See also: `bottom`, `left`, `right`, `top`, `z-index`

Value

This property may be set to any of the following constant values:

absolute

The element can be precisely positioned within the **positioning context** in which it resides. In other words, a (`top,left`) position of (0,0) will place the element against the top-left corner of the nearest ancestor that has a `position` setting other than `static`, or the `body` element.

Absolute-positioned elements do not occupy any space in the normal document flow.

fixed

This setting lets you position the element just as with `absolute`, but when the page is scrolled, the element maintains its position in the window instead of scrolling with the rest of the page.

relative

The element can be positioned relative to where it would appear if it were positioned normally with `static`. In other words, a (`top,left`) position of (50,-30) will place the element 50 pixels below and 30 pixels to the left of where it would appear if its position were left up to the browser.

Relative-positioned elements still occupy the space they would be assigned if they were not positioned to begin with. This may sound like a pain, but it comes in handy in some common page layout situations.

One common use of `relative` is to let an element act as a positioning context for one or more `absolute` positioned child elements, without moving it from its normal place in the document flow.

static

> The element is laid out according to normal document flow. The bottom, left, right, and top properties have no effect.

Initial value: static

Compatibility

CSS Version: 2

This property works in all CSS-compatible browsers; however, the fixed property is only correctly supported by Mozilla (including Netscape 6+), Opera 7, and Internet Explorer 5 (Macintosh) browsers. Internet Explorer for Windows (up to and including version 6 in standards-compliant mode) treats fixed exactly like absolute.

Example

This style rule places the element with ID logo 30 pixels from the top and right edges of the browser window (assuming the element is in the body's positioning context), and keeps it there even when the user scrolls the document:

```
#logo {
  position: fixed;
  top: 30px;
  right: 30px;
}
```

The chapters of this book that deal with page layout also contain plenty of examples with which you may experiment.

quotes

The content property of :before and :after pseudo-elements lets you specify **generated content** that should appear before and/or after any element. Among the types of content that can be added are quotation marks. The quotes property lets you define the format of those quotes.

Since you can have quotes within quotes, this property lets you set what the quotes will look like at each nesting level.

Inherited: Yes

See also: content

Value

A space-separated list of pairs of quote strings (see example below), or none. If pairs of strings are provided, the first pair will be used for the first (outermost) level of quotes, the second pair will be used for the first level of nested quotes, and so on. If the none constant is specified, the open-quote and close-quote elements of the content property will not generate any content.

The CSS2 specification does not cover how quotes should be rendered when they are at a nesting level for which quote strings are not provided; presumably, the final pair of quote strings would be used for all deeper nesting levels as well.

Initial value: A browser-specific series of quote strings.

Compatibility

CSS Version: 2

The best support for this property is provided by Opera 7; however, a bug in that browser does affect this feature. If you specify quote strings for n nesting levels, then any quoted elements at nesting level $n+1$ or deeper will have the close-quote string of the deepest specified nesting level as its open-quote string, and double quotes (") for its close-quote string.

Mozilla browsers (including Netscape 6) support this property, but the first pair of quote strings you specify are applied to all nesting levels.

Internet Explorer 5 for Macintosh supports the open-quote and close-quote elements of the content property, but it chooses the quote strings itself, ignoring this property.

Internet Explorer for Windows (up to and including version 6 in standards-compliant mode) does not support generated quotes.

Example

This example uses double quotes for the first (outermost) level of quotes, then single quotes for the second level (and presumably for all deeper levels). This setting is applied to the body element (it is inherited by all nested elements), and then quotes are added to blockquote and q (inline quote) elements:

```
body {
  quotes: '"' '"' "'" "'";
}
blockquote:before, q:before {
  content: open-quote;
}
blockquote:after, q:after {
  content:close-quote;
}
```

richness

For use by aural (speaking) browsers for the visually impaired, this property controls richness/smoothness in the voice that reads a selected element's content aloud (which affects the degree to which the sound "carries").

Inherited: Yes

See also: `pitch`, `pitch-range`, `stress`, `voice-family`, `volume`

Value

Any integer between 0 and 100, where 0 is a soft, mellifluous voice, 50 is an average speaking voice, and 100 is a strident voice.

Initial value: 50

Compatibility

CSS Version: 2

Not supported by any currently-available browser.

Example

This example causes aural browsers to speak elements of class `ominous` more softly than usual:

```
.ominous {
  pitch-range: 30;
}
```

right

This property lets you set the distance between the right edge of an `absolute` positioned element (including its padding, border, and margin)[11] and the right edge of the positioning context in which it resides. The positioning context is the content area of the element's nearest ancestor that has a `position` property value other than `static`, or the `body` element.

For `relative` positioned elements, this property sets a relative offset from the normal position of its bottom edge. So a setting of `10px` will shift the right edge of the box 10 pixels to the left, and a setting of `-10px` will shift it right by the same amount.

Inherited: No

See also: `position`, `bottom`, `left`, and `top`

Value

A CSS length measurement, a percentage value, or the `auto` constant. Percentages are based on the width of the parent element. The `auto` constant tells the browser to determine the position of the right edge itself, based on whatever other constraints may exist on the size/position of the element.

Initial value: `auto`

Compatibility

CSS Version: 2

Works in Internet Explorer 5 or later, Netscape 6 or later, and Mozilla browsers.

Often, the same effect can be achieved by setting the `left` property of a box. Since `left` is supported by more browsers than `right`, this should be done whenever possible.

---

[11]The CSS2 specification contains an error that suggests that the padding, border, and margin of the positioned element should not be considered. This has been acknowledged as a mistake by the CSS Working Group in the Errata document for CSS2.

Example

This style rule positions the element with ID `menu` against the right edge of the document (assuming it is in the body's positioning context):

```
#menu {
  position: absolute;
  right: 0;
  width: 100px;
  height: 200px;
}
```

ruby-align

Ruby text is a new addition in the XHTML 1.1 recommendation and is described by the Ruby Annotation Recommendation[28] of the W3C. Commonly used in Japan and China, ruby text generally appears in a smaller font over the main text as a pronunciation guide, or to provide some other explanatory annotation.

This property sets how the ruby text is aligned with the base text.

Inherited: No

See also: `ruby-overhang`, `ruby-position`

Value

This property accepts any of the following constants:

❏ `auto`

❏ `center`

❏ `distribute-letter`

❏ `distribute-space`

❏ `left`

❏ `line-edge`

---

[28] http://www.w3.org/TR/2001/REC-ruby-20010531/

❑ right

For the meanings of each of these constants, see the CSS3 Ruby module working draft[29] and the Microsoft Internet Explorer documentation for this property[30].

Initial value: auto

Compatibility

CSS Version: n/a

This property is supported only in Internet Explorer for Windows version 5 or later. In that browser, this property must be applied to the ruby element that contains the ruby text (rt) element for which you wish to set the alignment.

Equivalent functionality is planned for inclusion in CSS3, and the current working draft suggests that this property will be as documented here. To follow the work on this front, see the CSS Working Group Web site[31].

Example

This style rule centers ruby text over the base text:

```
ruby {
  ruby-align: center;
}
```

ruby-overhang

Ruby text is a new addition in the XHTML 1.1 recommendation and is described by the Ruby Annotation Recommendation[32] of the W3C. Commonly used in Japan and China, ruby text generally appears in a smaller font over the main text as a pronunciation guide, or to provide some other explanatory annotation.

This property controls whether ruby text is allowed to extend over adjacent text or whitespace, if it is longer than the base text it annotates.

Inherited: No

[29] http://www.w3.org/TR/css3-ruby/
[30] http://msdn.microsoft.com/workshop/author/dhtml/reference/properties/rubyalign.asp
[31] http://www.w3.org/TR/css3-ruby/
[32] http://www.w3.org/TR/2001/REC-ruby-20010531/

See also: `ruby-align`, `ruby-position`

Value

This property accepts any of the following constants:

☐ `auto`

☐ `none`

☐ `whitespace`

For the meanings of each of these constants, see the CSS3 Ruby module working draft[33] and the Microsoft Internet Explorer documentation for this property[34].

Initial value: `auto`

Compatibility

CSS Version: n/a

This property is supported only in Internet Explorer for Windows version 5 or later. In that browser, this property must be applied to the `ruby` element that contains the ruby text (`rt`) element for which you wish to set the alignment.

Equivalent functionality is planned for inclusion in CSS3, and the current working draft suggests that this property will be as documented here. To follow the work on this front, see the CSS Working Group Web site[35].

Example

This style rule allows ruby text to overhang whitespace adjacent to the base text only:

```
ruby {
  ruby-overhang: whitespace;
}
```

---

[33] http://www.w3.org/TR/css3-ruby/
[34] http://msdn.microsoft.com/workshop/author/dhtml/reference/properties/rubyalign.asp
[35] http://www.w3.org/TR/css3-ruby/

ruby-position

Ruby text is a new addition in the XHTML 1.1 recommendation and is described by the Ruby Annotation Recommendation[36] of the W3C. Commonly used in Japan and China, ruby text generally appears in a smaller font over the main text as a pronunciation guide, or to provide some other explanatory annotation.

This property controls where the ruby text is positioned in relation to its base text.

Inherited: No

See also: ruby-align, ruby-overhang

Value

In Internet Explorer for Windows version 5 or later, this property accepts the following constants:

❏ above

❏ inline

The current working draft of CSS3, however, proposes the following values:

❏ after

❏ before

❏ right

For the meanings of each of these sets of constants, see the Microsoft Internet Explorer documentation for this property[37] and the CSS3 Ruby module working draft[38], respectively.

Initial value:

❏ Internet Explorer: above

---

[36] http://www.w3.org/TR/2001/REC-ruby-20010531/
[37] http://msdn.microsoft.com/workshop/author/dhtml/reference/properties/rubyalign.asp
[38] http://www.w3.org/TR/css3-ruby/

☐ CSS3 draft: before

Compatibility

CSS Version: n/a

This property is supported only in Internet Explorer for Windows version 5 or later. In that browser, this property must be applied to the `ruby` element that contains the ruby text (`rt`) element for which you wish to set the alignment.

Equivalent functionality is planned for inclusion in CSS3, but the proposed property values differ from those supported by Internet Explorer for Windows. To follow the work on this front, see the CSS Working Group Web site[39].

Example

This style rule places ruby text inline with instead of above the base text in Internet Explorer for Windows:

```
ruby {
  ruby-position: inline;
}
```

scrollbar-base-color

This nonstandard property is provided by Internet Explorer for Windows version 5.5 or later to let the page designer control the overall color of the scrollbar(s) associated with an element. The browser will use the specified color as a basis for choosing the actual colors of all the parts of the scrollbars.

The colors of individual parts of the scrollbars can be controlled precisely with the `scrollbar-element-color` properties.

Inherited: Yes

See also: `scrollbar-element-color`

Value

Any CSS color value. See Appendix B.

---

[39] http://www.w3.org/TR/css3-ruby/

Initial value: depends on user configuration

Compatibility

CSS Version: n/a

This nonstandard property works only in Internet Explorer for Windows version 5.5 or later, and is disabled in Internet Explorer 6 when running in standards-compliant mode[40].

Example

This style rule sets the overall scrollbar color to blue on `textarea` elements:

```
textarea {
  scrollbar-base-color: blue;
}
```

scrollbar-element-color

This collection of nonstandard properties is provided by Internet Explorer for Windows version 5.5 or later to let the page designer control the colors of various parts of the scrollbar(s) associated with an element. The actual property names, along with their meanings, are listed in Table C.9.

---

[40] http://msdn.microsoft.com/library/en-us/dnie60/html/cssenhancements.asp

Table C.9. Internet Explorer scrollbar properties

Property	Affected area(s)
`scrollbar-3dLight-color`	outer top and left edges of the scrollbar buttons and thumb
`scrollbar-arrow-color`	up and down arrows in the scrollbar buttons
`scrollbar-darkShadow-color`	outer right and bottom edges of the scrollbar buttons and thumb
`scrollbar-face-color`	interior areas of the scrollbar buttons and thumb
`scrollbar-highlight-color`	inner top and left edges of the scrollbar buttons and thumb
`scrollbar-shadow-color`	inner right and bottom edges of the scrollbar buttons and thumb
`scrollbar-track-color`	background of the scrollbar, outside the scrollbar buttons and thumb

Inherited: Yes

See also: `scrollbar-base-color`

Value

Any CSS color value. See Appendix B.

Initial values: depend on user configuration

Compatibility

CSS Version: n/a

These nonstandard properties works only in Internet Explorer for Windows version 5.5 or later, and are disabled in Internet Explorer 6 when running in standards-compliant mode[41].

---

[41] http://msdn.microsoft.com/library/en-us/dnie60/html/cssenhancements.asp

Example

This style rule removes the 3D appearance of the scrollbars around `textarea` elements, displaying them in flat black and white instead:

```
textarea {
  scrollbar-3dLight-color: black;
  scrollbar-arrow-color: black;
  scrollbar-darkShadow-color: black;
  scrollbar-face-color: white;
  scrollbar-highlight-color: white;
  scrollbar-shadow-color: white;
  scrollbar-track-color: black;
}
```

size

This property, which can appear only within a @page at-rule (see the section called "At-Rules") lets you control the page size and/or orientation as needed.

Value

This property can take a number of constants, or specific page measurements.

Supported constants are:

❏ auto

❏ landscape

❏ portrait

auto tells the browser to use a page size/orientation equal to the printer settings, while landscape and portrait force the browser to rotate the page as necessary to print in the specified orientation on the printer's paper size.

Alternatively, you can specify an exact page size with either one or two CSS length values (separated by spaces). If only one value is specified, it is used as both the width and height; otherwise, the first value is the page width and the second is the page height.

Initial value: auto

Compatibility

CSS Version: 2

Not supported any current browser.

Example

This style rule specifies that the page should be printed in landscape orientation on a Letter-sized (8.5 by 11 inch) page:

```
@page {
    size: 11in 8.5in;
}
```

speak

For use by aural (speaking) browsers for the visually impaired, this property controls if and how an element's content should be read aloud.

Inherited: Yes

See also: speak-header, speak-numeral, speak-punctuation

Value

This property accepts any of the following constants:

☐ none: The element's content is not read.

☐ normal: The element's content is read normally.

☐ spell-out: The element's content is spelled out one character at a time.

Initial value: normal

Compatibility

CSS Version: 2

Not supported by any currently-available browser.

Example

This example causes aural browsers to spell out abbr and acronym elements:

```
abbr, acronym {
    speak: spell-out;
}
```

speak-header

For use by aural (speaking) browsers for the visually impaired, this property controls how table headers are read. As the browser reads out the contents of each cell in the table, it can either read all the headers for each cell before the cell's contents, or read only those headers that are different from the headers of the previously-read cell.

Inherited: Yes

See also: speak, speak-numeral, speak-punctuation

Value

This property accepts any of the following constants:

❑ always: For each cell, all the headers that apply to it are read first.

❑ once: For each cell, only headers that are different from the previously-read cell are read.

Initial value: once

Compatibility

CSS Version: 2

Not supported by any currently-available browser.

Example

This example causes aural browsers to read all the headers that apply to each cell in a table of class matrix:

```
table.matrix {
  speak-header: always;
}
```

speak-numeral

For use by aural (speaking) browsers for the visually impaired, this property controls how numbers are read. A number may be read either as a series of digits (e.g. "one two three") or as a whole number (e.g. "one hundred twenty-three").

Inherited: Yes

See also: speak, speak-header, speak-punctuation

Value

This property accepts any of the following constants:

❑ digits: The number is read as a series of digits.

❑ continuous: The number is read as a whole number.

Initial value: continuous

Compatibility

CSS Version: 2

Not supported by any currently-available browser.

Example

This example causes aural browsers to read numbers occurring in any element of class binary as a series of digits:

```
.binary {
  speak-numeral: digits;
}
```

speak-punctuation

For use by aural (speaking) browsers for the visually impaired, this property controls how punctuation is read. Punctuation may either be read aloud (e.g. "period") or represented by pauses in the reading of surrounding text.

Inherited: Yes

See also: speak, speak-header, speak-numeral

Value

This property accepts any of the following constants:

❑ code: Punctuation is read aloud

❑ none: Punctuation is implied by natural pauses

Initial value: none

Compatibility

CSS Version: 2

Not supported by any currently-available browser.

Example

This example causes aural browsers to read aloud punctuation occurring in any element of class spokenpunct:

```
.spokenpunct {
  speak-punctuation: code;
}
```

speech-rate

For use by aural (speaking) browsers for the visually impaired, this property controls how quickly (or slowly) the content of an element is read.

Inherited: Yes

See also: pause

Value

You can specify the exact speech rate in words per minute as a positive, floating-point number.

This property also accepts any of the constants in Table C.10.

Table C.10. speech-rate constants

Constant	Effect
x-slow	80 words per minute
slow	120 words per minute
medium	180 to 120 words per minute
fast	300 words per minute
x-fast	500 words per minute
slower	the inherited rate minus 40 words per minute
faster	the inherited rate plus 40 words per minute

Initial value: medium

Compatibility

CSS Version: 2

Not supported by any currently-available browser.

Example

This example causes aural browsers to read elements of class ominous more slowly than usual:

```
.ominous {
  speech-rate: slower;
}
```

stress

For use by aural (speaking) browsers for the visually impaired, this property controls stress in the voice that reads a selected element's content aloud. In English, for example, every sentence usually contains particular words that are emphasized more heavily than others. This property controls how great the difference is between emphasized and non-emphasized passages.

Inherited: Yes

See also: `pitch`, `pitch-range`, `richness`, `voice-family`, `volume`

Value

Any integer between 0 and 100, 50 is an average level of stress.

Initial value: 50

Compatibility

CSS Version: 2

Not supported by any currently-available browser.

Example

This example causes aural browsers to speak elements of class `ominous` with greater stress than usual:

```
.ominous {
  stress: 75;
}
```

table-layout

This property lets you accelerate table rendering by allowing it to take a shortcut in calculating the column sizes. When `table-layout` is set to `fixed`, the browser considers only the cells in the first row to determine the cell widths (and overall table width) for the table. This allows the table to be rendered one row at a time, instead of having to wait for the full table to load before any of it is displayed.

Be aware that wider content in subsequent table rows will be clipped to the column widths set by the first row when the fixed table layout mode is used.

Inherited: No

See also: `max-height`, `min-height`

Value

`auto` or `fixed`

Initial value: `auto`

Compatibility

CSS Version: 2

This property is supported by Internet Explorer for Windows version 5 or later and Opera 7.

Example

This style rule sets tables of class `thumbnails` to the quicker, fixed layout mode:

```
table.thumbnails {
  table-layout: fixed;
}
```

text-align

This property sets the horizontal alignment of text and other inline content within a block element.

If you're looking for a way to set the horizontal alignment of a block (e.g. to center it on the page), you should instead use the `margin-left`, `margin-right`, `left`, and `right` properties to achieve the desired effect (e.g. you can center a block horizontally by setting its left and right margins to `auto`).

Inherited: Yes

See also: `text-align-last`, `vertical-align`

Value

This property supports the following constant values:

- [ ] `center`

- [ ] `justify`

- [ ] `left`

- [ ] `right`

`center`, `left`, and `right` are self-explanatory. `justify` should be familiar to users of word processors; it causes the words on each line to be spaced out so that each line starts and ends against the edge of the content box, with the exception of the last line.

New in CSS2, you can specify a string for text in table cells to align on. E.g. the value `"."` would cause values in table cells to be aligned so that the decimal points all line up vertically. This type of value has only an effect on table cells; other elements will treat it as the initial value.

Initial value: depends on the language of the browser and/or the element

Compatibility

CSS Version: 1 (string alignment for tables added in CSS2)

This property is supported by all CSS-compatible browsers.

In older browsers (most version 4 browsers), `justify` behaves the same as `left`; however, this is allowable under the CSS2 standard.

String alignment in table cells is not supported by any currently-available browser.

Example

This style rule will justify text within the `body` and all child elements, unless otherwise specified (thanks to inheritance):

```
body {
  text-align: justify;
}
```

text-align-last

This nonstandard property, supported by Internet Explorer for Windows version 5.5 or later, lets you specifically set the alignment of the last line of text within a block element whose `text-align` property is set to `justify`.

This property is ignored when the `text-align` property is not set to `justify`.

Inherited: Yes

See also: `text-align`

Value

This property supports the following constant values:

- ❏ `auto`

- ❏ `center`

- ❏ `justify`

- ❏ `left`

- ❏ `right`

`auto` allows the last line to reflect the alignment set by the `text-align` property.

Initial value: `auto`

Compatibility

CSS Version: n/a

Supported by Internet Explorer for Windows version 5.5 or later only.

Example

This style rule causes the last line of a `blockquote` element to be right-aligned:

```
blockquote {
  text-align: justify;
```

```
    text-align-last: right;
}
```

text-autospace

This property lets you choose between a number of methods for increasing the space between ideographic characters (in Asian languages) and non-ideographic characters (non-Asian languages).

Inherited: No

Value

This property accepts any of the following constant values:

- ❏ `ideograph-alpha`: extra space between ideographic and non-ideographic characters

- ❏ `ideograph-numeric`: extra space between ideographic and numeric characters

- ❏ `ideograph-parenthesis`: extra space between ideographic characters and parentheses

- ❏ `ideograph-space`: extra space between ideographic characters and whitespace

- ❏ `none`: no extra space

Initial value: none

Compatibility

CSS Version: n/a

Internet Explorer 5 or later for Windows only.

Equivalent functionality is planned for inclusion in CSS3, but combinations of the above values will likely be allowed. To follow the work on this front, see the CSS Working Group Web site[42].

---

[42] http://www.w3.org/TR/2003/WD-css3-text-20030226/#text-autospace-prop

Example

This style rule adds extra spacing between ideographic and non-ideographic characters in paragraphs of class `mixed`:

```
p.mixed {
  text-autospace: ideograph-alpha;
}
```

text-decoration

This property lets you add one or more "decorations" to the text within an element. Decorations include overlining, underlining, striking through, and blinking.

Although this property is not inherited, specifying it on an element will apply the decoration through the whole element, including child elements.

Inherited: No

Value

This property can be set to `none` to remove any decoration specified in a lower-priority rule (e.g. to remove the underline applied to hyperlinks in the default style sheets of visual browsers).

Otherwise, it can take any space-delimited combination of the following constants:

☐ `blink`[12]

☐ `line-through`

☐ `overline`

☐ `underline`

Initial value: none

Compatibility

CSS Version: 1

---

[12]The author begs you not to use this.

This property works in all CSS-compatible browsers; however, the `blink` decoration type is (mercifully) not supported in Internet Explorer browsers.

Example

This style rule removes the underline from hyperlinks in the document and replaces it with a dashed bottom border:

```
a:link, a:visited {
  text-decoration: none;
  border-bottom: 1px solid dashed;
}
```

text-indent

This property sets the indent applied to the first line of a block element (and its children, thanks to inheritance).

A negative value will result in a hanging indent, with the text of the first line protruding from the content area of the block. You will usually want to balance a negative `text-indent` with a positive `padding-left` value of the same or greater size to keep all the text within the border of the block.

Inherited: Yes

See also: `padding`

Value

Any CSS length value (`px`, `pt`, `em`, etc.), or a percentage of the parent element's width.

Initial value: 0

Compatibility

CSS Version: 1

This property is supported by all CSS-compatible browsers.

Example

This style rule creates a one-centimeter hanging indent on all paragraphs by using a negative text-indent in combination with a padding-left value of the same size:

```
p {
  text-indent: -1cm;
  padding-left: 1cm;
}
```

text-justify

This nonstandard property, supported by Internet Explorer for Windows version 5 or later, controls the algorithm used to calculate spacing in blocks with text-align set to justify. This property is designed for use with Asian languages where "words" do not necessarily occur, and therefore the adaptive word spacing usually associated with justified text does not have a clear meaning.

Inherited: Yes

See also: text-align, text-kashida-space

Value

This property will accept any one of the following constant values:

- ❏ auto: allows the browser to choose which algorithm to use

- ❏ distribute: letter spacing and word spacing is increased by the same amount

- ❏ distribute-all-lines: same as distribute, but also applies to the last line

- ❏ inter-cluster: same as distribute, but does not add space between characters of Southeast Asian grapheme clusters

- ❏ inter-ideograph: same as distribute, but does not add space between non-Chinese/Japanese/Korean characters

- ❏ inter-word: the familiar method for Latin languages like English, adds only space between words

❏ `kashida`: uses elongated strokes in Arabic characters to justify text

❏ `newspaper`: same as `distribute`, but preference is given to inter-word spacing over inter-character spacing

Initial value: `auto`

Compatibility

CSS Version: n/a

Internet Explorer 5 or later for Windows only. The `kashida` mode is supported only by version 5.5 or later.

Equivalent functionality is planned for inclusion in CSS3, but final property names and values are likely to differ. To follow the work on this front, see the CSS Working Group Web site[43].

Example

This style rule specifies the `newspaper` justification mode for `div` elements of class `column`:

```
div.column {
  text-align: justify;
  text-justify: newspaper;
}
```

text-kashida-space

This nonstandard property, supported by Internet Explorer for Windows version 5.5 or later, controls the degree to which the browser relies on kashida expansion to achieve justified alignment. This property is designed for use with Arabic languages, where certain horizontal lines in the script can be extended to lengthen words.

For this property to have a useful effect, affected elements must have their `text-align` property set to `justify`, and their `text-justify` property set to a mode that allows kashida expansion (`auto`, `distribute`, `kashida`, or `newspaper`).

---

[43] http://www.w3.org/TR/2003/WD-css3-text-20030226/#justification-prop

Inherited: Yes

See also: `text-align`, `text-justify`

Value

A percentage ratio between kashida expansion and whitespace expansion, where 100% will result in only kashida expansion and 0% will result in only whitespace expansion.

Initial value: 0%

Compatibility

CSS Version: n/a

Internet Explorer 5.5 or later for Windows only.

Equivalent functionality is planned for inclusion in CSS3, but final property names and values are likely to differ. To follow the work on this front, see the CSS Working Group Web site[44].

Example

This style rule specifies that for every 2 units of whitespace that are added, 1 unit of kashida expansion is added:

```
div.column {
  text-align: justify;
  text-kashida-space: 33%;
}
```

text-overflow

This nonstandard property, supported by Internet Explorer 6 for Windows, lets you handle text that is clipped by the width of an element more elegantly. The portion of the string that would normally overflow the edge of the box is replaced with an ellipsis (...).

[44] http://www.w3.org/TR/2003/WD-css3-text-20030226/#kashida-prop

The element must have its `overflow` property set to something other than `visible` (although `hidden` is the only value that really makes sense) for this property to have any effect.

Note that this property affects only text that is clipped by the *width* of the element (or the height in vertical writing systems), either because word-wrapping is disabled with the `white-space` property, or because a long word or other non-wrappable text segment is too long to fit in the box.

Inherited: No

See also: `overflow`, `white-space`, `width`

Value

This property can be set to either of these two constants:

☐ `clip`

☐ `ellipsis`

Initial value: `clip`

Compatibility

CSS Version: n/a

Internet Explorer for Windows version 6 or later only.

Example

This style rule specifies that text within table cells should not be wrapped, and that text that does not fit within a cell should be shown with an ellipsis:

```
td {
  white-space: nowrap;
  overflow: hidden;
  text-overflow: ellipsis;
}
```

text-shadow

This property lets you create drop-shadow effects behind text. A drop-shadow is a copy of the text rendered behind the actual text of the element, usually offset from the element's position and in a different color, and possibly blurred, which simulates light hitting the text and casting a shadow against the element's background. This property lets you create multiple drop-shadows for a single piece of text to simulate multiple light sources.

Inherited: No

Value

The syntax for this is as shown here:

```
text-shadow: [color] xOffset yOffset [blurRadius][, [color]
  xOffset yOffset [blurRadius] ...]
```

Each shadow is declared in a comma-separated sequence from bottom to top (i.e. the shadow declared last will be rendered over all the others). For each shadow, you can specify an optional *color* for the shadow. If none is specified, the color property of the element is used. Next, you must specify horizontal and vertical offsets for the shadow (*xOffset* and *yOffset*, respectively) as CSS lengths (px, pt, em, etc.). Positive offsets shift the shadow down and to the right, while negative offsets shift it up and to the left. Finally, you may specify a blur radius (*blurRadius*), again as a CSS length, if you want the shadow to display a blurred appearance.

This property can also be set to none for no shadows.

Initial value: none

Compatibility

CSS Version: 2

Not supported by any currently-available browser.

Example

This style rule sets any element of class `phantom` to show white text against a white background and to have a highly blurred, black shadow that reveals the shape of the text:

```
.phantom {
  color: #fff;
  background-color: #fff;
  text-shadow: black 0.5em 0.5em 0.5em;
}
```

text-transform

This property causes the text of selected element(s) to be case-modified for display. Text can be displayed capitalized, uppercase, or lowercase.

Inherited: Yes

Value

This property may be assigned any one of the following constant values:

❏ `capitalize`: The first letter of each word is displayed in uppercase.

❏ `lowercase`: All characters in the text are displayed in lowercase.

❏ `uppercase`: All characters in the text are displayed in uppercase.

❏ `none`: The text is displayed unmodified.

Initial value: none

Compatibility

CSS Version: 1

This property is supported by all CSS-compatible browsers.

Example

This style rule displays all headings in capitalized text (the first letter of each word is capitalized):

```
h1, h2, h3, h4, h5, h6 {
  text-transform: capitalize;
}
```

text-underline-position

This nonstandard property, supported by Internet Explorer for Windows version 5.5 or later, controls whether underlines are drawn above or below text inside the selected element(s). This property is designed for use with Asian languages and other vertical writing systems.

For this property to have a visible effect, an affected element (or one of its children) must have its `text-decoration` property set to `underline`.

Inherited: Yes

See also: `text-decoration`

Value

This property will accept either of these two constant values:

- ❑ `auto` or `auto-pos`: The underline is drawn above the text if the language is set to `ja` (Japanese) and `writing-mode` is set to `tb-rl`.

- ❑ `above`: The underline is drawn above the text.

- ❑ `below`: The underline is drawn below the text.

Initial value:

- ❑ Internet Explorer 6 or later: `auto`

- ❑ Internet Explorer 5.5: `below`

Compatibility

CSS Version: n/a

Internet Explorer for Windows version 5.5 or later only. The `auto` and `auto-pos` values are supported only in version 6 or later.

Equivalent functionality is planned for inclusion in CSS3, but final property names and values are likely to differ. To follow the work on this front, see the CSS Working Group Web site[45].

Example

This style rule specifies that underlines should always be drawn below the text, even in vertical, Japanese text:

```
body {
  text-underline-position: below;
}
```

top

This property lets you set the distance between the top edge of an `absolute` positioned element (including its padding, border, and margin)[13] and the top edge of the positioning context in which it resides. The positioning context is the content area of the element's nearest ancestor that has a `position` property value other than `static`, or the `body` element.

For `relative` positioned elements, this property sets a relative offset from the normal position of its top edge. So, a setting of `10px` will shift the top edge of the box 10 pixels downward, and a setting of `-10px` will shift it 10 pixels upward.

Inherited: No

See also: `position`, `bottom`, `left`, and `right`

---

[45] http://www.w3.org/TR/2003/WD-css3-text-20030226/#text-decoration-other
[13] The CSS2 specification contains an error that suggests that the padding, border, and margin of the positioned element should not be considered. This has been acknowledged as a mistake by the CSS Working Group in the Errata document for CSS2.

Value

A CSS length measurement, a percentage value, or the `auto` constant. Percentages are based on the height of the parent element. The `auto` constant tells the browser to determine the position of the top edge itself, based on whatever other constraints may exist on the size/position of the element.

Initial value: `auto`

Compatibility

CSS Version: 2

Supported by all CSS-compatible browsers, including Internet Explorer 4 or later, Netscape 4 or later, and Mozilla browsers.

Example

This style rule positions the element with ID `menu` 10 pixels from the top edge of the window:

```
#menu {
  position: absolute;
  top: 10px;
}
```

unicode-bidi

Most western languages are written left-to-right (LTR). As you probably know, many other languages (e.g. Hebrew) are written right-to-left (RTL). Documents written with the Unicode character set[46] can contain text from both LTR and RTL languages. The Unicode standard includes a complicated algorithm that should be used for displaying such mixed text. It also defines special characters that let you "group" text.

For example, consider the following imaginary string of text, where the lowercase text represents LTR characters and the uppercase text represents RTL:

```
english1 HEBREW1 english2 HEBREW2 english3
```

---

[46] http://www.unicode.org/

Now, the obvious way to render this would be "english1 1WERBEH english2 2WERBEH english3", but what if we add some HTML tags to the mix?

```
<p>english1 <q>HEBREW1 english2 HEBREW2</q> english3</p>
```

As you can see, the text beginning with HEBREW1 and ending with HEBREW2 is intended as an inline quotation in Hebrew, which just happens to contain an English word. Since HEBREW1 and HEBREW2 belong to the same block of Hebrew text, "2WERBEH" should be rendered to the left or "1WERBEH". With this in mind, the complete paragraph should be rendered as "english1 2WERBEH english2 1WERBEH english3".

The HTML 4.0 standard (along with XHTML 1.0) defines the dir attribute and the bdo element to handle these complexities. To obtain the desired rendering in an HTML4-compatible browser, the code should be:

```
<p>english1 <q lang="he" dir="rtl">HEBREW1 english2 HEBREW2</q>
   english3</p>
```

The dir attribute of the q tag is what specifies the rendering order; the lang attribute won't have any actual visible effect. For full details on language and bidirectional text rendering in HTML, refer to Section 8 of the HTML 4.0 standard[47].

So, where does CSS come into play, you ask? Well, the direction property, in combination with a unicode-bidi property setting of embed, performs the same role as the HTML dir attribute. In combination with a unicode-bidi property setting of bidi-override, direction has the same effect as the HTML bdo tag. It is still considered best practice, however, to include bidirectional text attributes as part of the HTML code. The direction and unicode-bidi properties are intended for use in styling XML documents that do not have the benefit of HTML 4's bidirectional text features. Since the focus of this book is on Web development, I'll therefore refer you to the CSS2 standard[48] for full details on these properties.

Inherited: No

See also: direction

Value

This property will accept any one of these three constant values:

[47] http://www.w3.org/TR/REC-html40/struct/dirlang.html
[48] http://www.w3.org/TR/REC-CSS2/visuren.html#direction

- ❏ normal: The element is treated normally for purposes of bidirectional text rendering; LTR text is rendered LTR and RTL text is rendered RTL. The direction property has no effect on the element.

- ❏ embed: The element behaves as an embedded sequence of LTR or RTL text, as set by the direction property. This is equivalent to setting the HTML dir property on the element.

- ❏ bidi-override: All text inside the element, whether LTR or RTL, is rendered in the direction set by the direction property. This is equivalent to using an HTML bdo tag with the equivalent dir attribute value.

Initial value: normal

Compatibility

CSS Version: 2

Not supported by any currently-available browser.

Example

This style rule sets the text direction of an imaginary XML element named hebrew to rtl. The unicode-bidi property setting in this case ensures that all text within the hebrew element (even text that would normally be displayed LTR according to the Unicode standard) will be displayed RTL.

```
hebrew {
    direction: rtl;
    unicode-bidi: bidi-override;
}
```

vertical-align

This property sets the vertical alignment of text and other inline content with respect to either its parent element's font or the line in which it appears.

This value also lets you set the vertical alignment of content within table cells.

Inherited: No

See also: text-align

Value

This property supports a range of constant values as well as CSS measurements and percentages.

The majority of the supported constants for this property align text and other inline content with respect to the parent element's font:

baseline
> The baseline[14] of the content will line up with the baseline of the parent element's font. If the content has no baseline (e.g. an image), then the bottom of the content is lined up with the baseline of the parent element's font.

middle
> The content is aligned so that its vertical midpoint lines up with a point that is half the parent element font's x-height[15] above the parent element's baseline.

sub
> The content is aligned so that its baseline is positioned some distance below the parent element's baseline, suitable for subscript text. You will usually want to set a smaller `font-size` property for the content as well.

super
> The content is aligned so that its baseline is positioned some distance above the parent element's baseline, suitable for superscript text. You will usually want to set a smaller `font-size` property for the content as well.

text-bottom
> The content is aligned so that its bottom lines up with the bottom of the parent element's font. This position is independent of the actual line height.

text-top
> The content is aligned so that its top lines up with the top of the parent element's font. This position is independent of the actual line height.

As with the above constants, setting the vertical position with a numerical value gives a position relative to the parent element's font:

---

[14]The baseline is the imaginary line on which text is written. The bottoms of letters rest on the baseline, with descenders extending below it.
[15]The x-height is the height of lowercase letters in a font.

length

A CSS length (px, pt, em, etc.) shifts the content's baseline—or bottom, if no baseline exists—up or down from the parent element's baseline for positive or negative values, respectively.

percentage

A percentage (e.g. 50%) shifts the content's baseline—or bottom, if no baseline exists—up or down from the parent element's baseline by a percentage of the element's line-height property for positive or negative values, respectively.

Finally, two additional constants let you set the vertical position, with respect to the line in which the content appears. This may be considerably different from the parent element's font (e.g. if the line contains a tall image that increases the overall line height).

bottom

The content is aligned so that its bottom (not its baseline) rests against the bottom of the line area.

top

The content is aligned so that its top rests against the top of the line area.

When applied to table cells, this property does not support sub, super, text-bottom, or text-top—all of these behave like baseline. The constants bottom, middle, and top refer to the cell box, while baseline ensures that the first line of each cell shares the same baseline as the other cells in the same row.

Initial value: baseline

Compatibility

CSS Version: 1 (the *length* value format was added in CSS2)

This property is supported by Internet Explorer 4 or later, Opera, and Mozilla browsers (including Netscape 6 or later).

Internet Explorer for Windows supports only baseline, sub, and super in version 5 or earlier. Version 5.5 or later supports the other constants, but only on HTML elements that support the valign attribute (i.e. table cells). Internet Explorer for Windows does not support setting length or percentage values for this property.

Example

This style rule will align content within table header cells (th) to the vertical middle of the cell:

```
th {
  vertical-align: middle;
}
```

visibility

This property lets you set whether an element is visible or not. When an element is invisible, it is not displayed at all; however, it still occupies the space on the page that it would if it were visible. To hide an element so that it does not occupy any space on the page, set the display property to none instead.

Inherited: Yes

See also: display

Value

This property will accept any one of the following constant values:

❑ collapse: When applied to a row (tr), row group (thead, tbody, tfoot), column (col), or column group (colgroup) element, this setting causes the row(s) or column(s) to be visibly removed from the table, allowing the table to shrink accordingly. For other elements, this setting has the same effect as hidden.

❑ hidden: The element is not visible, but still occupies space in the document.

❑ visible: The element is displayed as normal.

Initial value: visible

Compatibility

CSS Version: 2

All CSS-compatible browsers support this property, but none yet support the collapse value.

Netscape 4 allows only the `visibility` property to be set on elements whose `position` property set to `absolute` or `relative`.

Example

This style rule hides elements with class `active`. Using dynamic HTML, these elements could be shown in response to some user event.

```
.active {
  visibility: hidden;
}
```

voice-family

For use by aural (speaking) browsers for the visually impaired, this property controls the **voice family** used to read the content of the element. A voice family embodies the vocal attributes of a particular character, and is the aural analogue to the `font-family` property.

Inherited: Yes

See also: `pitch`, `pitch-range`, `richness`, `stress`, `volume`

Value

A comma-separated list of voice names. Voice names that contain spaces should be quoted (e.g. `"Albert Einstein"`).

In addition to actual voice names, the list can contain any of the following generic voice names:

☐ `male`

☐ `female`

☐ `child`

Since browsers will always be able to find a voice for each of these generic voice names, it only makes sense for the last name in the `voice-family` list to be one of these.

Initial value: browser specific

Compatibility

CSS Version: 2

Not supported by any currently-available browser.

Example

This example causes aural browsers to speak elements of class `ominous` in the voice of Igor, or in any male voice if the Igor voice family is not supported:

```
.ominous {
  voice-family: igor, male;
}
```

volume

For use by aural (speaking) browsers for the visually impaired, this property sets the median volume (loudness) of the voice that reads a selected element's content aloud.

Inherited: Yes

See also: `pitch`, `pitch-range`, `richness`, `stress`, `voice-family`

Value

An absolute volume between 0 and 100 (inclusive), a percentage of the inherited volume, or one of the following constants:

- ❏ `silent`: no sound at all
- ❏ `x-soft`: the lowest perceptible volume, the same as 0
- ❏ `soft`: equivalent to 25
- ❏ `medium`: equivalent to 50
- ❏ `loud`: equivalent to 75
- ❏ `x-loud`: the maximum comfortable volume, the same as 100

Initial value: `medium`

Compatibility

CSS Version: 2

Not supported by any currently-available browser.

Example

This example causes aural browsers to speak elements of class `ominous` in a soft voice:

```
.ominous {
  volume: soft;
}
```

white-space

Experienced HTML designers will be accustomed to the fact that whitespace in HTML source code (sequences spaces, tabs, and line breaks) is collapsed to a single space character in the rendered output, and that line breaks occur only due to normal word wrapping performed by the browser or due to a hard break (`<br/>`) tag. Non-breaking space characters (` `), the `nowrap` attribute in table tags, and the HTML `<pre>` tag can be used to work around this behavior, when necessary.

The `white-space` property lets you assign the special properties of these work-arounds to other document elements so that the document code need not reflect the intended formatting.

Inherited: Yes

Value

This property will accept any one of the following constant values:

☐ `normal`: Content is rendered with the default HTML behavior. Whitespace is collapsed and word wrapping is performed.

❏ nowrap: Whitespace is collapsed as with normal, but word wrapping does not occur. Line breaks will occur only when specified with <br/> tags or when present in generated content (see content).

❏ pre: Whitespace is not collapsed and word wrapping does not occur. This type of rendering is the default for <pre> tags, except the font-family of the element is not set to monospace.

Initial value: normal

Compatibility

CSS Version: 1

This property is fully supported in Mozilla browsers (including Netscape 6 or later), Opera, and Internet Explorer 5 for Macintosh.

Internet Explorer for Windows supports this property as of version 5.5; however, the pre value is supported only in version 6, and then only when running in standards-compliant mode[49].

Netscape 4 supports this property with the exception of the nowrap value.

Example

This style rule will preserve whitespace and suppress word wrapping on div elements of class screen:

```
div.screen {
  white-space: pre;
}
```

widows

This property affects the position of page breaks when the user prints the page from his or her browser. With this property, you can specify the minimum number of lines that must remain in a block following a page break.

For example, if a paragraph element had six lines and the page size called for a page break to occur after the fourth line, then an orphans setting of 3 would

---

[49] http://msdn.microsoft.com/library/en-us/dnie60/html/cssenhancements.asp

force the page break to occur *before* the paragraph so that the last 3 lines could appear on the same page.

Inherited: Yes

See also: orphans

Value

A positive integer.

Initial value: 2

Compatibility

CSS Version: 2

This property is supported by Mozilla browsers (including Netscape 6 or later), Opera 7, and Internet Explorer 5 for Macintosh.

Example

This style rule indicates that page breaks must allow at least four lines of a broken paragraph to appear at the top of the next page after the break occurs:

```
p {
  widows: 4;
}
```

width

This property sets the width of the contents of a block or replaced[16] element. This width does not include padding, borders, or margins.

If the contents of a block require more horizontal space than the width you assign, the behavior is defined by the overflow property.

Inherited: No

---

[16]A replaced element is any element whose appearance and dimensions are defined by an external resource. Examples include images (img tags), plug-ins (object tags), and form fields (input and select tags). Another way to think of replaced elements is any element that can be displayed inline with text and that acts as a single, big character for the purposes of wrapping and layout.

See also: `height`, `max-width`, `min-width`, `overflow`, `text-overflow`

Value

Any CSS length value, a percentage of the parent element's width, or `auto`.

Initial value: `auto`

Compatibility

CSS Version: 1

This property is supported in some form by all CSS-compatible browsers. Current, standards-compliant browsers (Netscape 6, Opera 7, Mozilla, Internet Explorer 5 for Mac) support it fully.

Internet Explorer for Windows (up to and including version 6.0) incorrectly includes padding, borders, and margins in the width value. This is known as the **box model bug**. IE 6.0 corrects this in standards-compliant mode[50], but for all previous versions you'll need to use a separate, browser-specific style sheet or live with smaller boxes whenever borders, margins, or padding come into play (which is almost always). A third alternative is commonly known as the **box model hack**[51], and exploits a more obscure bug in IE6's CSS support to work around the box model bug.

In Internet Explorer 4, this property is supported only for a limited subset of block elements (`div` is a safe bet).

In Netscape 4, this property is really only supported for images and absolute-positioned elements.

Example

This style rule assigns a fixed width of 100 pixels to paragraphs within the element with ID `blurbs`.

```
#blurbs p {
  width: 100px;
}
```

[50] http://msdn.microsoft.com/library/en-us/dnie60/html/cssenhancements.asp
[51] http://css-discuss.incutio.com/?page=BoxModelHack

word-break

This nonstandard property, supported by Internet Explorer for Windows version 5 or later, lets you specify different word wrapping behavior for Chinese/Japanese/Korean (CJK) scripts than for other writing systems.

Inherited: Yes

Value

This property will accept any one of the following constant values:

- `break-all`: allows both CJK and non-CJK words to be broken by word wrapping at any point; ideal for CJK text containing non-CJK fragments

- `keep-all`: prevents both CJK and non-CJK words from being broken by word wrapping; ideal for non-CJK text containing CJK fragments

- `normal`: allows CJK words to be broken by word wrapping at any point, but prevents non-CJK words from being broken in the same way

Initial value: `normal`

Compatibility

CSS Version: n/a

Internet Explorer 5 or later for Windows only.

Equivalent functionality is planned for inclusion in CSS3, but final property names and values are likely to differ. To follow the work on this front, see the CSS Working Group Web site[52].

Example

This style rule sets the entire document to prevent arbitrary breaking of words in CJK and non-CJK text, in anticipation of the document being primarily non-CJK:

---

[52] http://www.w3.org/TR/2003/WD-css3-text-20030226/#wordbreak-props

```
body {
  word-break: keep-all;
}
```

word-spacing

This property lets you either increase or decrease the amount of spacing between words in an element.

Inherited: Yes

See also: letter-spacing

Value

Any CSS length, or normal. Percentages are *not* allowed.

Positive lengths increase word spacing by the specified amount, while negative lengths decrease it. In most cases, it is preferable to specify the spacing in ems (e.g. 0.5em), as this will preserve the relative spacing of words, even if you change the font size (one em is equal to the height of the current font).

Initial value: normal

Compatibility

CSS Version: 1

This property is supported by Mozilla browsers (including Netscape 6 or later), Internet Explorer for Windows version 6 or later, Internet Explorer for Macintosh version 4.01 or later, and Opera browsers.

Examples

This style rule sets all elements of class **spacy** to have extra spacing one half the height of the font between each word:

```
.spacy {
  word-spacing: 0.5em;
}
```

This style rule sets all elements of class `crowded` to display words one half the font size closer together than usual:

```
.crowded {
  word-spacing: -0.5em;
}
```

word-wrap

This nonstandard property, supported by Internet Explorer for Windows version 5.5 or later, lets you specify whether words that are too long to fit within the assigned width of an element should overflow that width (the default behavior) or be wrapped to the next line at the edge of the box.

Inherited: Yes

See also: `width`, `text-overflow`

Value

`break-word` or `normal`

Initial value: `normal`

Compatibility

CSS Version: n/a

Internet Explorer 5.5 for Windows or later only.

Example

This style rule allows long words throughout the document to be wrapped forcibly if they overflow the assigned width of their containers:

```
body {
  word-wrap: break-word;
}
```

writing-mode

This nonstandard property lets you choose between two common layout methods for text: left-to-right horizontal lines stacked top to bottom on the page (the usual layout for western languages like English), and top-to-bottom vertical lines stacked right to left on the page (the usual layout for East Asian languages like Chinese).

For scripts not designed to be displayed this way (e.g. Latin script as used in English text), the tb-rl setting rotates the text 90 degrees clockwise so that it can be read vertically.

Inherited: Yes

See also: layout-flow

Value

lr-tb or tb-rl

Initial value: lr-tb

Compatibility

CSS Version: n/a

Internet Explorer 5.5 for Windows or later only.

Equivalent functionality is planned for inclusion in CSS3, but final property names and values are likely to differ. To follow the work on this front, see the CSS Working Group Web site[53].

Example

This style rule sets the writing-mode of the body and all its children (unless otherwise specified) to the East Asian style:

```
body {
  writing-mode: tb-rl;
}
```

---

[53] http://www.w3.org/TR/2003/WD-css3-text-20030226/#Progression

---

z-index

For any element for which the `position` property is other than `static`, this property sets the stacking order relative to other positioned elements within the same **stacking context**[17].

Non-positioned elements are always beneath all positioned elements in the same stacking context; they effectively have a `z-index` of `0`. Elements in the same stacking context with the same `z-index` are stacked in the order they appear in the document, with later elements overlaying earlier ones.

Inherited: No

See also: `position`

Value

A positive integer, or the `auto` constant. The higher the integer, the higher the element's position in the stacking order.

The `auto` constant causes the element to behave as if it had a `z-index` of `0`, except that it does not create a new stacking context.

Initial value: `auto`

Compatibility

CSS Version: 2

This property works in all CSS-compatible browsers, including Netscape 4.

Example

This style rule positions the element with ID `mainmenu` near the top-left of the browser window and with a `z-index` value that causes it to hover over other elements of lower `z-index` values:

```
#mainmenu {
    position: absolute;
```

---

[17]The stacking context of any element is the closest positioned ancestor whose `z-index` property is set.

```
  top: 10px;
  left: 10px;
  width: 100px;
  height: 300px;
  z-index: 10;
}
```

zoom

This nonstandard property, supported by Internet Explorer for Windows version 5.5 or later, lets you magnify or reduce the size of an element and all its contents.

Inherited: No

Value

A magnification factor, either as a floating point number (1.0 is the normal size) or as a percentage (100% is the normal size), or the constant value normal.

Initial value: normal

Compatibility

CSS Version: n/a

This property is supported by Internet Explorer for Windows version 5.5 or later only.

Example

This style rule sets all images in the document to appear at half their normal size:

```
img {
  zoom: 50%;
}
```

Recommended Resources

This bibliography provides you with links to, and comments on, some of the better reference sources—online and off—that I've encountered in my adventures with CSS.

I'm absolutely certain that I've left out a lot of great stuff here. The universe of CSS information is too large for one person to know about, and certainly too vast for a single appendix in a book. What I've provided here is a list of the best books and Websites I've personally encountered and used. Each is accompanied by a few words—or paragraphs—of commentary to help you better decide which resources will work best for your needs in a given design situation, or for general background.

The resources appear in no particular order.

Books

Dynamic HTML: The Definitive Reference, 2nd Edition
By Danny Goodman. Published by O'Reilly. ISBN: 0-596-00316-1.

> This is the best comprehensive reference to DHTML, of which CSS is a crucial component. Goodman's writing is clear and concise. He's a real authority who not only writes about this technology, but uses it daily in his successful consulting business.
>
> While the book is pricey and weighty, it's all but indispensable. When the second edition came out, I bought it without hesitation, casting aside my well-thumbed and marked-up copy of the first edition of what is for me an absolutely essential reference.
>
> This is the first book I reach for whenever I have a question about how something works in CSS, HTML, JavaScript or the Document Object Model (DOM).

Eric Meyer on CSS: Mastering the Language of Web Design
By Eric N. Meyer. Published by New Riders. ISBN: 0-7357-1245-X.

> Meyer is among the best-known CSS authorities on the planet. This slick, oversized, highly illustrated book is an absolute treasure trove of teachings about CSS beyond the basics. This text consists of 13 separate projects

through which Meyer walks the reader step by step. From converting an existing page to CSS, through styling for print, and applying CSS to HTML forms, Meyer leads you carefully and precisely.

Learn to create an online greeting card, a multi-column layout, unusually shaped designs and translucent-looking scrolling areas atop fixed backgrounds.

Each chapter concludes with several challenges that stretch your skills as you attempt to build on what Meyer has taught in the chapter.

The only criticism I have of this book is its rather weak index, which reduces its value as a reference. But read through any of the projects and work them out on the screen, and I guarantee you'll learn something, no matter how sophisticated a CSS designer you might be.

By the way, if you buy this book, be sure to check out the companion Website (cited later in this appendix). There are errors in the first printed edition that you'll need to be aware of if you're to avoid total confusion at some points.

Cascading Style Sheets (CSS) By Example
By Steve Callihan. Published by InformIT. ISBN: 0-7897-2617-3.

This is the best CSS tutorial of which I'm aware. Examples abound and the code samples are, for the most part, correctly worked-out solutions. They are always readable and almost always properly formatted.

Callihan's style is brisk, friendly and very approachable.

If you're really new to CSS, and, having read this SitePoint title, you still feel shaky in your foundations, Callihan's title will give you a different take, and some reinforcement.

Useful Websites and Pages

The usual caveats about things moving around on the Web apply here. I've provided the URL for each site or page that was accurate and current as this book went into production. No guarantees.

Unfortunately, much of the CSS-related content you'll find by searching the Web via your favorite search engine is likely out of date before you see it. There was a flurry of articles in 1998-1999 when CSS was new, but very few sites (our own http://www.sitepoint.com/ is one exception) have continued their CSS coverage, or ever extended beyond basics.

A List Apart

http://www.alistapart.org/

A List Apart has been a cornerstone of the Web design community's online world since its inception. The brainchild of Jeffrey Zeldman, this site is chock-full of intriguing information. Zeldman shows how to do things, often by redesigning parts of his own site.

A really awesome repository of articles by many of the best designers and thinkers, this really is a list apart.

HTML Utopia – Designing Without Tables

http://www.sitepoint.com/article.php/379

This inspirational two-parter was largely responsible for the decision to write this book, and to treat the topic of CSS the way I have. It's a nice, condensed introduction to the issues in this book, and can serve as a decent refresher when you just want to remind yourself why you're going through all this!

Style Sheet Reference Guide

http://www.webreview.com/style/

This is the most comprehensive table of CSS compatibility analysis that I know about. It lists virtually every property and feature of CSS-1 and CSS-2, and indicates whether the feature is supported or not. The front page (which appears at the URL above) lets you select which chart you want to look at and work with.

I use this site extensively, because it's so accurate and complete that if I have any question at all about whether a particular CSS trick I'm about to try will work in most browsers, the answer is literally two or three clicks away.

The AnyBrowser Campaign Site Design Guide

http://www.anybrowser.org/campaign/abdesign3.html

This is one of the sites I love to support and visit. It's part of the "Viewable With Any Browser" Campaign that was launched to encourage Web designers and developers to be sure that their sites actually work in all the major browsers. It encourages the use of standards, and discourages relying on browser-specific tricks and techniques.

The page has a ton of links to places where you can validate, check, and get advice about conformance with standards and specifications. It's a good place to remind yourself how best to design Web pages using CSS to ensure maximum accessibility.

glish.com: CSS Layout Techniques

http://glish.com/css/

A brisk, chatty overview of CSS. The best feature of this site is the list of resources it includes. Although the site has some stale links and seems not to be currently maintained (or at least not very attentively), it nonetheless offers a wealth of information you'll potentially find useful.

The Layout Reservoir - BlueRobot

http://bluerobot.com/web/layouts/default.asp

This site is primarily a code repository for two- and three-column layouts, as well as some potentially helpful information about centering things in CSS.

Little Boxes at the Noodle Incident

http://www.thenoodleincident.com/tutorials/box_lesson/boxes.html

I find it helpful sometimes to sort of stumble through a series of design mishaps and blind alleys with someone who's been there and done that. This site is a bit like that. The UI is clean and well-thought-through, and each page gives you some useful information about a specific approach to a box layout design problem, how the author approached it, what worked, what didn't, and how he ultimately solved it.

CSS, cascading style sheets, HTML, Website Tips at Websitetips.com

http://www.websitetips.com/css/index.shtml

A fine repository of links with some commentary. There are lots of sites and other references listed here that I haven't included in this appendix. It may be a good idea to pop over to this site if you need something about CSS that either you don't find in this book, or you need more examples to clarify your understanding.

Complexspiral Demo

http://www.meyerweb.com/eric/css/edge/complexspiral/demo.html

This is a sub-site of Eric Meyer's, but it deserves its own entry because it was, as far as I can tell, the first place on the Web to teach the fixed-background trick that has become de rigeur on many modern sites. It's also an attractive design, and Eric gives you all the information and code you need to adapt it to your own uses.

Accessibility Features of CSS

http://www.w3.org/TR/CSS-access

Even though the entire W3C set of CSS sites is useful (and cited later), this page, in particular, is helpful when you're dealing with an accessibility issue and want to know what, if anything, CSS can do to help you make your site more accessible. Contrasted with most W3C recommendations (which are dry, hard to read, and terse to a fault), this discussion is readable and helpful.

Eric Meyer on CSS

http://www.ericmeyeroncss.com/

This site is the supplemental/support site for Eric's book of the same title as the site. It offers errata (very helpful; some of the stuff that slipped through the cracks of the editing and production process are embarrassingly wrong) as well as some information that didn't fit into the book.

Real World Style

http://realworldstyle.com/

A very nice, cleanly designed, and helpful site by Mark Newhouse that's full of tips, insights, opinions, and other goodies. Be sure also to follow the links to his blog, where he holds forth regularly on CSS-related topics.

This is one of my favorites. I visit it often.

NYPL: Style Guide

http://www.nypl.org/styleguide/

The esteemed New York Public Library's site, where styles and rules about the use of XHTML and CSS are linked. Every once in a while, I'll wonder about the proper way to do something (as opposed to the technically correct way) and when I do, this site has been quite useful.

W3C Recommendation for Cascading Style Sheets, level 1
W3C Recommendation for Cascading Style Sheets, level 2

http://www.w3.org/TR/REC-CSS1

http://www.w3.org/TR/REC-CSS2

These are the definitive sites for explaining exactly how CSS is supposed to work. The W3C's recommendations appear here in their entirety, are searchable, and are well-organized, too. The main idea is that browser manufacturers memorize and internalize these recommendations, and then make their browsers behave correctly.

But, as a friend of mine likes to say: "In theory, there's no difference between theory and practice, but in practice, there is."

Still, it's a good idea to be familiar with the contents of these pages and to at least know your way around them.

W3C CSS Validation Service

http://jigsaw.w3.org/css-validator/

This is the site for the validation service I talk about in Chapter 12.

Image Overflow Trick

http://people.opera.com/jax/buzz/css/imagepos/

A good example of the image overflow trick I demonstrate in Chapter 9, with a more fleshed-out and interesting example (hey, he had big pages to work with!).

A CSS based "Frames" simulation

http://css.nu/exp/nf-illustration.html

The site is slightly mis-labeled. It's actually about how to use CSS to avoid the frames/tables otherwise necessary to create modern layouts. It offers some suggestions and tidbits I didn't find easily elsewhere, and it's quite entertaining.

Fancy Paragraphs With CSS

http://www.sitepoint.com/article.php/942

This article on SitePoint offers good explanations and insights into some of the topics I cover in Chapter 9. Examples are clear, large, bold and in color, so there is value in reading them even if you feel you understand the topic well.

CSS Is Easy!

http://www.sitepoint.com/article.php/309

A SitePoint article that offers a quasi-interactive tutorial in CSS. You might find this useful primarily because it takes things in very small doses, and doles them out carefully.

What is Liquid Design?

http://www.sitepoint.com/article.php/951

A well-organized SitePoint article that teaches the basics of using CSS and tables for liquid (aka "stretchy") design. I found its primary value to be in the clarity with which you could see the distinction between using tables and CSS for this kind of project.

Introduction to CSS Shorthand

http://www.sitepoint.com/article.php/966

As you've learned in this book, many groups of related CSS styles have a shorthand identifier that collects all the individual properties into a single one. For example, `font` is shorthand for `font-family`, `font-size`, `font-weight`, and other, related properties.

This brief article discusses shorthand in CSS, how it develops, and how to use it properly.

Index

U

underlines, 215

V

validating CSS code, 275
visible width/height, 91

W

W3C (see World Wide Web Consortium)
Web Content Accessibility Guidelines (WCAG), 80
Web Design Group (WDG)
   CSSCheck validator, 279
Web Standards Project (WaSP), 45
width (see content width/height) (see properties, width)
World Wide Web Consortium (W3C), xii, 5
   CSS validation service, 275

X

x-height, 69

Z

z-indexes (see CSS Positioning (CSS-P), z-indexes)

Books for Web Developers from SitePoint

Visit http://www.sitepoint.com/books/
for sample chapters or to order!

sitepoint

Build Your Own

Database Driven Website
Using PHP & MySQL

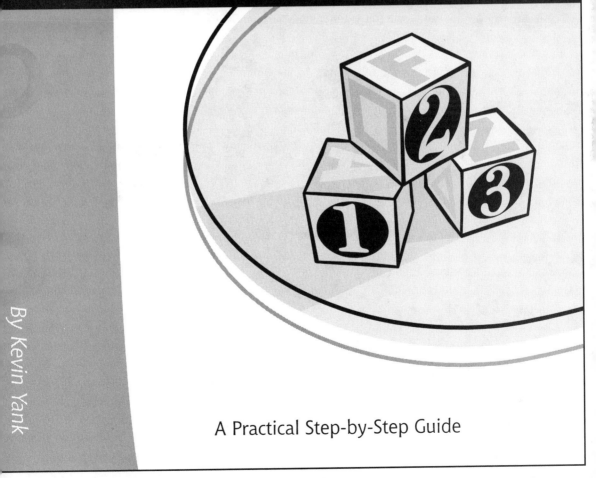

By Kevin Yank

A Practical Step-by-Step Guide

HTML Utopia:

Designing Without Tables

Using CSS

By Dan Shafer

A Practical Step-by-Step Guide

HP 5 Ready

sitepoint

The PHP Anthology

Object Oriented PHP Solutions
Volume I

By Harry Fuecks

Practical Solutions to Common Problems

PHP 5 Ready

sitepoint

The PHP Anthology

Object Oriented PHP Solutions

Volume II

By Harry Fuecks

Practical Solutions to Common Problems

Build Your Own

ASP.NET Website

Using C# & VB.NET

By Zak Ruvalcaba

A Practical Step-by-Step Guide

The CSS Anthology

101 Essential Tips, Tricks & Hacks

Practical Solutions to Common Problems

By Rachel Andrew

Kits for Web Professionals from SitePoint

Available exclusively from
http://www.sitepoint.com/